REPUBLICAN LIKE ME

REPUBLICAN LIKE ME

infiltrating red-state, white-ass
and blue-suit America

HARMON LEON

Prometheus Books

59 John Glenn Drive
Amherst, New York 14228-2197

Published 2005 by Prometheus Books

Inquiries should be addressed to
Prometheus Books
59 John Glenn Drive
Amherst, New York 14228–2197
VOICE: 716–691–0133, ext. 207
FAX: 716–564–2711
WWW.PROMETHEUSBOOKS.COM

09 08 07 06 05   5 4 3 2 1

Library of Congress Cataloging-in-Publication Data

Printed in the United States of America on acid-free paper

CONTENTS

1. MY DINNER AT APPLEBEE'S
   WITH WHITE SUPREMACISTS!

2. I SWING BOTH WAYS

3. ARNOLD MEIN GOVERNOR!

4. I WAS AN ABORTION CLINIC PROTESTOR!

5. ANGRY ABORTION LETTER

6. LEGENDS OF THE CONSERVATIVES—
   CELEBRITY EDITION!—VINCENT GALLO

7. FOR THE LOVE OF GOD, COUNTRY,
   AND CHEERLEADING!

8. YOUNG DEMOCRATS VS. YOUNG REPUBLICANS

9. REPUBLICAN POLITICAL MERCHANDISE TIE-INS

10. LEGENDS OF THE CONSERVATIVES—TOBY KEITH

11. BAD JOBS THAT INVOLVE WEARING COSTUMES

12. MASTER OF CORPORATE MANNERS

13. ACTION ALERT! A MESSAGE FROM THE
     AMERICAN FAMILY ASSOCIATION

14. NEW URBANISM MON AMOUR

15. ACTION ALERT! A MESSAGE FROM THE
     AMERICAN FAMILY ASSOCIATION

16. MY PART IN HOMELAND SECURITY

17. DO YOUR PART-HELP FIGHT
     THE WAR ON TERRORISM !

18. WHAT PART OF *ILLEGAL*
     DON'T THEY UNDERSTAND?

19. WHAT WILL YOU DO WHEN
     THE ILLEGAL ALIENS COME?

20. LEGENDS OF THE CONSERVATIVES-TED NUGENT

21. I SPY ON THE FBI

22. YOUR CONSERVATIVE HOROSCOPE!

23. ANGRY TALK RADIO CALLERS-UNITE!

24. JOKES ABOUT THOSE TRAITORS, THE FRENCH

25. I'M A LITTLE ANGEL
     WITH THE GUARDIAN ANGELS!

26. MY RIGHT TO BEAR!

27. LEGENDS OF THE CONSERVATIVES MEL GIBSON

28. CHRISTIAN IS THE NEW LATINO

29. HOW TO BE A CHRISTIAN VENTRILOQUIST

30. ONWARD CHRISTIAN EX-GAYS

31. SLAMMIN' FOR JESUS

INTRODUCTION

In the Deep South of the 1950s, journalist John Howard Griffin decided to go undercover and cross the color line. Using medication that darkened his skin to deep brown, he exchanged his privileged life as a Southern white man for the disenfranchised world of an unemployed black man. His audacious, still chillingly relevant eyewitness history is a work about race and humanity that, in this new millennium, still has something important to say to every American.

Griffin's breakthrough was in enabling a white person to read about what it might be like to be black in America during the era that predated Civil Rights. He accomplished this feat by going undercover, and holding a mirror up to an ugly side of Southern culture. Rather than editorialize, he documented attitudes, opinions, and a collective state of mind.

Let's jump ahead. In the 21st Century, America is still split in half. Only now, it's between Republicans and Democrats, Red Staters and the Blue Staters, and each side is completely alien to the other. I live in Northern California, the land of the peace-loving, true BLUE liberal. We hate the Republicans and they seem to hate us. We yell and hurl accusations at one another across every communication medium. And we're only moving further apart.

In *Republican Like Me!*, I seek to emulate the social science of Mr. Griffin (maybe with tongue a little more in cheek), and go over yet another line that needs to be crossed—the conservative line! Through a drastic change in my looks, style of clothing, and attitude, I will become a Republican. That's right Johnson, I will infiltrate and live the life of America's Bush-loving extreme Right. It will be a daring, anthropological romp into finding out how the other half lives.

One might also say my mission is like that of Jane Goodall, living amongst the chimps, but that would be insulting to the chimps. My subject is far more savage, and, in some cases, much hairier (especially around the knuckle region).

I can't beat them, so I'll join them. I'm going to cut my scruffy hair, put on an Armani suit, and become a Republican for one year. I'll fear God and salute the flag. From my new home base in Orange County, California (home of John Wayne Airport), I'll infiltrate the underbelly of Republican life. I want to see what makes these people tick. Are they as bad as they seem? Are they for real? Because to me, their views seems unfathomable.

Once, disguised, I will be able to observe Republicans in their nature habitat, getting a true insider's view, and a sense of these characters, who, at this writing, pretty much run the country.

Just to make it fun, I'm going to go the extra mile. As the situation dictates, I will work to inhabit the most extreme, grotesque caricature of the particular right-wing group that I'm infiltrating. While feeding them their own meat, I will hold up a mirror and record how they react to my absurd stereotype of their behavior.

How far is *too far*? Where does the patriot end and the extremist begin? Only by working without a net will I be able to know for sure.

Onward!

1.
MY DINNER AT APPLEBEE'S WITH WHITE SUPREMACISTS!

First off, I highly recommend you not try this at home. I decide to infiltrate a white supremacist hate group by posing as an eager new recruit, a new hater, if you will. I want to put a face on extreme hate, to find out the hobbies of haters, what haters find hot and what haters find not. I want to learn what someone in a hate group really loooooooves. Ice cream? Everyone loves ice cream. I love ice cream. Maybe hate groups love ice cream, too?

SO MANY HATE GROUPS, SO LITTLE TIME

I go online, trolling for hate groups. Who knew there was so much organized hate around? Which one to choose? Why there's The Aryan Nation, The World Church of the Creator, and the National Socialist Movement, not to mention the White Aryan Resistance, the White Power Liberation Front, and, of course, the kooky and lovable Ku Klux Klan.

After sending out many emails under the pseudonym of

hater-to-be Hal Haterman, I find my hate group. And believe me, it's a good one! Its Web site rails on about "the Negroid filth churned out by MTV and the other Jewish promoters of anti-White music intended to demoralize, corrupt, and deracinate young Whites." My, someone certainly has got their panties in a bundle!

It gets better. The founder of the organization wrote a whopper of a book, called *The Turner Diaries*, that's an awesome detailed blueprint for race war and is credited with inspiring young Timothy McVeigh to bomb the Federal Building in Oklahoma City. Hurrah for hate!

Since they're not known for great sense of humor, and in order to protect the innocent (namely me) I'm reluctant to reveal the hate group's name, being I wouldn't want the next time they see me be through the scope of a rifle. Cut me some slack, I mean these guys DO hate for a living. Dedicating a whole organization to hating leaves little room for a greeeeeeeat sense of humor (unless, of course, you're the Carrot Top of racist jokes). Besides, why give them the extra publicity.

After emailing the hate group about its next meeting, I'm truly paranoid. I'm not only a member of the number one religion that they want to wipe off the planet; once I push SEND, I get the uneasy feeling that I've immediately been put on a FBI watch list. Terrific, my email will now be monitored!

Day turns to night, then back to day again. Pages fall off my calendar (not really). The seasons change (still not really). A week later, eerily sitting in my in-box is an email from my prospective hate group:

"We should have our next meeting coming up mid to late January. I would like to meet with you in person before then."

The next hurdle: a little new-potential-hater questionnaire I'm asked to fill out. I start by answering with extreme sarcasm:

Ethnic background: "What do you think! Come on!"

Profession: "Children's birthday party entertainer"

What prompted you to want to become a racial activist or at least look into it? "I really want to get more involved in activism in my community. I work well with others and have good organizational skills. I have a pickup truck if that's needed at any events."

Then I throw in for good measure: "Also, I hate the Jews! Lol"

And in closing I add, "Where shall we meet?

The local leader of the hate group — an organization that is a direct spin-off from the old American Nazi Party and that sees itself as carrying on Hitler's dream to purify the white race and prevent Jews and blacks from degrading "our" culture — responds:

"How about Applebee's? I'll be coming with my wife, baby, and one other member. We can meet in the reception area. I'll be coming with two women and a baby?"

Bingo! I got a date with hate! And who doesn't love Applebee's? It has quality dinners and a wide selection – and all at budget prices!

A little preparation is in order.

MY HATEFUL DISGUISE: Trucker hat, jean jacket, camouflage army pants. Balancing everything out is a Mickey Mouse T-shirt. (Mickey Mouse wasn't Jewish, was he?)

HATEFUL BACKSTORY: As a new recruit, Hal Haterman is a bit confused on whom exactly to hate. Hal's attitude about hating is very cheerful and enthusiastic.

HATEFUL BACKUP: A large friend planted by the entrance of Applebee's to watch my back and have his finger ready to punch 911, in case anything weird happens.

APPLEBEE'S MOTTO: Eatin' Good in the Neighborhood

They Put the "Ha" in "Hate"

I'm nervously sick to my stomach at the prospect of the entire evening as I drive the one and a half hours from San Francisco, purposely making sure that I'm 40 minutes late for my white supremacist rendezvous at Applebee's. They're going to absolutely hate me. It's Friday night at Applebee's, and the place is packed, filled with clean-cut couples, carefree college students, families with happy little kids, as the perky waiters and wait-resses bounce with big smiles from one table to another, glee-fully taking food orders. Being purposely late presents a problem: How will I find my white supremacists in this packed medium-priced eatery? Will they be wearing matching hats? Will they have similar haircuts? Will they already be picking on minorities bussing the tables?!!!

Approaching the perky Applebee's receptionist, I explain that I'm supposed to meet a guy named Kevin, his wife, a baby, and another member of their group.

"They promote *our* culture you know," I say with a wink

"Right this way," she answers with a bubbly smile, not com-puting my meaning and leading me past dining joyful families right to the table of three white supremacists – and a baby. I'm actually taken aback. They look normal: a guy with short hair and buttoned-down shirt, his wife, who wears glasses and looks like a soccer mom, their baby, and a dumpy, blond college girl (calling her such to prove how not nice it is to generalize about people). The white supremacists are already eating their appe-tizers; they have frowns on their faces.

"Glad to see that you made it," says unsmiling Kevin, a guy who works as a computer software technician. The normality isn't just dumbfounding; it's disturbing. Maybe the joke's on me. Maybe they're not as extreme as I imagined!

I find myself apologizing to the haters.

"There's nothing I hate more than traffic," I present as an excuse. "Except, of course, the Jews." Surprisingly (or not sur-prisingly), they agree.

There's initial nervousness all around; they try to feel me out, yet, at the same time, they also try to impress me with the merits of their hate group. I, meanwhile, ponder whether my fork will work as a weapon in a situation of self-defense.

"Can we get a menu?" the white supremacist soccer mom asks the bubbly waiter.

"I forgot, how did you find out about our organization," inquires white supremacist Kevin.

"I work on weekends as a children's birthday party clown," I explain with enthusiasm. "The new guy who plays SpongeBob told me about you guys."

"I'm glad that he referred you to us," hater-Kevin says, then asks how long I've been a "race-activist."

I tilt my head back and reflect, "I started to dislike Canadians, then moved on from there." Under my breath, I mutter, "Fucking Canadians."

Three blank white supremacist stares.

"What made you want to get involved?" Kevin asks.

"It's either complain or do something. It's better to do something than complain," I say, throwing something from their Web site right back at them. They seem pleased.

After some arbitrary small talk, without fanfare or a segue, white supremacist Kevin starts laying out hate literature on the Applebee's table, bearing such bold headlines as "White Identity" and "Our Jewish Keepers," under the publication's title, *Free Speech*. Families around us enjoy their dinners.

"This tells a little bit about our organization, our ideology," Kevin explains as the table's baby gurgles. "We also have our application on the back if you decide to sign up."

"Wicked!" I exclaim. I read:

I am a White person of good moral character, with no ineligibility. I want to build a secure and healthy future for my race by becoming a member.

"This is another of our publications," white supremacist Kevin says, doing so while avoiding eye-contact; his voice fills with pride. "It deals with current issues. It deals with historical issues." He pulls out a magazine geared towards "A New Consciousness; A New Order; A New People." "It's kind of like *Time* magazine, except it's for *us*."

Yes, it's true. This would be just like *Time* magazine, if *Time* magazine ranted on endlessly about hating Jews. This version of *Time* is a little short on subtlety, though. I note some of the whimsical headlines:

"Jews Run Hollywood"

"Homosexuality as a Weapon"

"News from the Homeland"

"Jews a Different Race"

"Survival Manual for the White Race."

Just like *Time*, this magazine's entertainment section reviews *Saturday Night Live* skits that feature Jewish performers (need I tell you their take?). A review of Ann Coulter's book, *Slander*, reads, "*Slander* is fast, funny and factual. Although, unless you know the code, it can also be frustrating. The secret code is this: Almost every time you read the word, 'liberal,' think 'Jew.'" (Sounds like a crazy racist drinking game.) By not stating the real problem, Ann is aiding and abetting the enemy."

Just then our overly cheerful Applebee's waiter comes over.

'OK, who had the salad?" he bellows with a big, Eatin'-Good-in-the- Neighborhood Applebee's smile.

"Can we get another menu?" the white supremacist soccer mom asks the perky waiter as race-hater Kevin tries to subtly cover up the hate literature with his forearm.

"You bet! And here's some napkins for you." He bubbles off.

As the menu is being sought, we, the men of the table, get down to the business of hate discussion while the racist womenfolk make cutesy baby-talk to the gurgling infant.

"Crazy baby, boy," coos his racist mom, who recommends reading David Duke's book *My Awakening* because it changed her life. "You're such a good boy,"

Race-hater Kevin asks where I live. I tell him I'm about to move up from the Bay area.

"It's really horrible about the Asian problem there," the dumpy blond girl chimes in, speaking for the first time tonight, matter-of-factly, as if making small talk about the traffic or baseball scores.

(Long pause) "Uh, yeah. (Pause.) The Asian problem. (Pause.) That's why I'm planning on moving up here."

A Hispanic couple at the next table shoots a surprised—no, shocked—look, thinking they must be hearing things at cheerful Applebee's. I'm taken aback. As a first blatant racist comment of the evening, it's almost surreal. It's like someone you've just met loudly farting at a quiet, fancy dinner party, making no apologies, and then continuing to do so, completely unconcerned with the reaction of those around her. My point, without a hint of a suggestion of concern, this woman just loudly farted racism.

"It's probably a lot better up here," she spews with a vicious, hate-filled laugh. "At least you won't have to see a lot of Asians. But I'd recommend staying away from the University."

(Pause.) "OK." (Pause.) "So where would you suggest moving?"

"You're not safe anywhere," hater Kevin throws out.

"I have a friend who lives in Oakland," the soccer mom adds. "She used to be really, really anti-racist when she moved there. She's now so much more reasonable. Do you know what I mean? She's not one of us, but she's so much more level headed about the whole thing."

We grow silent. I fiddle with my water. The baby starts gurgling. (I imagine his first words will be, "Mamma," and then, a few days later, "America for white people!")

"How's that salad?" I ask, to break the silence.

"I haven't tried it yet," says the hate-filled soccer mom. "But I'm sure it's really good."

So, it seems, she hates Asians but loves Caesar salads.

DO HATE GROUPS LIKE TO ROCK?

I crane my neck, looking toward the door, hoping to spot the friend who is supposed to be watching my back. Where the hell is he?! He's not back-watching.

"This is our music magazine," racist Kevin interrupts, laying on the Applebee's table a publication that would look like any other indie/hipster music magazine, except that the music it's writing about glorifies, Germany's Third Reich and denigrates blacks and Jews.

"We also have a record company," Kevin boasts, in a manner that seems to say, "Even though we're white supremacists, that doesn't means we can't ROCK!" "We have over 750 CD titles."

"Oh yeah. What kind of music?" I ask. The group's Web site, after all, describes exactly what ideal white utopian music involves: "In specific terms, this means a society in which young men and women gather to revel with polkas or waltzes, reels or jigs, or any other White dances, but never to undulate or jerk to negroid jazz or rock rhythms."

"All kinds of music," racist Kevin boasts again. I almost expect him to strike a racist air-guitar pose.

"Yeah, well, your Web site said the kind of music you guys are into is polkas," I note, raining on his hate-filled music parade. "It said not to listen to rock and roll and instead listen to polkas. Yeah, it said the music to listen to is polkas. Do you listen to polkas?" I ask, directing the question at hate-filled Kevin.

He seems mildly embarrassed, professing with a shrug of the shoulders and a slight trace of what seems to be a blush, "Uh, sometimes we have the wrong people working on the Web sites."

"I swear it said the only music you guys should listen to is polkas," I say again, rubbing his nose in the fact. "I think it was suggested by the founder of your organization."

"What kind of music do you like?" asks the dumpy blond girl, quickly changing the subject. Fortunately I did a little Web research in case the question of white supremacist music popped up.

"I loooooooove Skrewdriver," I exclaim with girlish glee, letting out a squeal, nodding my head as I spout the name of one of the most popular Aryan Nation skinhead bands. The white supremacists at my Applebee's table acknowledge the reference with a headshake.

(For those not familiar with Skrewdriver, a brief sampling of the group's feel-good lyrics involve how all men aren't equal. The reason being that those who aren't white live in mud huts, run around throwing spears, and also eat other men. Meanwhile the Aryan race lives in houses and aren't a gang of Semitic bankers. (But here's the crux they pose: the teachers say we're just the same as them!)

"Yeah, we have Skrewdriver in our music catalog," race-hater Kevin confirms. "We're trying to branch out in other genres of music. There's a little bit of country, a little bit of heavy metal, a little bit of classical. All kinds of music."

All kinds of music indeed. In fact Kevin's hate organization puts on an annual "pro-white" music festival. One of the headlining acts this past year was a pair of blond, 12-year-old twin girls clad in matching plaid skirts with braided Heidi-hair. Here's the twist, they perform folk versions of classic racist songs by bands like Skrewdriver. Aaaaah, that's so fucking cute. They croon racist lyrics, obviously with their parents' urging like two little racist windup monkeys thrown on stage to applauding white supremacist approval. Kind of like the Olsen twins—but with blatant racism. It gets cuter though. These adorable minxes take their band name, Prussian Blue, from the Zuklon B residue that Holocaust revisionists claim was not found in the "so-called" gas chambers in concentration camps. These Neo-Nazis claim that this should make people question the accuracy of the "Holocaust myth." Now that, my friends, is absolutely fucking adorable!

"I have an article in this month's new issue about my experiences going to school at UC Santa Cruz," the dumpy blond racist girl proudly proclaims, nibbling at her Caesar salad, gesturing towards the magazine.

I feign faux shock. "You went to Santa Cruz?!" I question with a sour look on my face in regard to her neo-Nazi experiences at one of the hippy capitals of America. This should be good.

"It was pretty much a liberal freak show," she scorns with angry bitterness. "It totally transformed me," she slowly explains with strong eye-contact. "I went their not really knowing anything. It changed my perspective for the better [better?!]. It made me a much better person," she adds with reassuring smile.

The ironic crux, by "better person," she actually means "racist-to-krazy-Ku-Klux-Klan-proportions." Example, she was shocked when her roommate's "wigger traits" started to emerge, obviously a person, as she puts it, who hated herself for being white and partook in such atrocities as singing *black music* and inviting over black friends on a regular basis (gasp!). She in turn, decided to decorate their dorm room with iron crosses and Nazi swastikas. Oh yes, those zaaaaaaaany college roommate pranks. Believe it or not, her promotion of the white race caused concern with the "liberal-loving" housing authorities and the Chancellor of the University (probably Jewish), especially with all the Nazi recruitment flyers she tacked everywhere causing extreme eye-brow-raising-what-the-fuck concern amongst the good people of Santa Cruz (those crazy college days). The dumpy girl (again, only calling her such to prove how not nice it is to generalize about people), claims her efforts have "opened eyes by saying all men *aren't* created equal." You go racist girl!

I ask the dumpy blond girl (see how not nice it is to generalize about people) where she's originally from. Believe or not, I learn she hails from Orange County.

"The *OC*," I say, making a small attempt at humor by referring to the TV show.

She laughs for a moment. Then laughter stops. "Do you know the main family on the OC is Jewish?!" the dumpy girl spits in disgust.

"You mean the actors or the characters they play?" I ask.

"Probably both," she adds with revulsion. "I have no interest in watching that!"

(Pause.) "Yeah, me too."

"What do you do now?" I inquire to the dumpy racist girl.

Digging at her salad, she says, "I'm a graduate student."

"What do you study?"

"Child development," she says proudly. "I'm four credits away from graduating."

Holy shit. Pray for us all.

"How is everything?" the bubbly Applebee's waiter asks, popping out of nowhere.

"Can we please get a menu?" the racist soccer mom asks once again, turning increasingly hateful towards the cheerful Applebee's waiter. It's a good thing he's white.

I go to the bathroom, splash water on my face, and look deeply into the mirror. There's a message on my cell phone. It's from my large friend, the large friend who was planted by the door at Applebee's in order to watch my back. He's no longer planted by the door. He had to take off to meet a girl. He is sorry. I hate him.

I return to the table, presenting the white supremacist with a nervous smile; a smile of one who's no longer having his back watched.

"Have a chance to check out our Web site?" Kevin asks as I sit back down ready for round two.

"Yeah, I was checking it out today," I reply uncomfortably. The same Web site that advocated polka dancing, was veeeeeeery informative. It calls for what they term "A White Living Space" and complains about "the sickness of multiculturalism" that is destroying America and other good Aryan nations. There's a call for "a racially clean area of the Earth for the further development of our people. We must have White schools, White residential neighborhoods and recreation areas, White workplaces, White farms and countryside. We must have no non-Whites in our living space."

As a call to battle-arms, it trumpets, "We will do whatever is necessary to achieve this White living space and to keep it White. (That's a hell of a lot of white.) We will not be deterred by the difficulty or temporary unpleasantness involved, because we realize that it is absolutely necessary for our racial survival."

With that in the back of my head, I sit at Applebee's with the local crusaders for the cause, who hungrily pick at a plate of spicy Buffalo wings, deeming them delicious. (They *are* delicious!)

"We're getting a lot of hits," racist Kevin remarks. "Our link is up in the top 10,000 in the World Wide Web. I believe we got even more hits than *USA Today*, so that's a real positive thing."

"Now, about this white living space," I ask. "How do you suggest one tries to go about achieving this?"

"How are we going to achieve a white living space?" Kevin repeats without making eye-contact. "In a small way you can start doing your part by doing business with white businesses and let them know why you are doing business with them."

The perky Applebee's waiter appears again from nowhere, presenting a menu and scaring the hell out of me. "How is everything?" he asks.

"Can I get some nachos please. They look delicious," I say, wanting to see if a hate group loves nachos, even though they are Mexican in origin. I also order the Oriental Chicken Rollup.

"So do you have any other friends who are into this?" racist Kevin asks when the bouncy waiter departs.

'Oh yeah. I sure do," I insist, explaining that I have a friend who would be a really great member, because not only does he have interest in being a white racialist, but he is also an albino, which makes him extra white.

How Do Hate Groups Recruit Fellow Haters?

So what goes on at a meeting?" I ask. "I just want to be a better racial activist. Do we organize protests? Do we have bake sales?"

"Every unit varies. There're some units who are more active. We go out to demonstrations and stuff like that. We have gone to demonstrations against Israel."

"Do you do anything with immigration?" I ask.

"You know we really should, especially in California. It really would attract a lot of new members.

"Our Las Vegas unit decided to put a huge billboard up in the middle of the street that said Stop Immigration. They got it taken down," Kevin says, blaming the removal on some Jewish professor who complained.

"San Francisco would be the place for a billboard," I advise. "You got to go where the trouble areas are." (I'm scaring myself.)

"We're going to be doing some flyering," Kevin explains, picking at his food. "We're going to be doing some big flyering this weekend; race flyers. It says (hate group's name) with this picture of this blond woman and it says LOVE YOUR RACE. I know the media is going to jump all over that."

"I'm sure they will," I reply, knowing at least one member of the media who will be writing about it.

Along with the Love Your Race catchphrase, the flyers will denounce Martin Luther King and include anti-Semitic quotes from Richard Nixon and Henry Ford. It will be the largest literature distribution that this unit has ever undertaken, printing up over 10,000 flyers.

The leafleting is done in what they call drive-bys; the flyers are launched out of car windows onto random residential driveways. (Imagine waking up one Sunday morning, going out in your bathrobe for the paper, and finding that this has come to your neighborhood.)

"We try to put out a positive message that people can go out and promote their own race," Kevin says.

"Yeah, why can't we," I add, throwing fuel on the fire and pounding the Applebee's table with my fist. (I'm scaring myself again.)

"Exactly," Kevin says, smiling. He thinks we think alike. He thinks I'm hate-filled enough to be allowed on the hate bandwagon. "If you're eager to help out, there's plenty of work."

"Yeah, I'm eager," I respond to his recruitment call-to-arms. "I like keeping busy. I can drop some off at the birthday parties when I'm entertaining. SpongeBob can help me."

Next shocker! Gun shows, it seems, are a big recruiting arena. But lately the gun show crowd hasn't produced the type of quality hate group candidate as in days of old.

"We put flyers on cars at Oz Fest," the racist soccer mom says, wiping her baby's chin. "We also did that Metallica concert." (Good move, guitarist Kirk Hammett is actually part Filipino—adding to "the Asian problem.")

The group also gives out recruitment DVDs at "European" cultural events. "It gives some background into the group and what's going on in the world," white supremacist Kevin explains, handing me a copy.

I make my most hate-filled face. "I know what's going on in the world; that's why I'm here!" I say with a cold, dead look in my eye.

"Exactly!" Kevin says, smiling again.

"You can talk," I add, repeating propaganda I found on the group's Web site, "or you can take action! I take action!"

Now, I'm really scaring myself.

IT'S A FAMILY AFFAIR

My Applebee's nachos finally arrive, and let me tell you, they are absolutely delicious.

"So, how many members do you got?" I ask white supremacist Kevin like I were rushing a college fraternity (Phi Delta White Power) and he needs to sell me on the idea of joining.

"Nationwide? Worldwide? I don't have the exact figure. But we are the largest racial-activist organization of its kind in the country," he says, explaining that Hal Haterman would pretty much have a racist friend in every major city. "It could be a couple thousand. We have a good size unit here. Each meeting we have 30 to 40 people.

The local unit has been around since 1993, and white supremacist Kevin has been along for the hate-mongering ride since the beginning, working his way up the ranks. They have a weekly broadcast on shortwave radio. ("It has to do with pretty much every topic that has to do with our race."), and there's plans to spread their message further through a fun-lovin' public access show news program.

"Most of our other members in their early 30's and late 20's," explains the racist soccer mom, bouncing her baby on her knee. "There's a lot of couples with kids. We're very family-orientated. In our unit there's about 14 kids, total. At the meetings, there will be little kids running around everywhere. Yeah, we're really family-orientated."

"Yeah, that sounds like a good atmosphere," I add, biting my lower lip.

"So we'll go and spend about a half an hour having the meeting and then a half an hour just playing with the kids."

The racist baby starts screaming.

"Nancy is the only one who isn't married," the soccer mom says, and the dumpy girl makes a sad face (perhaps secretly eyeing Hal Haterman as a potential future racist white supremacist husband?).

Besides meetings, the group also sponsors social events, camping trips, outings to European cultural fairs, and, of course, protests in front of the Canadian consulate for their treatment of Ernzt Zundel, leading Holocaust denier and the world's largest distributor of Nazi propaganda and memorabilia in the world. ("That's why I hate Canadians!" I explain.)

"Are there any celebrities members of the group?" I inquire with hope.

"There are, but they don't want to make it public."

"Come ooooooooon. Who?" I plead. I throw out a few to see if there react (Roger Ebert? Tara Reid?! Will Smith? the guy on the Quaker Oats box?!!).

"There's quite a few people from mainstream bands. You'd be surprised; in really popular bands."

"Who? Justin Timberlake?"

"We have all kinds of members. Doctors, lawyers, professors," he says, going on to list several other occupations, and to note that a hate group is a really good place for professional networking. "We had some members who were on the ballot for the Reform Party. Until the press found out and made a big deal about it."

"Stupid press," I add, "You should be careful of them." Then, "So where are your meetings at?"

"We usually have them at the public library or different restaurants. The last one we had to have at our house. It varies."

This month, believe it or not, it's going to be in the backroom of a German restaurant. Claiming I'm an amateur video buff, I ask if I can film the meeting for their website.

"That wouldn't be a good idea. Like if we're planning a certain event and the opposition (non-racists) sees it they might plan a protest."

"Yes, you shouldn't let the opposition know what you're up to," I agree while heaping salsa onto a chip.

"We want to be as open as possible. But there's also people out there who hate us, and they want to do anything possible to destroy us," racist Kevin says almost with a hint of sadness.

"How do you deal with that?"

"We try to stay private as possible."

"That's a good idea. You guys shouldn't tell your secrets to anyone outside the group you can't trust," I add, adjusting my tape recorder. "They could spread the secrets.

"Hi baby! You've been a good baby."

DO HATE GROUPS HATE OTHER HATE GROUPS?

The perky Applebee's waiter with the big Applebee's smile describes the desserts.

"If I order something will you split it with me," the white supremacist wife says, nudging her husband. "We want to get one of those sweets with the brownies and the chocolate and the ice cream," she tells the smiling waiter.

I knew they would love ice cream!

I have an idea.

"Know what we should do? We should start a softball team!" I throw out with a big smile in order to generate enthusiasm for the idea, while grabbing a heaping of nachos. I explain we could take on other white supremacist groups in athletic competition. "I could even design the T-shirts."

Kevin ponders the notion, (not catching on how utterly ridiculous that actually would be) and only answers back with "So you like softball, huh?"

"Do you guys do things, like have get-togethers with other groups like the Klan?" I ask. "You know like throw picnics or bowling night?"

"We tried it in the past but it just didn't work out." Kevin admits solemnly.

"It wasn't our ideology; it was more personal conflicts. Some members had a little too much to drink and started arguing. We like to present the best representation of the white race that we can."

Kevin knows about the Klan. He did a two-year stint in Texas but wasn't happy about the experience.

"The Grand Wizard was on welfare," he recalls; his voice contains as much distaste as if he were commenting on Mexicans. "He was about 50 and lived with his mother. It was really depressing. We had to go with him to get his welfare check."

Still in the mode of a popular kid during fraternity rush week, I puff out my chest and state with an air of cockiness, "You know I've been kind of looking around at a lot of other white racialist groups. I'm still deciding which one to join. The Church of the World Creator doesn't look that bad."

My Applebee's table collectively rolls its eyes. I stare off towards the kitchen and run my finger up the side of my fork, acting like I'm starting to get bored, to make them work harder at recruiting.

"Will I have to wear a stupid hood?!" I complain out of nowhere. "I just want to wear normal clothes. I don't want to wear a stupid hood."

"No. We're just normal, you know," the racist soccer mom explains. "A lot of those other people are just like caricatures."

"There's lot of hobbyists," the dumpy blond girl leans in and adds. "I think overall our organization has a higher level of intelligence. I don't want to sound snotty but it's true. I think we attract the best of the best."

Kevin explains the protocol of the business of racial-hating. "At our meetings we make sure everyone wears shirt and tie. We make sure of that. We want to represent our race in the best possible manner," he says. "We try to eliminate the cheese factor."

Everyone laughs and repeats. "Cheese factor." (Ah, white supremacist-humor). The racist baby loudly gurgles.

Kevin goes on, "We just want to give people a good impression. We want to change people's impression of what a white racialist is. We're all not evil people," he utters with an air of sensitivity. "We're all not sickos and weirdos."

I jump in to help make his point. "Yeah, just normal people. Just people who are normal. It's a cultural thing!"

"Is there a special topic or agenda for the next meeting?" I ask.

"We go through our monthly bulletin," Kevin explains. "Usually our meetings are two to three hours."

At the meetings, Kevin continues, they usually go over what's happening generally with the organization, cover old business, and host a speaker or speakers on relevant issues, such as a lawyer talking on freedom of speech. They're also planning a big

European cultural festival for April. The baby starts screaming.

"We generally put the agenda together the weekend before. Then we open up the floor so we can have a group discussion," Kevin says. "Maybe we'll discuss the Iraqi war?"

"What's our group's take on the war?" I ask, expecting him to use the word *towel-head* or *camel-jockey* somewhere together in a sentence. "I just want to make sure we're on the same page."

"You're allowed to have your own opinion," he replies.

"They're taking our money and getting our *white soldiers* killed," the racist soccer mom says scornfully, giving her baby its bottle.

"Like how many of our *white soldiers* are over there and have died? Like thousands," the dumpy girl chimes in.

The racist soccer mom insists her husband should try some of the chocolate brownie ice cream dessert. Her husband, though, is lost in a train of thought about the next meeting.

"Yeah I don't think we'll be talking too much about the tsunami," he says with a sarcastic smirk.

"Oh yeah, what's your opinion on that?" I ask. After all, more than 170,000 human beings did die.

"Tsunami?" he repeats.

The dumpy blond girl immediately jumps in with her position: "It's natural population control."

"What's that?" I reply, hoping I'm not hearing correctly.

"It's natural population control," she says once again without hesitation as the hairs on the back of my neck stand on end.

White supremacist Kevin voices concern over her statement, noting, "Well, there were a lot of Europeans who died in there too."

This knocks some sense into her dumpy racist head.

"Yeah, you're right. There were a lot of Swedish people who died."

"I just think it's kind of sad," adds the racist soccer mom while playing with her baby "All those kids are going to be homeless, and we're going to have to pay for them all!"

We grow silent. Under his breath, Kevin mumbles, almost as if solely for the benefit of himself, "Yeah, I wish one of those tsunamis would hit Mexico!"

Waiter, check please!

DO HATE GROUPS PICK UP THE TAB?

When the bill comes, I make no offer to pay my part. In fact, I even grunt, "You're going to get this, right?" If I had to spend an entire meal listening to pure racism — not cultural pride, mind you, but pure racism — I'm definitely not going to pay for my meal. Race-hater Kevin, after a moment of hesitation, agrees to flip the bill.

As other Applebee patrons, sit laughing, enjoying their meals I sit here wanting to get the hell home as Kevin asks one final question.

"What religion were you raised?"

I'm caught off guard. I forgot to look on their Web site to see which religion they attest to. I know they hate Catholics.

I throw out, "Jewish!" just to see their expression. Their faces turn whiter than a Klansman's sheet. "Just kidding," I state as the table breathes a sigh of relief and let's out a nervous laugh. "I was raised Christian."

That should go much better, I think. But I'm wrong again; they also hate Christians (who do they like?!). I quickly make excuses and change the topic.

Since my large friend, rather than watching my back, has ditched me for a girl (I hate him), I do not want to leave with this group; being ambushed by other members hiding in the bushes, flitters through my mind. As we head towards the door, I say, "I'm going to go back and use the bathroom, but it was *really* nice meeting you."

"We'll wait," says unsmiling Kevin, now making full eye-contact. "Nancy's going to go to her truck and get you some stickers to hand out."

(Pause.) "Ok."

I try to spend as much time as possible in the men's room, hoping the white supremacists will go away. As I walk out to the parking lot, I pray there is not a waiting van that I'm going to be thrown into as part of the initiation. Instead, the dumpy girl hands me a stack of crude, homemade stickers from her truck. They read: "Earth's Most Endangered Species: THE WHITE

RACE. Help preserve it."

"I put these on the back of chair lifts when I go snow-boarding!" the dumpy blond racist states proudly. Nearby, a young Hispanic woman starts talking in Spanish on her cell phone.

"That really ruins the mood," remarks the dumpy girl, who hates Hispanics, but loves snowboarding—carving turns on snow as white as the society she wishes she lived in.

Before leaving, I ask Kevin, "What made you decide to join the organization?"

He pauses, turning a bit reflective, almost philosophical. Perhaps he is about to provide a true meaningful insight into the complex psychology of white supremacy.

"I always hated minorities," he states bluntly. "I've always never really liked being around them. They always made me feel uncomfortable. So when I was 14, I decided to do something about it."

"We were old school skinheads from way back," the racist soccer mom says perkily.

Now I see it. This is what happens to skinheads when they grow up, have kids, and move to the suburbs. They become fatherly, respectable, racist white supremacists, the kind you'd wave to at the company picnic.

"What were you expecting?' asks Kevin about my precon-ception of the evening.

I ponder for a moment. I was looking for depth, and this is all I got. It's as simple as this: hate groups hate. That's exactly what they do, in a cult-like way, expanding their ranks by preying on the lonely and isolated. There's no great intellectual explana-tion for it.

"This was different, a lot different than I was expecting," I say.

I'm given a handwritten address for the next meeting, which is going to be at a German restaurant. I can't make it, but I'll pass on the information to some friends of mine at The Anti-Defama-tion League.

2.

I SWING BOTH WAYS

Republican or Democrat? Kerry or Bush? These crazy kids sure dominated the news around election time. Every time I turned on my TV, there were their leering mugs on news shows, commercials, debates, late-night talk shows and even MTV. But there was still more I needed to know. That's why I stepped away from my TV, walked out of my living room, down my hall, past that old antique vase, and out my front door into my community to find the answers. I wanted to be fully prepared to watch the elections, with exclusive inside knowledge on both candidates, in order to make the right choice inside the voting booth.

In my mind, there was a great debate. Not who would make a better president. I wondered which campaign was better for being a volunteer. That's why I went to both the Kerry and Bush headquarters in San Francisco in order to solve this head-to-head debate. These were my findings.

GOAL: To know my candidate and his party better by working for him completely devoid of pay.

MY CRITERIA:

I believe the following criteria should be fulfilled in comprising a good campaign volunteer program:

1) There must be free food involved.
2) There must be cool pamphlets
3) Other volunteers must show a mild to heavy interest in kickboxing.

PERSONA

In order to properly infiltrate these hallowed, political grounds, I created two suitable personas:

KERRY PERSONA

Name: Dusty Turnip—As "Dusty," I wear Birkenstocks, shorts and a Grateful Dead T-shirt. I also use the word "radical" way too often.

BUSH PERSONA

Name: Trevor Goebbels III—As "Trevor," I wear a clean, white buttoned down shirt, khaki dress pants, and a bowtie. I look like an off-duty waiter. I also have the falsely-created bad habit of blinking too much.

DEBATE ROUND 1: WHO HAS THE BETTER CAMPAIGN HEADQUARTERS?

KERRY

A large former car showroom. High ceilings. Lots of old people, minorities, and women, hustling and bustling for the cause. Everyone is in casual dress. A life-size, cardboard Kerry is prominently displayed by the entrance. For some reason, an old woman is dressed like a rabbit, selling Kerry buttons and t-shirts outside the headquarters. I find this disturbing.

BUSH

The headquarters is actually a small office in a rigid-looking building. It's a bit pathetic. There's only three volunteers. With the addition of me, I reminded of the frat house in the movie *Revenge of the Nerds*. For the upcoming weeks, the volunteer schedule boasts a total of five rotating supporters.

The wall has a large poster which reads "Proud to be a Republican." For some reason, there's a drum in the corner of the room.

DEBATE ROUND 2: WHO TREATS THEIR VOLUNTEERS BETTER?

KERRY

People I Encountered: An old woman (name unknown), Igor, Danny.

I walk into the headquarters. I meet a man named Igor. He immediately asks if I want to be Precinct Leader. He tells me it's very prestigious position. I tell him I think being a Precinct

Leader would be "radical."

I'm given a list of phone numbers to call for supporters. The old woman sitting next to me leans over.

"Did you see the debates last night?"

"Yes!"

"That Bush is a big-time loser."

"Yeah!" I exclaim, adding my two-cents. Then I elaborate, "I think *Bush* is a Bozo!"

We smile. We laugh. We have shared a moment. This is what's called campaign camaraderie. As the fun dies down, It's time to lay the cards on the table. I puff out my chest.

"I am Precinct Leader you know!" I didn't mean to pull rank like that, I just don't want her to pull any shenanigans with me!

BUSH

People I Encountered: James, Randell, and two guys who didn't trust me.

My first attempt at volunteering is at an orientation meeting. Down a long, industrial-looking hallway, there's a small table with a cardboard sign that reads "Bush/Cheney in '04," written in Magic Marker. There's about four or five blown up balloons attached to the sign. Two young, clean-cut guys are sitting behind the table. I assume it was their job to mount the balloons on the sign. I walk up. Only one guy introduces himself. The other looks at me like I'm the enemy. Though I'm dressed like an off-duty waiter, I still look scruffy by Republican standards.

"Are you a registered voter?"

"Yes."

The other guy pipes in.

"Registered *Republican*?"

I blink at him for a moment. Is he trying to catch me off-guard?! The two look at each other. I remind them that Ted Nugent is also a Republican, and he ROCKS! I'm told I can volunteer next week, but under certain conditions:

"When you come in next week, can you......look different!"

You mangy-one-tooth-Republican-motherfucker! You're getting my services for free! I'm volunteering you Republican-fuck. Why should it matter what I look like! (despite the fact that I'm only volunteering for the sake of a journalistic comparison).

I come back on Friday. An uptight woman is dissing Kerry.

"......they need to open up those FBI files. It's the only way people will see him for what he is."

A clean-cut man called James momentarily takes me under his wing. He says I can do some phone work. I ask for a better volunteer job than that. James assures me that all volunteers start out by doing phone work. I'm about to tell him that the Democrats made me Precinct Leader—a very prestigious position, but instead I let out a huge sigh and say "whatever." I'm given a brief run-down on what to do. I ask again for a better volunteer job. Again I'm denied.

DEBATE ROUND 3: WHO HAS BETTER FOOD?

KERRY

Lots of potato chips and a variety of generic soda. A man called Danny is giving me some further phone pointers. Suddenly Danny's speech gets slower and he starts looking over my shoulder. Sandwiches are being brought in. Danny must like sandwiches.

BUSH

There are two bowls. One filled with cookies. The other with M&Ms. An hour into the phone work, a man comes in and says "Who wants pizza?" Hooray! It's going to be a Republican pizza-party! Like a bunch of Pavlovian morons, we all raise our hands. Randell, my new Republican volunteer friend, leans over and whispers, "We had pizza last week."

After 45 minutes, there's still no sign of pizza. Is this a reflection on the false promises of the Republicans?!

DEBATE ROUND 4: WHO HAS THE BETTER PHONE SCRIPT?

A good way to read a phone script in an uneasy manner is to use a monotone voice, speaking rapidly and avoiding all punctuation. Here's a sample of each script.

KERRY

Hi, my name is "Dusty" and I am a volunteer with the United Democratic Campaign working to re-elect President Kerry and the Democratic ticket. Can John Kerry and all of the Democratic candidates count on your support when you vote on November 5th?

Wow, that's a lot of responsibility and power riding on these phoned upon citizens' shoulders. Most are happy to vote for Kerry. So to pass the time, I do a little improvising on the speech.

"Will you be voting for Kerry?"

(Old lady voice) "Yes."

"Radical! Did you know Kerry is thinking of buying some baby deer and opening a petting zoo on the White House grounds for visiting children."

(Delighted) "No, I did not know that."

BUSH

This is "Trevor," I am a volunteer with the San Francisco Republican Party. Are you planning to vote for George W. Bush this November?

No foreplay here. It's direct and to the point. Being a Republican in San Francisco is as popular as eating a baby-seal entree at a vegetarian fund-raising dinner. I encountered a lot of angry or confused people.

"Will you be voting for George W. Bush?"

(Long pause) "I speak Russian."

"(Louder) GEORGE W. BUSH! WILL-YOU-VOTE-FOR BUSH!"

"Aaah.. I speak Russian."

"Bush! George W. Bush. Son of George Bush. Will you vote for him?!

"......I speak Russian!"

"Will you vote for George W. Bush?"

"No, I'm going to vote for my man Kerry!"

(Confrontational) "Oh! Are you! Big deal!"

"I think Bush is a Republican son-of-a-bitch."

-click-

I wait thirty seconds and call the number again.

"No really, will you being voting for Bush this November?"

-click-

For no apparent reason, in black Magic Marker I scawl the words "Bush Wears Panties!" in the middle of the phone list and leave.

DEBATE RESULTS:

I would have to say, it was much better to be a campaign volunteer for Kerry. Even though I basically did the same thing for each campaign, I was impressed with being knighted the title "Precinct Leader." See, Democrats want to build self-esteem amongst Americans by creating new jobs, whilst Republicans are worried more about their own image. When they take power, their first concern is to be suspicious of people who "look different" and fuel them with a false promise of pizza that never materializes.

3.
ARNOLD MEIN GOVERNOR!

Some say science fiction writer L. Ron Hubbard started his religion/cult, Scientology, in order to win an arrogant bet amongst his peers. That's my theory on the genesis of the Arnold for Governor campaign, ("I can do anything I want, I'm Arrrrrrnold!"), which has led him to become the leader of the 5th largest economy on the planet. Oh yes, I, like many, love it when my governor drives a Hummer! Now Arnold's aspirations are set on changing the Constitution with his sights set on the White House.

Is it vastly wrong (on many levels) to have a big arrogant Austrian bodybuilder/action star wanting to lead the country? After all he leads our state as a puppet representative (he's good at memorizing lines) for the Bush/Cheney Republican party! What Mickey Mouse is to the Disney Corporation, Arrrrrrnold is to the Republican party—a cute, child-friendly mascot.

Sure Arrrrnold moans on about the children ("We have to do it for the children"…etc….), is a great cheerleader, but what the hell does he stand for besides, as stated in his campaign motto, wanting to give California Back (or Baaaaaaaack!). Then again in *Terminator*, Arrrrrrnold uttered only eighteen lines (and look how successful that movie was!) Simply star-struck, I don't think people can even decipher *movie-Arnold* from *political-Arnold*—the huuuuuuuuge man who would be president!

Questioning who the man behind the body truly is, even before he was "running" for president, I decided to venture to LA, go undercover, and become a volunteer at the Arnold Schwarzenegger for Governor campaign headquarters.

Yes, I wanted to look past the political circus sideshow, and instead, hopefully see qualities reminiscent of a young, idealistic Jack Kennedy..........WHO COULD SQUASH YOUR HEAD LIKE A GRAPE!

So I'll share my meticulously recorded story from the beginning in volunteering for Arnold, just as it happened, in all its hairy detail.

Remember, please don't hate Arrrrrrrnold because he's beautiful!

PREPARATION

In order to fit in, I'm going fully undercover using the pseudonym of John Kimble (Arnold's character in the movie classic *Kindergarten Cop*). My reasoning, it was during the demanding shooting of the film *Kindergarten Cop*, that Arnold had an epiphany—his stand on education was formulated. For my m.o. I'll also adopt the catchphrase *"I'll be baaaaaaack!"* As John Kimble, I'll compensate for my lack of political knowledge by mouthing a vast amount of Arnold movie trivia.

After filling out an information form on the *Join Arnold* website, I receive an email giving the impression Arnold himself personally answered it!

Dear John,

Thank you for signing up to volunteer with Californians for Schwarzenegger. Together, we will bring California back!
There is an enormous disconnect between the people of Cali-

fornia and the politicians of California. We the people, are doing our job—working hard, paying our taxes and raising our families. They, the politicians are not doing their job. They fiddle, they fumble, and they fail. It is time to return California to the people.

We will keep you apprised of ways in which you can help with this campaign. Again thank you for joining the team.

Sincerely,

Arnold Schwarzenegger

I imagine Arnold lumbering over a keyboard with big sausage-like fingers hitting against the keys. After reading and rereading the *fiddle, fumble and fail* line, I push *reply*, acting highly honored.

Hey Arnold! -

Thanks for emailing me back! Wow! I can't believe it's you!
No problem, I'd love to help you out, buddy
By the way, I really like your movies. I've seen
    Terminator over 23 times.
    Hey, I got an idea, let's say HASTA LA VISTA BABY to Gray
Davis! You can
    use that in one of your speeches if you want.

Your pal forever,

John Kimble

ARRRRNOLD FUN FACT: Did you know Arrrrnold underwent a genioplasty-a procedure in which his jaw has been moved back so it no longer juts out. Way to go Arrrrrrrrnold!

I'm giggling, actually giggling like a schoolgirl with a silly crush at my first sight of the ridiculous Arnold for Governor headquarters in Santa Monica. Yes, I'm truly giddy because this *actually* exists in America, situated right in front of me. Pee-sha! to pesky foreigners who laugh at our country!

"You've stolen my identity!" mocks a delighted homeless

man, spouting a line from an Arnold movie (where one's identity was stolen). He notes the huge (or huuuuuuuuge) banner of Arnold in the window, perched in front of the American flag and pointing as if to say, "I am Arrrrrnold!" But which Arnold is it— *Collateral Damage* Arnold? *Running Man* Arnold?! *Predator* Arnold??! The homeless man shakes his head as if to say, "Man this is crazy!"

What the outside was to conjuring giddiness, the inside is even more so. In the world of Arrrrrrnold, everything is big; big balloons, big American flags, big, big, big! The only thing missing is a massive close-up of Arnold's flexed bicep. Large pictures of Arnold with children (*"We have to do it for the children!"*) are scattered along the walls. In one picture, sausage-fingered Arnold hovers over a child playing chess (*"You are playing a game that totally screwwwws with my mind!"*) On another, he's hunched over a child typing on a computer ["In *Terminator*, I was a T-800 much like a compuuuuuter!"]

I approach a man moving a table. He is large, but large in a soft oversized baby sort of way. For some reason this man's eyebrows are singed off (did Arnold do that?!). He is a Republican campaign *specialist* brought in especially from Ohio to whip the Arrrnold headquarters into shape.

"This is the first election I've ever been excited about," I state, then add "I've seen *T2* over 23 times!"

I ask the man who is large (but in a big baby sort of way), if I, John Kimble, can be an Arnold Schwarzenegger for Governor campaign volunteer.

"I want to be a part of history!" (True because nothing as asinine as this has ever happened.)

"What do you do for a living, John?" he asks with a fixed grin that hides stress. His goofy demeanor makes me think it's his first time outside of Ohio.

"I'm a kindergarten teacher," I proclaim, then add, "But I also work in law enforcement!"

He fails to get the reference, leaving me in doubt of his competence in being a Schwarzenegger specialist. But I'm told to come back tomorrow at noon to help get the campaign headquarters ready for the big rally—featuring, you guessed it, Arrrrrnold! I think he likes me; I think he really, really likes me.

Making an excited face, I add, "OK! (pause) I'll be baaaaaack!"

ARRRRNOLD FUN FACT: Did you know Arrrrrnold objects to his wife Maria (a niece of the Kennedy's) wearing trousers? Way to go Arrrrrrrrrnold!

GAME DAY

Noon. The place is bustling, bustling, and extremely hot. Several large TVs blare inane Arrrrnold speech clips with his thick guttural Austrian voice frequently mispronouncing words:

"This is a takeover by the people! I want to be the people's governor!"

I hope other Hollywood celebrities will be on hand as volunteers—Steven Segal blowing up balloons, Ned Beatty making coffee. Rob Lowe, suffering mild megalomania, already offered his services as a *political adviser* (*"When I'm on a movie set, I want to know who the director is!"*). He's qualified, yes, for he starred on a *TV show* about politics. Yes, I love it when celebrities, not the brightest tools in the shed, take up political causes.

I've returned wearing a T-shirt that has Arnold as *The Terminator* holding a large gun. Earlier, at a coffee shop, noting reactions, I see that Arrrrrnold's Terminator image has now taken on political significance, in the same manner as, say, that of Che Guevara.

The headquarters' activity is centered around placement of red, white and blue balloons by a large group of men, who look like body builders of past and present—each wearing identical *Join Arnold* T-shirts. They scurry about like busy worker ants on steroids.

I'm delighted once again to see the man who is large (but in a big baby sort of way). He's more stressed than before, but still grins madly. Looking down at my *Terminator* T-shirt, I can see the wheels of his mind trying to decipher whether the image of his gubernatorial candidate with a large gun is a positive thing or not.

Before reaching a conclusion, he gets mocked by a large volunteer for wearing the collar of his polo shirt up.

"That's how they wore their collars in the movie *Aliens*," teases one of the body builders of the past and present. Embarrassed, the large, baby-soft man quickly puts down his collar.

Joining the fun, I get things going on the right track.

"Now *Aliens*," I inquire while pointing, "Wasn't that directed by James Cameron?"

"Yes," answers one of the body builders. He makes an excited face.

"Was that *before* or *after* he directed *TERMINATOR*?"

"It was right after!"

He progressively gets more excited. We digress into a lively discussion on the intricacies between *Terminator* and *T2*. This is great; just fucking great! My career as an Arnold for Governor campaign volunteer has only been 5 minutes and already I'm discussing a shared affinity for *T2* ....WITH AN ADULT!

Since I arrived early, I'm given one of the most prestigious volunteer tasks. Yes, standing by the entrance, I get to be the public's face (and representative) of the Arnold Schwarzenegger for Governor campaign headquarters!

If anyone (and I do mean anyone) comes into the headquarters with a question concerning the recall election (and hopefully *T2* trivia), I'm there to answer it and direct him to a table full of Arrrrnold brochures and mailing lists. Well, fuck me sideways!

"Why don't you put on a *Join Arnold* T-shirt," the man who is large (but in a big baby sort of way) says, pointing to the backroom.

"OK!" I perk up. Then, "I'll be baaaaaack!"

We chuckle at my "clever" reference (he chuckles a lot less than I do).

While placing on my stylish red, white, and blue *Join Arnold* T-shirt, the campaign headquarters phone rings. I look around. No one's there to answer it. It keeps ringing. I clear my throat. I pick up the phone.

"*Ja! This is Arrrrrnold!*" I answer, putting on my best Austrian accent (giving the impression that Arnold's just hanging out answering phones). Whoever's on the other end seems confused. Once again I forcibly state "*JA! I AM ARRRRRNOLD!*" and then add another *T2* tribute, "*Come with me if you want to live!*"

I quickly hang up the phone. Upon returning (in my new Arnold-wear) the man who is large (but in a big baby sort of way), directs me towards a box of pamphlets that read "*I Want to Be the People's Governor.*"

"Be sure to give everyone one of these and a Join Arnold sticker," he instructs.

I look at the material then add, "OK! (long pause) I'll be baaaaaaaaaack!"

We again laugh (this time, he isn't really laughing).

I'm beginning to think it's fun to support Arnold. He *should* be president! Yes, the most powerful man in the world, teamed up with *True Lies* costar Tom Arnold as vice president, making them a mismatched-buddy presidential pair. Because they're so mismatched, they'll always be shouting lines like, "*I'm getting too old for this shit!*" whenever another Republican-based war is launched against a defenseless country whose policies we don't agree with. And then, through a chain of events, president Arnie will be sent to the frontlines, firing missiles and uttering cute catchphrases.

I, on the other hand, am teamed up with another *Join Arnold* volunteer named Eddy, who used to be a cop for 31 years. Eddie invades my personal space when he talks, and tells me he often saw Arnold eating breakfast at the I-Hop back in the '70's.

"He's a real good guy!" says Eddy, moving in closer, on his reason for supporting Arnold.

In San Francisco, I have NEVER come across a SINGLE person who has shown even the remotest iota of support for Arrrrrnold. Now I'm in an entire building full of them. Who the hell are these people?! Recently, on *Jimmy Kimmel Live*, when asked if he would support Arnold, guest Jim Belushi answered, "Yeah, he's got some good ideas!" So that's what I think the demographic of supporters will be like—Jim Belushi! I want to shake them and go, "Please! Open your eyes for the love of God!"

People, mostly tourists with cameras, walk by generally intrigued by this whole oddity. Some give double-takes. Others have a sense of disbelief; all are intrigued.

"JOIN ARNOLD!" I shout in the doorway like a circus barker. "COME JOIN ARNOLD! My role as representative and (public face) of this fine operation, evokes complete cute-girl-repulsion. A pair of hotties walk by and look at me as if I'm spouting the ramblings of a village idiot. White middle-aged men, on the other hand, love me.

"I think he's a good leader," explains a white middle-aged man, wanting a handful of stickers.

"Are you going to vote for him?" I ask.

"You bet I am," he exclaims like a little boy granted the chance to vote for the Green Lantern. "I just want to hear what he stands for." (DUH!)

I get a little irritated.

"Arnold doesn't *have* to stand for anything," I snap. "He's Arrrrrrnold!"

"Well," the man adds, "tell him he's doing a good job,"

"OK, I will tell Arnold," I confirm (like somehow I'll see him in the breakroom by the watercooler).

Before the man leaves, I add with snorting laughter, "Hey! Let's say *hasta la vista, Gray Davis*!" I wish this man knew how much I hated Arnold.

"JOIN ARNOLD!" I once again, bellow. "COME JOIN ARNOLD!"

Several Austrian tourists come by to show support for one of their country's favorite sons.

One bug-eyed Austrian wanting Arnold stickers, tells me, "We think it's great he's running. It's Bush we don't like."

When I hear him speak, I get mildly excited that he might be related to Arrrrrrnold (sadly he is not).

I nod my head, then add, "Hey, did you know OJ Simpson was originally considered for Arnold's role of the *Terminator*?"

There's a short discussion on what that would have been like along with the differences between the T-800 and the T-1000, interrupted only by two women who look like they shop for a living. I assume they are really old but have gone to great lengths to look much younger.

"Will you tell Arnold that Sheryl and Debbie stopped by?" coyly asks one of the two women (who I assume is actually really old), with the enthusiasm of a teenage girl entering the Justin Timberlake's fan club headquarters

"Yes, Sheryl and Debbie," I exclaim like a Motley Crue roadie with access to Tommy Lee's dressing room. "Are you voting for him?"

"You bet," she says in a flirty Mrs. Robinson manner, then winks.

Members of the press, with extensive camera gear, start filtering in, setting up for the 4:00 rally. Since positioned at the headquarters' entrance, they ask me for official information.

"Can you tell me exactly what will be happening here today?" asks a man with video equipment from CBS News.

Standing up straight, I tell CBS News, "At 4:00 the rally begins. Arnold will be arriving at 5:00. At 5:30 Jean-Claude Van Damme will be joining him on stage to make a political endorsement and give a martial arts demonstration."

I nod my head with authority.

ARRRRNOLD FUN FACT: Did you know for his role in *Junior* Arnold spent time in doctors' waiting rooms in order to learn how pregnant women behave! Way to go Arrrrrrrrnold!

Before things get too crazy, I break for lunch (*"I'll be baaaaaack!"*). I make DAMN SURE to remove my *Join Arnold* T-shirt in order to walk amongst civilians on the 3rd Street Promenade, especially those in front of a political booth supporting reactionary presidential candidate Lyndon LaRouche. These well-meaning kids resemble a bunch of political skater punks. Unlike the pomp (or pompous) and circumstance of the Schwarzenegger headquarters, their small table has a handwritten sign that reads, *Stop the Terminator!* along with *Arnie's Flabby Arms Will Destroy Californians!* These are the lone Don

Quixotes stabbing at the giant action hero windmill with their little handwritten signs.

It's time to stir things up!

Approaching, I make DAMN SURE I'm not being spied on by Arnold's goons taking numerous snapshots which I'll be presented with at the headquarters right before a blanket goes over my head and I'm hit with large sticks, as they shout, "No one makes Arrrrrnold look stupid!" (He can do it on his own!)

"Hey!" I say to one of the political skater punks. "Do you know that Arnold Schwarzenegger is going to be appearing at a rally one block away at 4:00?"

"No way," exclaims the political skater punk. "Hey guys!" he yells to the rest of his ragamuffin crew, sharing the news.

"Yeah, Schwarzenegger's going to be there at 4:00," I restate, scribbling on a piece of paper. "Here's the address!" I then add, "But remember, if you see me, you got to act like you don't know me!"

I hand the one-I-assume-is-the- leader the address of Arrrrnold's campaign volunteer headquarters. For the second time this week, I feel giddy. I conclude my lunch break by temporarily *switching teams* and helping handout *Arnie's Geek Act Is Falling Flat* leaflets.

ARRRRNOLD FUN FACT: Did you know childhood friends of Arrrnold stated that he often said his goals in life were to move to America, become an actor, and marry a Kennedy. Arrrrnold has done all three! Yay Arrrrrrrnold!

Slightly paranoid, I apprehensively return to the Join Arnold headquarters.

"We have to be more security conscious!" exclaims the man who is large, (but in a big baby sort of way), who I think knows of my recent double-life on the La Rouche campaign trail.

I'm about to hand in my *Join Arnold* T-shirt, when he points to a velvet nightclub rope. "Don't let anyone past here!" he exclaims, instead, knighting me with added power amongst other volunteers.

I nod incessantly, repeating aloud what he just said.

"Watch everyone who comes in. If they say they are here to

volunteer but didn't check with me yesterday, don't let them in. *We need to keep out the riffraff!"*

It's interesting there's concern about riffraff, yet there's NO concern on background checks for their very own volunteers. I AM THE RIFFRAFF!

"This is a very controversial election," he continues. "There'll be women's groups picketing later. Yesterday, someone threw an egg at Arnold!"

"Arnold was cool about it," adds one of the large body builders of the past and present. "He just threw off his jacket and said, *'Where's the bacon!'"*

Of course Arrrrrrnold said that; that's how Arrrrrrnold speaks—in asinine catchphrases.

As it gets closer to 4:00, the carnival rolls in for the circus sideshow. The already hot headquarters is much hotter. A multitude of TV cameras are set up on one side of the room (I think *Entertainment Tonight* is here!). A hot dog stand and popcorn booth are put into place. This has all the excitement of a *Planet Hollywood* opening! The large TVs continue spewing Arnold's political philosophy.

"This is a takeover by the people! I want to be the people's governor!"

As I stand at the entrance, arms folded, it's reassuring to know they have put *me* in charge of security. I can put that on my resume: *Security for Arnold Schwarzenegger*! I seize the opportunity to go completely *Mad with Power!*

"Can you *please* get on the other side of the rope!" I bark at a guy who's obviously been working here all morning. With others, I take a more apathetic approach. "Go right on in," I tell some French tourists wanting to take photos.

Slowly, Arnold supporters start lining up down the block, along with the arrival of the first Schwarzenegger protestor trying to find the others. She holds a sign that reads, *All Robot. No Human Parts!*

With the appearance of a professional-looking security team (suit jackets and earpieces), I'm relinquished of my duty as security chief for the headquarters. I'm told to wait in back with the rest of the volunteers and help myself to some chicken wings, ironically donated by *Hooters* (It's good to see *Hooters* supporting a political cause). What controversy!

The newly arrived campaign volunteer staff is a sad bunch. One older, effeminate man wearing an ascot, holds a bouquet of roses with a card on it that reads *Arnold* (I think he has a crush).Another concerned man asks his wife if his *Join Arnold* T-shirt should be worn tucked-in or not. Others slightly resemble Arnold in haircut and build.

While yet others frantically prepare for Arnold's arrival, I take the opportunity to explore, unhindered, every damn nook-and-cranny of the campaign headquarters. I go down a long hallway where Arnold will enter through the back alley. It's reassuring to know that any buffoon (or terrorist) could show up early, claim to be a campaign volunteer, and then get free reign of the place. (It's a darn good thing I'm on the side of good!) The security team should know this. Even Arnold's idiotic movie plots are more cunning than this.

I make it to the end of the hallway, right by the very door where Arrrrnold will be entering, noting the many places I could hide if I wanted to. Just then another door swings opens. A large member of the security team comes out. He has a look of concern. (Am I busted?!)

"I wouldn't use that bathroom unless you can find a plunger!" he tells me. He then walks away.

ARRRRNOLD FUN FACT: Did you know that Arnold has a soccer stadium in his hometown of Graz Austria named after him? Wow Arrrrrrnold!

A marachi band (Arnold show's affinity for the Latino community!) assembles on stage and starts playing. More protestors organize outside with varied and imaginative signs.

I, along with a woman wearing two carpal tunnel wrist guards, and a middle-aged lady who used to be mayor of a town close by, are given the most prestigious volunteer position—manning the front table filled with Arnold propaganda. Everyone who enters the building has to interact with us. We are a team! We are the "A" team! We are Arnold!

"Let security know if you see anyone acting suspicious or bad-mouthing Arnold," briefs the security chief (Great, I won't look in a mirror). "This is still a private party and we don't have to let them in!" He makes a line with his arm right in front of me. "Right now, no one gets passed here!"

Outside, Arnold's large goons openly mock the scrawny protestors like schoolyard bullies.

"He's the Terminator! Who the fuck are you going to vote for," yells a goon at a petite woman.

"Gary Coleman!" she shouts sarcastically.

"What a bunch of kooks!" exclaims the middle-aged former mayor (who actually uses the word "kooks."). She doesn't share my inner-delight with the now large number of protesters (bless their hearts). She points to a sign that reads "Arnold's Daddy Was A Nazi!"

"Oh, yeah! Well you are a bunch of commies!" she retorts, applying my favorite personal pet peeve: Republicans who accuse those who don't agree with their policies as being un-American.

"Yeah, commies!" I echo her sentiments, in order to gain her confidence.

The sign is eclipsed by another reading "Governor Gang Bang!" This is enough to make the carpal tunnel sufferer, now sweating profusely, steam.

"Oh yeah, well where were you when Clinton was in office!" she says, looking towards me for support.

"Yeah!" I reply, fully enjoying the voyeuristic aspect of hearing Republicans when they are angry.

"Are those 'goonbas' still at it?!" interjects a clean-cut man with an Armani tie.

"Yeah. What a bunch of kooks!" I state. "A real bunch of kooks!"

The man in the Armani tie confides in me (Me!) his conspiracy theory, "You know, the unions hired those people to come down here. They did the same at the Bush election!"

"What a bunch of goonbas," I exclaim, using their 1950's slang as the Marachi band kicks into La Bamba.

In groups of threes, people start filing in, as security looks through everyone's bags (except the volunteers). The supporters are white, and *very* white.

They are requested to fill out forms, the majority having sojourned from open-minded Orange County. An animated man, trying to get his college professor wife to be Arnold's education adviser, intensely talks to me like I can personally pass on messages to Arnold. I nod my head, then add, "Did you know that a young Bill Paxton appeared in *The Terminator* playing a punk with purple hair?"

He stops babbling his diatribe, and looks at me with a crazed look in his eye, interrupted by, an old man in an Uncle Sam hat being escorted out.

"Tell him all the shirts they're wearing are from China!" he screams.

"I've been to a protest before," remarks a 12-year old kid from Manhattan Beach, who, along with his brother is wearing a blue button down shirt and khaki pants. How cute—young protestors who look like they were probably dragged here against their will by their cranky Republican parents.

Almost wanting to tussle his hair, I ask the little rapscallion, "What did you protest?" He looks at his brother and smiles.

"We protested CNN for their biased coverage of Bush!"

So much for wanting to tussle his hair.

A TV camera is shoved in my face.

"Hi, we're from Fox 11 News. If it's Ok, can we ask you a few questions?"

"You bet you can!!!!!!" I exclaim, knowing that I'm going to reply with the stupidest answers known to humanity.

"Why do you support Arnold Schwarzenegger?"

I look directly into the camera.

"You know, I must have seen *Terminator 2* over 23 times!" I nod. "How often do you get to vote for your favorite movie stars! Robert De Niro isn't running, so I'm voting for Arnold!"

Then a throw in a few chants of "Arnold! Arnold! Arnold!" I ask the cameraman if I can add one more thing.

"Sure."

"Hey,! I think it's time we said......HASTA LA VISTA, GRAY DAVIS!"

The Channel 9 News, a documentary crew, and several photographers follow them, as I continue spewing inanities.

"Why do you think Arnold will make a good leader?"

"I like what Arnold represents, and that is a man with huge muscles and a big gun! It's time we had a governor that can really kick serious ass!"

I throw in another "Hasta la vista, Gray Davis!" also mentioning that character actor Lance Henriksen was the first choice for the role of the Terminator.

"Hey! I think it's time we said......HASTA LA VISTA, GRAY DAVIS!" I add.

Republicans continue to pile in. It's getting even hotter. The carpal tunnel sufferer starts complaining she's going to pass out. The Marachi band plays with added frenzy. Something is about to go down soon.

I look out from amongst the crowd of protestors. Well sodomize me with a crusty pirate's hook! By complete coincidence, one of my best friends in the whole world, Johnny Hardwick, is among them, screaming into a bullhorn about lying Arnold's taking campaign funds from large corporations.

I stand glaring with the other stoned-faced, *Join Arnold* goons. I finally make eye contact with Johnny. It takes a moment for him to register why I'm inside Arnold Schwarzenegger's campaign headquarters wearing a *Join Arnold* T-shirt. He momentarily thinks I might be a Schwarzenegger supporter. Not wanting to blow my cover, I wink. It sinks in exactly what I'm up to. This is followed by large volumes of laughter on his part.

Just then, from across the street, in full view of everyone, a large 2-story banner is dropped down the side of the building that reads, *ARNOLD YOU'RE TERMINATED!*

It's simply beautiful. This pisses off the sweaty carpal tunnel sufferer.

"What a bunch of kooks!" she cries. "How would you like to be Arnold and come to your headquarters and see THAT!" (Poor Arrrrrnold!)

"What a bunch of *goonbas*," I add.

"I wish I had my Glock!" she shares, giving insight into her personal weaponry.

"I'd put that infra-red scope right on them!" "Yeah!" I knowledgeably agree. "TERMINATED!" Then, for no reason I add, "HASTA LA VISTA, GRAY DAVIS!"

ARRRRNOLD FUN FACT: Did you know that Arrrrnold was the first private citizen in the US to own a Humvee? Way to go Arrrrrnold!

On stage, a multi-ethic special interest group assembles, including an African American body builder wearing a World's Gym tank top (he keeps flexing his grotesque muscles). They are pretty much the only minorities in the joint. I guess this shows that Arrrrrrnold knows minorities and likes them (particularly bodybuilders!).

The assembled crowd starts chanting, "ARNOLD! ARNOLD! ARNOLD!"

I wonder how Arrrrnold will make his big entrance? Will he drive his Humvee through the plate glass window dressed in commando gear? Or will he pulley down from the opposite building, wearing night goggles and dodging bullets? I'm wrong on both accounts.

"Please welcome, Maria and Arnold Schwarzenegger!"

The crowd goes apeshit.

"ARNOLD! ARNOLD! ARNOLD!"

Arnold Schwarzenegger (star of *Last Action Hero*) and his wife Maria (Is she wearing trousers?!) both in casual wear, simply stroll on stage to a sea of flashbulbs. Arnold is huuuu-uuge! They both look like two tan androids. Actually seeing Arnold in person puts in perspective the multi-levels of how utterly ridiculous this freak show is.

"ARNOLD! ARNOLD! ARNOLD!"

The protestors outside are now making loud chicken noises. Some pound on the glass. I look out. YES! There's the political skater punks! They sing their rendition of *Edelweiss*, involving Arnold's link to Enron and how it screwed all of California.

I feel proud as they scream into a bullhorn, knowing I'm

fully responsible for their presence, as we hit 'em from both the outside and the inside.

The protesting bullhorns and chicken noises are so loud, that they have to close the doors, as things are kicked off by a prayer (of course) from Arnold's monsignor. All the Republicans lower their heads.

"Oh strong and faithful God.....blah, blah, blah, etc....."

Then Arnold speaks! This is history in the making, similar to what others felt hearing Jack Kennedy or Martin Luther King speak for the very first time.

"It's an honor to be here with you!" he says in broken guttural English. "Thanks to all the volunteers, this is your home!"

"ARNOLD! ARNOLD! ARNOLD!"

And then Arnold's android wife (a member of the Kennedy family mind you) says a few supportive words. She's one of those women who are beautiful to the point of creepy.

"I'm glad to be here on behalf of a candidate who I know would make a difference in this country.........ARNOLD SCHWARZENEGGER!" (I could almost hear Ted Kennedy turning in his grave, if he happened to be dead.)

Someone yells out something about Enron. Hurrah! It's one of the political skater punks (how did he get in?!). He's quickly escorted out of the building by Arnold's goons.

Arnold talks more about the issues.

"My wife, she is the greatest mother in the world. She was here for days, putting up balloons, helping decorate this place."

Wait?! Arnold is lying. I saw all the balloons being put up and his wife (in trousers or not) wasn't here at all. Arnold philosophizes.

"When I was bodybuilding, my wife always said don't eat more pie. [Huh?!] She would read every script to every movie I've done." He turns his huuuuuge body towards her. "Maria I love you today more than ever!"

Arnold then decides to rally his supporters. He does this by showing how smug and arrogant he is.

"People say to me, Arnold, you have the greatest job in the world. You make so much money. You have the most beautiful wife. You own so many businesses. Why do you want to do this?"

He pauses for dramatic effect.

"Because I could no longer watch and.....TAKE IT ANY-MORE!"

Poor Arnold! Have things gotten that bad where the man with the greatest job in the world, so much money, and the most beautiful wife, could no longer TAKE IT ANYMORE!

If he' so concerned why doesn't he offer California one of his over-inflated movie salary checks? He could do a sequel to *Kindergarten Cop* and that would $40 million right there! Or perhaps he could tell his Republican buddies not to spend another $87 billion on a pointless war?!

"It's time to give back (or baaaaack), this is why I'm running for governor of this great state!"

"ARNOLD! ARNOLD! ARNOLD!"

The crowd has been blindsided into thinking they've heard Arnold speak about the issues?! I would love to see someone like James Carville tear Arnold a new one. I want to shake these people and wake them up. Here's a man, who when asked how he'd deal with the states $38.2 billion dollar deficit, said, " Maria and I teach our kids basic principals. We teach them: don't spend more money than you have....I promise that's what I would teach Sacramento!"

That, my friends, is a final nail for the dumbing down of America.

He concludes by saying his usual diatribe about the children, ("We have to do it for the children"...etc....)

"ARNOLD! ARNOLD! ARNOLD!"

Before departing, the star-struck Republicans rush the stage. Arnold shakes hands. Many simply want his autograph. A large guy next to me, in a sleeveless T-shirt, holds a copy of Arnold's bodybuilding book for him to sign. I make my way up front, sticking out my hand. Arnold's jutting jaw smiles down at me. Arnold's hand is huuuuuuuuge. I hold up a photo of Arnold carrying a big gun for him to sign. I madly wave it in his direction, shouting my favorite line from *Kindergarten Cop* ("*I don't have a tuuuumor! I don't have a tuuuumor!"*).

But both the guy with the bodybuilding book and I are sadly disappointed; Arrrrrnold and his tan, android wife, make for the exit, leaving people swapping stories on what it was like to see movie star Arnold Schwarzenegger.

My volunteer compatriot, who used to be the mayor of a town close by, is clearly star-struck. Her face is blushing.

"He shook my hand! He actually shook my hand!" she utters with a dreamy look on her face. Now, this is a woman who was a *mayor*, an actual mayor of a city, and she's star-struck!

"Was his hand huuuuuuge?" I ask.

"Yes," she replies like a hyperventilated 'N Sync fan. "It was!"

When the rally ends, the two Republican kids, the ones who protested CNN, caught in the joys of childhood, are out on the street waving *Join Arnold* signs at passing cars. I'm asked if I want to join some of the campaign volunteers for chicken wings down at *Hooters.* I decline.

The man who is large (but in a big baby sort of way) looks like a stressed, but proud, father. His collar is back up. He tells me to come back tomorrow, excitedly explaining the agenda of making phone calls, handing out pamphlets, and other great campaign volunteer activities. I nod my head vigorously, then hold up the photo of Arnold carrying a big gun.

"That sounds great. (Pause) Hey, can you sign this for me. It would mean a lot!"

He seems confused, especially when I then run over and unite with my protestor friends, leaving him with the photo in his doughy hands. Yes, this is the side I need to belong on and fight for. Perhaps California wouldn't be in so much debt if we didn't have to put up with the likes Arnold, Gary Coleman, Larry Flynt, and a cast of countless other buffoons wasting our hard-earned tax dollars for a momentary ego trip, when the millions spent on this ridiculous recall could be used for, say, education......for the children!

I turn to the man who is large (but in a big baby sort of way). Picking up a banner, I cry, "I'll be baaaaack!"

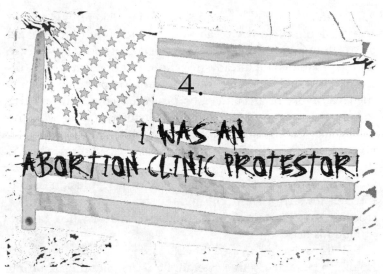

4.
I WAS AN ABORTION CLINIC PROTESTOR!

"**P**eople will be driving by, flipping you off," Charlie explains over the phone. "If you can take that sort of thing, then you're our kind of guy!"

"People flip me off all the time," I enthusiastically respond. "So yeah, I can take it."

"OK, we meet Saturday mornings at 8:30 in front of the *Temple of Moloch.* Or, as I like to call it, *Plan Deathhood!*"

"Can I bring my own protest signs?" I ask Charlie

"What kind of signs do you have?" he responds with what could be mistaken for slight giddiness.

"I made some with poster board and markers."

"Don't worry," Charlie assures me. "We have plenty of signs here!"

Going by the American-sounding name, Monroe Peterson, I gain sympathy with Charlie by claiming that I was an aborted fetus who was reincarnated back to spread the word that abortion is wrong. Yes, the best way to know how extremists think is by becoming one of them. Time to match their fanaticism with my fanaticism!

Saturday morning I venture to Planned Parenthood in San Jose for a fun-filled day of abortion clinic protesting. Situated across from a YMCA in a very quiet neighborhood, my intense fellow protestors are already in action, stationed in front. Following the ever-interesting aspect of abortion protests, which is the creative use of arts-and-crafts projects, I got a little creative myself. I arrive carrying a baby doll floating in a jar with the words *Stop Now!* written on the outside, while I'm adorned in an elaborate outfit with more, tiny baby dolls taped to my shirt to drive home my point.

"Charlie sent me!" I proclaim to avoid confusion as I'm directed towards a short guy manning a street corner, with a stocking cap, mustache, dark sunglasses, and a video camera around his neck.

"I think I only missed one Saturday," Charlie professes, holding a large sign; a true veteran, he's been picketing abortion clinics every weekend morning for the last seventeen years.

Charlie was right. It's so true. They DO have signs; a million times more elaborate than I could ever fathom. Their signs are huge. Some are rigged to the back of a truck with large American flags. In bold, graphic colors, these signs are the most disturbing images I've ever seen. Subtlety is not the order of the day in the abortion-clinic-protesting-arena. Looking like a blender accident gone array, bloody, mangled twisted fetus images are far more frightening than anything in the movie *The Seed of Chucky* (5th installment in the *Child's Play* horror film series).

Sheepishly, I hide my homemade sign with a hand-scrawled, "HEY-HEY! HO-HO! ABORTION HAS GOTTA GO!," feeling like a complete amateur.

"We're just a fellowship of guys who feel it's the Lord's calling to do this. We do it for the Lord and we do it for the babies," Charlie explains, seeming generally pleased to have me on board, as I feel slightly scared shitless.

"Let's save two lives at a time," I weakly smile, letting out a nervous laugh.

"Are you Catholic or Protestant?" Charlie asks (as if these are the only two options for protestors).

"*Catholic,* "I find myself trumpeting (since my religion option was not made available). Its explained that *Dave* is in charge of showing the Catholics the ropes, while Charlie breaks in the new Protestant recruits. If the goal is non-abortion-ness, why don't they throw down their differences and protest as one united force? Instead, pro-life-ers are as segregated as a Northern Irish neighborhood.

"I met many women who have had abortions," Charlie admits. "I met one woman who's had four abortions, and I told her, when you get to heaven, you'll get to hold those babies."

I nod my head vigorously. Around the corner, a group of roughly 35 people, on their monthly excursion from a local Catholic Church, are on the sidewalk in the midst of an intense prayer hymn. Some have brought their small kids, making it a family outing.

"It's a bit of a slow day," professes Dave, a soft-spoken older man with glasses and a crew neck sweater, almost apologetically before he shows me the protesting ropes. "On Saturdays, we usually go to the Planned Parenthood in Santa Clara first."

"What's the deal with the dogs?" I inquire, noting several stern-looking Planned Parenthood workers, adorned in Planned Parenthood smocks, suspiciously looking on while monitoring the facility's parking lot. Several have vicious German Shepherds on leashes, who are running and jumping around, ready for action if a protestor crosses the line.

"They're there to intimidate us," Dave explains. He points to a large man with a graybeard, knowing all the Planned Parenthood workers by first name, "One time *Curtis* let his dog jump *at* us, and then he said, *there's your dinner!* Can you imagine the mindset of that?"

I shrug my shoulders, not being able to imagine this. Meanwhile, on the sidewalk a frowning man holds a large sign that reads *Unborn Jesus,* with an illustrated version of exactly what Unborn Jesus would look like. Unborn Jesus (not to be confused with *Kung-Fu Grip Jesus* or *Sporty Spice Jesus*) has a full beard (quite a feat for one who is unborn). A Planned Parenthood worker, an older woman, comes over to the edge of the parking lot and starts humming loudly in order to disrupt the protestors and their hymns. Soft-spoken Dave shakes his head in disapproval.

"That's Lilly," Dave gestures, introducing a new cast member. He then, inquires why I want to become a sidewalk counselor. I feed Dave exactly the answer he wants to hear.

"I want to save two lives at a time!"

Soft-spoken Dave looks pleased.

Then I add, "Also, I think it would be a great way to meet women," elaborating, in a subtle way, the obvious aspect that I already know they put out. Before Dave can fully compute this, I once again quickly add, "Yeah, that's it, I want to save two lives at a time."

Dave assumes the Mr. Miyagi role in our *Karate Kid* training. "We can't block the driveway. When you see a car pulling into the parking lot, go up to the window and say, "Can I give you some literature." He explains in a soft-tone, motioning towards a pamphlet that reads "*Simply* get up *and* walk away," with a *God Bless America* sticker on the back.

"One woman read the literature then drove away. That's one child I've saved, and I feel pretty good about that," he states, then refers to Planned Parenthood as an "*abortion mill.*"

A beat-up late model car, driven by a scared-looking teenage guy, pulls into the driveway. Soft-spoken Dave saunters over and hands him some literature through the driver's side window. Minutes later a teenage girl gets into the beat-up car. Dave comes back over to me.

"The Hispanics, you'll find, are usually quite respectful," he softly states in reference to the interaction. As the beat-up car drives away, Dave suddenly snaps, snarling, "Yeah, but he still went and had it killed!"

Handing me a cross that's attached to some beads, Dave asks, "Do you do the Rosary?"

I respond, "Oh, you bet I do. You bet I do, indeed!"

I join the others, filing into one of the two parallel lines on the sidewalk. Some eye me with mild suspicion, so I start mouthing the words to "For He's A Jolly Good Fellow," since I'm clueless to knowing the Rosary, as a microphone is passed down the line to allow each person to do a verse (Don't stop on me, please!). Our prayer vigil is concluded how? With a rousing chorus of *God Bless America!* (I shit you not!). I DO know the words to that song. Piping in with added fervor, I include an arm-swing to my singing presentation.

"GOD BLESS AMERICA..........."

I personally *love* the patriotic connection. (But isn't trying to deny people their rights pretty much a fascist attribute?) The song continues:

"GOD BLESS AMERICA............."

"Here comes Carl," someone yells as everyone smirks. The focus shifts. A man rounds the corner dressed in, I again shit you not, A GRIM REAPER OUTFIT! Carl has gone all out for the Saturday morning abortion protest—he's the clown prince of abortion protests! The antsy little kids' attention goes from *Unborn Jesus* to Carl. They go wild. The kids are thrilled. Here comes Carl in his skeleton mask, long, black hooded robe, carrying a sickle and holding two large signs that read *Death Sold Here* and *The Killing Place*.

"Mommy! Mommy! Can we go talk to the skeleton? Can we go talk to the skeleton?! Can we Mommy?!" screams the excited little kids who, in the midst of childhood, run over to the Grim Reaper. With the addition of costumes, I did not know abortion protests could be sooooooo much fun.

"Do a lot of people dress up in costumes at these protests?" I inquire of Dave.

"Sometimes."

"In general," Charlie adds, coming over from the Protestant side to see the spectacle, "It takes a little bit of guts to do this, so it's part of it."

"Is it okay if I come back in costume next week?" I ask.

"Sure. What do you have in mind?"

I make an excited face. "Well, I have this great Ninja costume!" Making a few Ninja moves, I demonstrate how that could be a benefit to the entire operation.

Dave points at Carl. "I one time saw an abortion mill worker dressed in the same costume for Halloween. Think of the mindset of that," he adds pointing to his head. Dave can be such a downer sometimes.

The families from the monthly church group slowly depart, leaving behind the no-nonsense hardcore abortion protestors, comprised entirely of slightly hardened middle-aged men. The kid stuff is over!

Glen, one of the hardened men with an intense look of a prisoner of war camp survivor, pulls out a large, yellow tape player, cranks up the volume, and points it directly towards the Planned Parenthood parking lot.

"That's something Glen likes to do," Dave explains softly.

"This is my prayer medallion!" Glen sarcastically expresses, pointing to a photo of Planned Parenthood worker Curtis pinned to his jacket, throwing a nasty glare towards real-life Curtis in the parking lot. "Have fun voting for Kerry," he mockingly adds since this is the moral dividing line between which presidential candidate their friends will vote for. Glen cranks up the tape player louder, as if we were US troops trying to get a South American warlord out of his compound by blasting rock music. The tape methodically explains how to pop the head off a fetus.

"This is one of their very own tapes. It's a doctor explaining the procedure of how to give a partial abortion." Dave adds with disgust, "They actually applaud at the end. Can you believe it? Think of the mindset of that?"

"Fuck off!" someone suddenly screams from a passing car, flipping us the finger. Glen quickly grabs his camera and starts snapping photos of the vehicle.

"I usually take a picture of anyone who flips us the bird," Glen explains while I pull out my camera and also start snapping away. "It's for our own protection."

"Just remember, it's against the law to take a picture of anyone going into the abortion mill," soft-spoken Dave calmly advises, correlating the law to his other passion. "Just like you can't take a picture of someone going into a dirty bookstore. We used to take pictures of guys coming out of the dirty bookstores and then send it right to their homes," he says with a smirk.

Soft-spoken Dave continues, "Back in '89, I was with Operation Rescue. We used to block the doors of an abortion clinic. One time we had 800 people out there! A few of us ended up going to jail," he adds with a smile and hint of nostalgia. He recalls the golden age among the most radical pro-life groups. They used to employ bicycle locks along with human chains and sometimes automobiles to keep people out of abortion clinics.

"It's now a felony to block the entrance of an *abortion mill,*" Dave spews with revulsion. "You can block an animal testing clinic, but you can't block an abortion mill. Think about the mindset of that?"

"Are you reminiscing about the good old days?" Glen pipes in, as we all share a hearty chuckle. The moment's short-lived. A San Jose police car pulls into the Planned Parenthood parking lot. Glen pulls out his camera and snaps a photo of the patrol car.

"That's not a good idea, Glen," soft-spoken Dave advises. This is going to be good. A direct police confrontation! With both hands kept on his belt, an officer gets out of the squad car, giving a "here we go again" look.

"How many times do I have to tell you, you can't have your signs on public property," he sternly proclaims, gesturing at the numerous graphically horrific, *Seed of Chucky* blender accident signs, resting against trees and wired to street traffic signs for all the peaceful neighborhood residents to enjoy.

Glen immediately gets in his face. Soft-spoken Dave tries to calmly mediate.

"Well, how come you can hang political signs on traffic signs," Glen angrily retorts. He *actually* starts arguing. "We're expressing our right to freedom of speech!" What about that sign," hotheaded Glen proclaims, pointing across the street to a *YMCA Construction Parking* sign, posted in front of, well, the YMCA parking lot.

Soft-spoken Dave suddenly snaps, screeching in an angry tone, raising his voice for the first time today, "WE DON'T WANT TO BE DISCRIMINATED AGAINST!"

Whoa! The Grim Reaper and I look at each other in disbelief. Glen storms off to get some reinforcements. Minutes later he returns with a stack of legal papers from the *Life Legal Defense Foundation* and presents them to the officer.

"What are you showing me here?" asks the annoyed officer. Glen points to various sections. The annoyed officer shakes his head. "This says nothing about having the right to post your signs on public property."

Showing a little Fifth Amendment spirit, I help out the cause, by bellowing a chorus of "GOD BLESS AMERICA!"

Dave advises me to save my singing for later. The police officer sternly lays down the law. "You can have your signs, but you have to carry them, do you understand?" He goes back to his patrol car, waiting, in order to assure that this actually happens.

"Can you hold this sign?" Glen sharply requests, handing me a very large, horrific sign with a very disturbing graphic color image and words reading *"The 8th Week!"*

"Sure, no problem," I cry with new enthusiasm, as I grab the highly disturbing sign and take my place on the side of the road. (If anyone's interested, graphically, horrific abortion protest signs can be ordered from a company in Dousman Wisconsin.) I now find myself manning a street corner, side-by-side, next to the guy in the skeleton mask dressed like the Grim Reaper. Whoever Carl is, inside the Grim Reaper costume, he seems to be talking to himself. Peering inside his mask, I notice yellow bloodshot eyes. Two Planned Parenthood workers seeing me in action, start animatedly whispering, clearly putting me on their *crazy-list*. For their benefit, I throw in some loud, screaming chants with the spirit of a 49ers fan:

"2, 4, 6, 8!
WHO DO WE APPRECIATE?
JESUS! JESUS! YAH, STOP ABORTION"

Drivers passing give double-takes at my sign. Not so much in a manner that we've changed their opinion on the hot abortion issue, but more in a manner that my sign is of a bloody, hacked up fetus projected in a quiet neighborhood; they're not tickled pink about our overbearing presence. The aforementioned flipping off by passing cars continues, along with various shouts of disapproval.

"Kids can see that, you know," screams an angry bicyclist.

"Well, what about all the kids who *can't* see it," I retort, seizing abortion protestor logic.

Children being picked up from the YMCA, perhaps from a tap-dancing class, look highly disturbed. Perhaps it's my sales pitch? I add a big, hearty smile and a wave to my protesting approach, enthusiastically lifting my horrific sign up higher, gesturing to cars as if beckoning them to a junior high charity car wash.

"Can you move your sign?" screams a woman with a teenage daughter in an SUV, trying to depart Planned Parenthood.

"Hey! Free Speech," I yell, taking a cue from Glen, then burst into another chorus of "God Bless America."

"You're blocking the view of the traffic," Dave explains, motioning me out of the way.

"Can I give you some literature?" I shout at another car, filled with a distraught passenger, in the millisecond window of opportunity as they pull into the driveway.

Somehow I have that uneasy feeling that I'm suddenly going to get a lead pipe to the back of my head, either from being discovered as an imposter pro-life protestor, or from some angry boyfriend with a newly traumatized girlfriend. Regardless, a lead pipe to the back of my head seems not out of the question.

Still, Glen invites me down for next weekend.

"I usually get down here at 7 am."

"Oh, yeah. Well, I'll be down here at 6:30 am," I state, topping him on his fanaticism. Getting ready to leave, I grab my jar with the baby doll floating in water. The jar accidentally slips between my fingers and falls to the ground. It smashes. My eyes well up with tears as I give Glen a beaten look.

5.
ANGRY ABORTION LETTER

H ere's a news flash. The entire abortion issue is very controversial in our country. No I'm serious. If one writes a story about the abortion issue, and takes a very strong side on the matter, he is bound to letter of dissatisfaction from those who support the complete opposite viewpoint. Seriously! In fact, here's an actual letter I got when the Abortion Protest story first appeared:

> **Go to hell. Go straight to hell. Do not pass Go. Do not collect one damned thing:** I can't quite figure your article out. Are you pro-life, pro-abortion, or just pro-stupid? These people who were protesting this clinic have the right to do so, under the Constitution, just the same as you do.
>
> Obviously you are so self-absorbed and brainwashed by the liberal left deathmongers and satanic, atheistic secularists that you would jeopardize your eternal soul by blaspheming the name of Jesus! You should thank God Almighty that your mother didn't abort you! However, after giving that some thought, I kind of wish she had. Then there would be one less idiot in this world who thinks he knows more than God.

I hope you like warm weather, 'cause where your [sic] going, it's going to be HOT! HOT! HOT!

I pray for your enlightenment, sir. That you might come out of the darkness and into the light that is Jesus Christ.

Weather [sic] you believe it or not, he suffered and died for you. He loves you more than anyone can — even yourself.

Ronald Emanuel

Bishop

6.

LEGENDS OF THE CONSERVATIVES- CELEBRITY EDITION!

(Brought to you by
The League for a Greater Right Wing Tomorrow)

Legends of the Conservative salutes................Vincent Gallo!!!! Who-the-hell would have thought underground film iconoclast, Vincent Gallo, would be one full-fledged conservative mofo? Yes, the one-time indie-film "It-boy" is a Ronald Reagan-loving, full-blooded right-wing reactionary, or as he likes to describe himself, a "Constitutionalist."

Hat's off to you Vincent Gallo; glad to have you on board the conservative bandwagon.

BORN: April 11th, 1962

BIRTHPLACE: Buffalo, New York

OCCUPATION: One-time heroin chic Calvin Klein model, actor/director

VINCENT GALLO'S PET PEEVES

While addressing a Young Republican Club, Vincent Gallo expressed to the group, he loves President Bush and loathes "self-serving" lefties, particularly "that commie crawfish, Al

Franken," and that "destructive hog," Michael Moore. Vincent Gallo wrapped up the fun-filled evening, expressing he thinks politicians spend too much time pandering to special interests like "the gays, the AARP, handicapped groups."

Yay, Vincent Gallo!

EARLY CONSERVATIVE GALLO

Vincent Gallo is the real deal when it comes to conservatism. "There's a picture of me at 6 years old campaigning for Richard Nixon. I've always been the same. Always. I was against hippies."

DID YOU KNOW?

Did you know when Vincent Gallo sees Pat Buchanan speak on TV, he gets "thrilled"? "He's one of the brightest, cleverest, funniest people I've ever heard speak," Gallo said in an interview. "I like so many right-wing politicians. I idolize Reagan and Nixon."

VINCENT GALLO FUN FACT

Vincent Gallo used to play in a band with Jean-Michel Basquiat, the famous artist who dated Madonna, and overdosed on heroin.

VINCENT GALLO HAS A WOODY FOR THE CONSTITUTION

"When I'm reading James Madison, he speaks for me. I don't feel disenfranchised. When I read Madison or the Constitution, I relate to the broad-mindedness, the bigger picture. There isn't anything in my life that's oppressed me in a real way or was beyond my control."

GALLO ON GALLO

"When I say I'm conservative, that's being radical, that's moving forward in a real way. Liberals are small-minded manipulators; they pander to special interest groups just for the sake of power. Don't you find it odd that if you segregate women, blacks, homosexuals, and Jews, they vote in such radical numbers in one party? Where's the balance there?

Way to go Vincent Gallo!

VINCENT GALLO FUN FACT

Vincent Gallo was a friend of Studio 54's Steve Rubell!

GALLO'S BIG OBSESSION

Vincent Gallo is obsessed with Bill O'Reilly. As he puts it, he's "dying - dying - to go on Bill O'Reilly's show."

Can't wait to see it!

GALLO'S CONSERVATIVE DREAM WOMAN

The star of *Buffalo 66* considers ultra-conservative political radio commentator Laura Ingraham his "dream woman."

"I'm seriously in love," Gallo once gushed about the blonde author of *Shut Up and Sing: How Elites from Hollywood, Politics, and the UN are Subverting America*. "I'd love to go out with her. Ann Coulter is too scrawny. Laura is so much brighter, and she's beautiful."

Wow, Vincent Gallo!

VINCENT GALLO FUN FACT

Vincent Gallo once got into a verbal feud with film critic Roger Ebert. "I had a colonoscopy once, and they let me watch it on TV. It was more entertaining than *The Brown Bunny*," Roger Ebert said of Vincent Gallo's last film. Gallo went on the defensive, and wittily lashed out at Roger Ebert by calling him a "fat pig." Ebert responded with, "It is true that I am fat, but one day I will be thin, and he will still be the director of *The Brown Bunny*."

Vincent Gallo we salute you! We love your independent movies, your wry abrasive sense of humor, but most of all we love you because you are one conservative mofo!

7.
FOR THE LOVE OF GOD, COUNTRY, AND CHEERLEADING!

Oh my God, they're having Raiderette tryouts! OH MY GOD! I know this, because several billboards around town read "Raiderette Tryouts!" This begs the question, what kind of cheerleader talent pool does one attract when billboards are randomly put up trumpeting auditions. This is the conservative girl all-American dream—to become a NFL cheerleader. Yes, it's the chance for every American young woman to get out there and rally some USA-style spirit, while representing our country's favorite pastime, which is KICKING SOME ASS!!!

The story starts. I phone the number on the billboard and explain to a really bitter woman that I'd like to write a story about the Raiderette tryouts (Oh my God!).

"I've seen every scam there is," she snarls. "Guys have claimed they're writing a magazine story just so they can come down and get girls' phone numbers."

This lady's a piece of work. That is not my intent. No. I don't want girls' phone numbers; I simply want to berate the whole entire proceedings. Boy, she pegged me wrong.

After jumping through a million hoops, I'm finally granted

a press pass. Why so sphincter-tight about Raiderette cheerleader tryouts? Does it involve a topless pillowfight? Perhaps Raiderettes are trained to be hired assassins who terminate world leaders during football games? That's why I now need to infiltrate these tryouts from all angles. I enlist my trusty girlfriend.

"I want you to tryout for the Raiderettes!"

"Do I have to?" she pleads.

"Yes!" I demand.

After much coaxing (more or less begging), she finally relents. My direction for her:

1) Dress slutty.
2) Wear more makeup than a Ringling Brother's clown.
3) Make sure things go terribly wrong.

TRYOUTS-SUNDAY 8:AM OAKLAND AIRPORT HILTON

This is the East Bay at its East Bay best. It looks like a "College Girls Gone Wild!" convention. Though this is supposed to be the crème of the crop, if this were a nightclub, you'd go elsewhere. Instead, it's like the type of chicks you'd find in a sports bar dispensing Jager shots.

"You're not supposed to be in here," a bitchy woman behind the check-in desk barks at me.

"As a matter of fact, I am," I assert, flaunting my press credentials in her face. I'm lucky. Earlier a photographer from Salon was turned away. He was told, "We're used to pimps and perverts like you!"

I'm given a black garter belt to wear around my arm as a press pass. The bitter woman informs me this lets people know I'm not "a pimp."

A mammoth security guard, who's the head coach's bodyguard, with large, hulking posture, takes me to the tryout prep area, relaying how things have changed through the years. I hope he doesn't hurt me.

"The women are more open, they're more liberal. And their

style is different. You see a lot of tattoos now," he says. "I think girls are willing to go the extra mile and get personal trainers.

Out of today's 450 potential Raiderettes, only about 10 will actually make it on the 49-cheerleader Raiderette squad.

"Do they have to be a Raider's fan?" I ask.

"Nah, we can change them over," he smirks, hiding his grandmaster plan for Raider world-domination.

ON THE SCALE LADIES!

A huge line careens down a hallway as women of various shapes and sizes, with slutty outfits—looking as if bought at the same slutty shop—wait to check-in. Huge fake boobs reign supreme, along with big hair and padded bottoms.

Others show as much skin as possible. One girl was sent home to change, shamelessly showing up wearing *pants*! She later came back in short-shorts. My undercover girlfriend is the only one wearing thigh high boots and a granny sweater. Some have failed to hit the mark, dressing like office workers at a failing insurance company.

"I came up from LA," says a potential Raiderette who works in marketing for U-Haul and wears more makeup than a drag queen. "It's a three day weekend so I figured, why not! Have fun, get a drink, meet a couple of new people.....take somebody to my room. You can scratch that."

I don't.

My undercover girlfriend gets to the table. She fills out a form stating, something to the effect, she won't sue the Oakland Raiders. Also answering if she has ever committed a crime. (I'm sure some have, for a few here have STOLEN MY HEART!)

"I think it would be a very hard decision to be a judge," states an older woman who registers a contestant whose shorts ride right up her butt-crack.

"I think I would go for the enthusiasm and the smile," she adds. "Some just stand out, and I think they would make the crowd enthusiastic at the games."

With more large fake boobs than funny hats at a Pope convention, I assume this is her definition of "making the crowd enthusiastic." Some are even "super-sized."

Butt-crack is checked in, and a number is pinned on her. And then it's time to check Butt-crack's weight.

"I weigh the girls in," clarifies a short guy with glasses, standing by a scale.

"Do you weigh the players in during the season?" I inquire. "Is that why they appointed you in this position?"

"No, I work field security on game day."

I don't really see the connection but, given his diminutive stature, I assume he's more than qualified for the task at hand.

THE CUT!

I run into the bitter woman from the phone. She looks exactly how I expected her to look—bitter.

"I'm really protective of *my* Raiderettes," she stresses. "This is my 16th year," she explains, giving a little insight into her mindset.

"We have mothers, we have dental hygienists, sales people. They're just women you'd meet at work or the grocery store."

Yes, women with huge fake boobs have to eat just like you or I. But what about the scams?

"I've heard it all," she stresses. "It's a long day so people don't want to hang out to see if they made finals. They might say 'my grandmothers died,' that's the most popular. One year I had 5 grandmother's die."

"A bad day for grandmothers!" I add.

"Guys will take pictures of the women and say do you want a copy, I'll send it to you. I will not give their name and address to anybody. That's an absolute no-no."

She's cut short by a sudden sea of Raiderette candidates spilling out into the foyer. The numbers of those who made the cut from the morning group is about to be posted.

"Hey judges, let's go," demands the bitter woman.

I'm about to experience cheerleader social Darwinism.

"Can I get everyone's attention."

The potential Raiderettes become instantly quiet.

"For those of you whose numbers are not on the list, we're going to ask you to leave, and thank you so much for trying out," the bitter woman coldly explains as no love is lost. "If you can keep the noise down and very quietly exit if your number's not up there."

The snotty, popular girls stand with confidence. We all wait nervously, wondering, who will be one step closer to Raiderette-dom. The list goes up.

"Be patient, don't push!" she says as some girls plow others out of the way like defensive linesmen.

Excited girls see their numbers on the list.

"Ashley made it!"

Dreams have been realized, dreams have been crushed, it's the best of times, it's the worst of times as there's a sea of shrills, hugging and squealing—like high-pitched speed drill at a dentist office (It makes my teeth hurt).

A few, near tears, choose to walk silently away with a sad face, whilst surrounded by the victors clapping and hugging. "Oh well, I'll know what to do next year," remarks a trooper with a stiff upper lip. "Where is that! Where is that!" a girl clad in some type of homemade cheerleading cape screams, clearly pissed off. She keeps repeating, "I'm still looking! I'm still looking!"

Others cry, but tears of Raiderette cheerleader joy! There's nothing sadder though than a potential Raiderette walking dejectedly to her car in her slutty outfit with a look of defeat on her face. Conversely, there's nothing worse than a shrilling Raiderette with big hair jumping up and down clapping after seeing her number on the list.

"I'm so excited," screams a scantily clad woman in a leopard skin dress, laughing outrageously into her cell phone. "I love the Raiders," she shouts at random.

An ESPN camera crew filming the two hour special, *A Season of Raiderettes*, gathers deep insights. (Wouldn't one hour tell the whole story?!)

"I was the last one up. I looked on the list and I screamed. I said, 'I made it!'" pontificates a girl with her pierced midriff into the camera, which is filming the special that I assume many men will watch with the sound down and their pants off.

I conduct my own interview with a girl in a low cut dress and huge fake boobs. For added creepy effect, I continually apply too much Chap Stick to my lips while talking to her.

"What do you think put you over the edge with the judges?"

"Because I think I was really natural when I went up there. I wasn't like faking it," she says with astute insight. "Yeah, like my smile was kind of fake, but I was being natural and giving them a huge smile."

Then she starts hugging somebody.

"Who is your favorite Raider?" I ask, shoving my face between the huggers, as I apply another thick layer of Chap Stick.

"Um, my favorite, I don't know," she says, mentioning how one recently tried to hit on her.

"I was working at a bar in Berkeley and he was like 'oh come with me and we can go watch a movie.' And I'm glad I didn't go."

"Would dating a Raider disqualify you?"

"They don't allow it. I wouldn't want to jeopardize any part of my Raiderette career!"

AND TIME DRAGS ON!

There's plenty of downtime before the afternoon session starts. Creepy guys lurk on the outskirts of the parking lot. Disgruntled boyfriends in baseball caps, sit with their primping girlfriends.

"You watchin' the Raider cheerleading tryouts," asks a man missing several teeth."

"Yeah," I say.

"They're bad, huh?"

"When you say 'bad,' do you mean 'good'?"

"It's all good!" he confirms.

One, and only one, Raiderette candidate smokes while

waiting. I call her "Bad Raiderette." She looks Goth, dressed in an all black Vamperella dress—but she's hot. Aah, yes, potential Raiderette #637.

I point to her cigarette.

"Are you shunned by the other Raiderettes for smoking?"

"Actually everyone's been really nice. But I'm here by myself and everyone else is in groups," she says, taking another puff, then explaining how she got "discovered."

"I ran into one of the Raiderettes at Starbucks. She said 'I'm sorry to bother you but I think you're very beautiful, and you should try it out.' She gave me her card."

Then my questions get tougher.

"How would it affect your viewing of the new Spiderman movie if you were voted a Raiderette?"

Vamperella thinks for a moment.

"I would enjoy it a lot better because I wouldn't think of the movie as a depressing way out of life. I would think of it as I made the first cut so far and I get to watch Spiderman!"

"One last question. Real or fake?" I ask pointing to the chest area. Smoke is blown in my face.

The ESPN crew has a more professional approach, as they question a nineteen-year-old hottie.

"My dream is to write for a fashion magazine. I'm a good writer and that's my dream," she states into the camera with her mom standing close by. "I went to every mall in the Bay area to choose my outfit. In case another girl is wearing the same dress, I've added straps." She then has trouble spelling her name out loud, and has to repeat it several times until she gets it right.

Another girl, about to get her "big break," gets really pissed because her strap breaks right before being interviewed.

"It's my turn next," she whines as her mom coaches her right back in there.

ON AND ON AND ON

The afternoon session starts. In groups of twenty-five, the numbered contestants sit in a long row of chairs, waiting for their turn to enter the inner sanctum where the balance of their entire Raiderette future lies in the hands of the judges.

"My name is Debra, I'm a former Raiderette," prompts a big sister-type in a conventional yellow dress. "I started in 1977 and went to the Super Bowl in '80. Now I'm a 43-year-old stay at home mother of three. I still have my number from my tryout. It was an experience of a lifetime," she solemnly explains to the attentive group of twenty-five. "When I tried out, there were six of us who met that day and hooked up. And we all made it."

Four girls sitting next to each other shriek and hug. That's soooo damn cute.

"Be confident. Be poised. Shoulders up, back down, project. If you have gum, get rid of it. Don't lie about your weight because it says it on your form," she prompts. "Some judges had to tell girls to smile. Don't be one of those!"

The previous group files out.

"Your smiling was kicking! You got a great smile," says one contestant encouraging another. A girl gives a sigh of relief.

"You're so nervous, your smile starts twitching."

A woman with huge Godzilla boobs to the point of zany, clearly mistakes me for someone else,

"You were there, how did I do?" she asks.

"Yeah, it was great," I say, trying not to stare at her creatures that destroyed Tokyo.

"Did I trip on anything?"

"Are you too nervous to remember?"

"Did I seem nervous? Tell me! Tell me!" she screams like the paranoid, hyperventilating schoolgirl she is. "You're a judge, right," she asks.

"No."

With that she walks away.

After a long, long, and I mean long, eight hours (when the hell will this end), it's finally time for my undercover girlfriend's group. She goes in the bathroom for "preparation." The others use the opportunity to practice spinning and smiling.

"Did you see someone take a purse," a scantility clad woman

asks the group.

"No."

Aah, the ugly side of Raiderette cheerleader tryouts.

My girlfriend returns. The granny sweater is off. To get a competitive edge, she stuffed her bra with wads and wads of toilet paper. She's now attained Godzilla proportions. Some immediately notice the difference.

"Your stuff is showing," a girl whispers, noting large bits of toilet paper purposely hanging out of her cleavage. "And you got lipstick on your teeth," she adds, not catching on.

They file in. Twenty-five nervous Raiderette candidates sit with their best posture perched on one side of the room. On the other side, two long tables of judges, comprised of former players, ex-cheerleaders, writers, and local TV personalities, casually eat breakfast rolls and read the sports page between groups.

"Honest to god, this is painless," briefs a man who looks like a cross between Burl Ives and Santa Claus.

With a wave of nervous energy and clenched hands, the girls come up on stage one right after the other. In front of a huge Oakland Raider backdrop, they state their name. Then they spell their name. Some have names (Sharccka, Eriaa, Kistalyn) I've never heard of outside of Raiderette cheerleader tryouts.

Others mumble, having trouble with the spelling portion. There's a glimmer of hope in their smiles, that occasionally drops due to lack of full confidence.

They give their eye and hair color, and, most importantly, their weight. Remember, no lying, THEY KNOW! Both spelling your name and honesty are two key Raiderette attributes.

And then comes the booty. They spin around, not once, but twice, holding it for a few beats, giving the judges two glimpses of their backside. I gather this is the "ability to excite a capacity crowd."

"Let's go!" someone yells the moment there's hesitation.

It's complete silence between contestants as the judges scribble down their scores. There's no joy in the judges' faces; this is serious goddamn business.

My undercover girlfriend is up. I'm weirdly nervous. She

purposely trips up the stairs. I can see toilet paper hanging out of her shirt.

"Bon jour," she says with a bad fake French accent, immediately striking several overtly provocative poses.

"Je m'appelle Renee," she says, pointing to her head. "That's spelled

F-U-C-K Y-O-U."

The room, already quiet, is now much quieter. A few judges let out nervous laughs. The bitter woman is not happy. A mockery is made of this sacred ritual.

"I am 6 foot 7. My eyes are plaid."

Then it's the booty time. My fake French girlfriend spins around and sticks the booty out there for way too long. The judges wait. The booty stays. Then she firmly slaps the booty like a nasty girl.

"Go Bears!" she yells, throwing in a cheerleader jump.

Steam is coming out of the Raiderette den mother's ears, as the judges shift uncomfortably. The entire group is brought up on stage. They stand there smiling for several minutes; I assume it's a test to see if any will crack. My undercover girlfriend uses the opportunity to glare angrily at the judging panel to see if they, in turn, will crack. All around her are huge plastered All-American fake smiles. I have a strange feeling she didn't make the cut. C'est la vie.

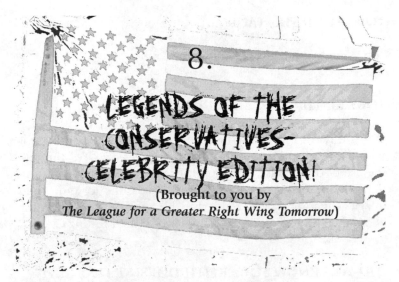

8.
LEGENDS OF THE CONSERVATIVES—CELEBRITY EDITION!

(Brought to you by
The League for a Greater Right Wing Tomorrow)

Legends of the Conservatives salutes................ Toby Keith!!!!!!!! He's been called, by some, quite possibly the most ignorant, prejudiced, unsophisticated ignoramus that has ever graced country music. If you love Rock 'n Roll Country, sometimes "in your face" content, and a singer that seems bigger than life—you'll love Toby Keith! Straight-shooting, with a "gotta be me" attitude, Keith brings this same style to the songs he chooses to record. And a good style it is! His patriotic, flag-waving lyrics have pumped up many a redneck's jugular, inspiring them to go out and KICK SOME ASS! To us, he's simply a legendary conservative mofo.

BORN: July 8, 1961

BIRTHPLACE: Clinton, Oklahoma.

OCCUPATION: Straight-shooting country musician who is not afraid to speak his mind.

TOBY KEITH FUN FACT

Toby Keith's real name is Keith Toby Covel?

TOBY KEITH ON CAMEL RIDERS

Did you know one of my favorite parts of The Taliban song is when he refers to Middle-Easterners as *camel-riders*? Yes, through the use of one phrase, Toby Keith has destroyed the work millions of Southerners and Westerners have done to undo their image as ignorant, racist rednecks who basically know nothing about the Middle East or anything beyond their rotting Chevys?

DID YOU KNOW TOBY KEITH DOESN'T TAKE SHIT?

After capitalizing on hit-songs about 9/11, Toby Keith has become Nashville's most controversial personality. "I just don't take shit," says Toby Keith. "I'll rear up on you and say what I feel. Of course, the press loves that stuff and it's easy to get me going."

TOBY KEITH WILL PUT A BOOT IN YOUR ASS!

Did you know one of Toby's Keith's biggest hits was *Courtesy of the Red, White, & Blue (The Angry American)*? Sure, pansy liberals will dismiss this song as one of the xenophobic reasons why everyone in the rest of the world now hates America. But Toby is not afraid to speak, what conservatives like to call, the truth. The controversial, patriotic song tells of a veteran who lost his eye in a combat training mission and also features a number of confrontational verses, where the US of A will put a boot in the ass of anyone who messes with it.

SORRY LADIES, HE'S TAKEN

Sorry Ladies, Toby is married. He and his lucky wife, Tricia, have three children, daughters Shelley and Krystal, and son Stelen.

TOBY KEITH TAKES ON THE DIXIE CHICKS, LOOK OUT!

When Natalie Maines of the Dixie Chicks had the audacity to question and speak her displeasure about our nation's great leader, George W. Bush, it caused a feud to erupt with Toby, who, as we know, has a fire-from-the-hip attitude. In response to Maines's criticism, Toby, always the creative thinker, projected a photoshopped picture of her and Saddam Hussein during his live performances. His crowd of free-thinkers, who also possess a fire-from-the-hip attitude, simply loved it. Little word to the Dixie Chicks: don't take on Toby Keith because you fight like a bunch of girls! Not to mention the potential boot that might be put into your ass! Way to go Toby Keith!

HOBBIES OF KEITH

Toby loves golf, fishing, and collecting sports memorabilia.

TOBY KEITH TAKES ON NEWSCASTER PETER JENNINGS, LOOK OUT!

Toby Keith doesn't mind taking a stand when it comes to the good of our country. He even had a spat with news anchor Peter Jennings when he wouldn't include the confrontational "Courtesy of the Red, White & Blue," in a Fourth of July network special. Keith fired-from-the-hip at Jennings—who is CANADIAN! "I find it interesting that he's not from the U.S," remarked the straight-shooter, adding, "I bet Dan Rather would let me do it on his special." Dan Rather, as you all know, is an American (who went on to be pounded by the Religious Right). Stupid liberal bias media. Way to go Toby Keith!

IS TOBY KEITH PATRIOTIC?

Yes. Let there be no doubt, Toby Keith is patriotic. He even once said, "When nobody really thought you needed to fly a flag and patriotism was gone, we flew one in our yard."

Congratulations Toby Keith for being one who fires from the hip, and whose boot is ready to be put in the ass of anyone who crosses his conservative path!

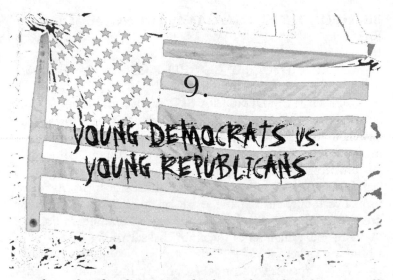

9.
YOUNG DEMOCRATS VS. YOUNG REPUBLICANS

The cult of politics is indeed a cult. Political parties all require a group of rabid supporters trying to be persuasive, intruding on your personal space with intense eye contact, insisting on you becoming a follower of their leader. Meet the Young Democrats and Young Republicans. Each party sets up its own special club for young zealots who are total ass-kissers thirsting to be on the political fast track. With the zeal of former high school class presidents, these youthful overachievers take themselves way too seriously, as they're tantamount to being cannon fodder for the political fat cats—about sixty rungs on the ladder above them. Yes, these earnest young putzes are played by the political system in order to consolidate each party's power base for it's own ill gotten gains.

That's why I decided to become a cult initiate for both of the big teams. Posing as an extreme stereotype of each, I went undercover and became a member of both the Young Democrats and the Young Republicans, to see who will push harder for me to drink from their political fanatics' tub of Kool-Aid.

BRING ON THOSE CRAAAAAZY YOUNG DEMOCRATS!

MY CLICHÉ DEMOCRAT CATCHPHRASE: "Where are those weapons of mass destruction, huh?"

"DEMOCRATS! DEMOCRATS!" I chant with my arms in the air, as I enter a sterile, white room with chairs in neat rows in the basement of a government building—for my indoctrination meeting to the San Francisco chapter of the Young Democrats.

I'm wearing a cunning liberal disguise: a tie-dye shirt, torn jean jacket, and recently grown extra thick sideburns. As heads turn, I've totally missed the mark on how Young Democrats dress. They dress, well, as conservatively as Republicans do.

"Are you a member of the club?" asks a Young Democrat in a blue suit jacket.

"Yes!" I answer with pride. Hoping to immediately bond, I add, "Hey, where are those weapons of mass destruction, huh?"

Tonight, the Young Democrats, with roughly eleven members present, is almost strictly a boy's club. The one hot Democrat babe (with nice Democratic booty) among the bunch, surprisingly, gets a lot of attention from the male Dockers-wearing crew. These are the smart kids from high school, who were on the student council, and always kissed the principal's ass.

"The San Francisco Young Democrats endorsed Dean and he withdrew from the campaign this morning," announces the club president, a man resembling a high school social studies teacher. Everyone in the room makes a sad face. "We will fight hard to support whoever the party endorses in order to defeat George W. Bush!"

When the obligatory Young Democrat Pavlovian applause dies down, I cry out "YEAH, WHERE ARE THOSE WEAPONS OF MASS DESTRUCTION!"

He continues to work the room with a few crowd-pleasing jokes about Bush's questionable National Guard duty. "In November, let's kick Bush's ass back to Crawford Texas!" More Pavolian idiotic Young Democrat applause.

When the cheerleading ends, I stretch for another clever

Democrat cliché, poking the guy next to me in the ribs, "Yeah, *Mission NOT Accomplished!*" (Pause). "Hey, where's those weapons of mass destruction?!"

One astute Young Democrat ladder-climber, with a blue button down shirt and crossed legs, keeps asking way too many questions to politicians who've come tonight to give endorsement speeches. He annoyingly bursts in with a comment on everything that is said in order to show how smart a Young Democrat he truly is.

"Proposition J is supported by the affordable housing *alliance*."

"Don't you mean the affordable housing *coalition*," he smugly corrects, showing he's a big mister smarty pants. He then grills a political representative on the Patriot Act, and even steals my *weapons of mass destruction* catchphrase (the bastard!).

The meeting abruptly ends with the high school social studies teacher announcing, "We normally go to 9:00, but we seem to have finished twenty minutes early. No one brings up the notion that we, as Young Democrats, maybe should go and consume some alcohol. Instead, like being let out early from social studies, we all quietly dispense from the sterile, white room.

TO THE DEMOCRATIC CONVENTION!

To further infiltrate the Young Democrats, I venture to the State Democratic Convention to gather among Young Democrats from all over California. Walking toward the San Jose Convention Center, I pass several grown adults who are covered with dozens of politician-supporting buttons endorsing candidates whom, I assume, they must like. These are political-convention junkies. It's going to be interesting to see how the political cheerleading and positive rhetoric will play out. For, as you might have read, it's kind of a *building year* for Democrats.

I make my way towards the entrance, passing a small contingent of the reactionaries supporting conspiracy theorist,

LaRouche for President. Hey-hey, I met their crew at the *Join Arnold* headquarters. Candidate LaRouche seems to be very popular amongst 18 year-olds who have access to bullhorns.

"Stop acting like Republicans! Get a spine!" a supporter screams into a bullhorn. To emphasize this point, several LaRouche supporters have taped a paper spine to the back of their clothing (roughly around the spine area). This is followed by yelling something about Hitler and Dick Cheney (and the insightful, comparisons thereof). The pesky LaRouche *Children of the Corn* use persuasive campaign tactics that involve simply annoying people.

Making my way toward the concourse, filled with numerous booths trumpeting each of this year's democratic candidates, I first notice, it's not unlike, say, a comic book convention.

"Hey, Dad! Dad! C-SPAN is here," exclaims a geeky and delighted 13-year-old kid to his similar-looking father, as the interior is filled with an abundance of fanboys, flyers, and just plain political nerds mingled among a lot of older politicians with hot, young female apprentices following at their heel. Democrats, rabid as Britney Spears fans, frantically wave signs touting their favorite (Kerry is the cutest!). Some immediately get in my face and try to sway me to their viewpoint. More fliers than I'd like to be holding are shoved into my hand. This is already turning into something, not unlike, irritating.

The afternoon general sessions have commenced already in the main hall, filled with a large majority of old people wearing mostly blue and gray. The projected word "Democrats" blazes behind the large stage, where a man conducting the proceedings repeats, "They broke the mold. They broke the mold," referring to the speaker who just departed (apparently stressing that somehow a mold was broken to create that person).

How do you fire up the losing side? With each speaker—including the mayor of Los Angeles and various Congressional members—it's a sea of empty rhetoric, clichés and cheerleading for the Democrat troops, all aimed at evoking vigorous applause. Yes, it's like a football pep rally for the team that has had several consecutive losing seasons, especially, now, months later, in the wake of the whole Arrrrrnold coup d'état.

As a political speaker, one combats this malaise by pimping for applause with crowd-pleasing sound bites.

"This is the best time to be a Democrat!"

(Clap clap clap.)

"These may be difficult times for our party right now. But during difficult times, we need to hold true to our values."

(Clap clap clap.)

"We need to be in this together to make California a state we can be proud of!"

(Clap clap clap.)

"As Democrats, we're going to fight! We're ready for the fight. Let's get to work!"

(Clap clap clap.)

Yes, it's the empty sound of one hoof clapping.

I'm again accosted by one of the annoying LaRouche minions. He shoves, in my direction, some campaign propaganda. These people looooove to talk about their candidate as if he were L. Ron Hubbard. They also looooooove to invade your personal space by talking way too close. Out of all the presidential candidates' campaign materials, LaRouche's is the only one that has a man wielding an ax on the front.

"He's the only candidate with a spine!" states the intense LaRouche supporter, showing me the taped paper spine on the back of his clothes (roughly around the spine). He tells me that LaRouche is the only candidate trying to impeach Cheney. I mention that if, say, Kerry wins, there would be no reason to impeach either George Bush or Cheney. We grow silent. When the silence ends, I'm told boastfully that LaRouche is the only candidate here with a sea of supporters, as evidenced by those outside with bullhorns. I conclude by suggesting that, next time, it might be more politically effective to get a booth actually inside the convention. We grow silent once again.

Authoritatively in front of the Young Democrat hospitality suite is a girl around nineteen, wearing way too much makeup, to orange-face proportions. She's in charge of letting people in. This fast-tracker, and surely former high school class president, is the living incarnation of Tracy Flick from the movie *Election*. There's a problem; I didn't bring my official Young Democrat membership card.

"I don't know if we can have you in here," she indignantly tells me with a snotty mad-with-power attitude from her sudden stamp of authority. Sadly, I'm sure she, and her stupid orange face, will be pulling in six figures in three years time as an assistant to some horny, old congressman in Washington. Orangeface goes over to an adult Democrat, after I make a stink, who comes over and immediately says it's okay for me to enter.

Once inside, the Young Democrats are doing a lot of "Wooing!"

"This is the best time to be a Democrat," California State Treasurer Phil Angelides also stretches the truth, disregarding the fact that Bush is in office, the Republicans hold all of Congress, and their downtrodden elected Governor was ousted from office by the star of *Kindergarten Cop*.

"Woo! Woo!" enthusiastically cries the Young Democrats.

DEMOCRAT PARTY TIME

The State Treasurer invites all the Young Democrats to a party he's throwing later tonight. I'm told with great assurance, that the Democrats "love to party hard." Good. I want to run into a scenario that would make Bill Clinton blush. At 10:00 pm I venture to the hospitality suites for Phil Angelides' "Big Fat Greek Party!" (Note: the name of his party is "funny" because it's similar to that popular movie *My Big Fat Greek Wedding* and the short-lived TV spinoff, *My Big Fat Greek Life*.)

Outside the hospitality-suite doors, it's a sea of blue- and gray-colored clothing, making the Democrats look as conservative as, well, the Republicans. After much anticipation, and a half-hour wait, the packed crowd filters in through the door. Phil's *Big Fat Greek Party* turns out to be *Phil's Big Fat Pay-For-Your-Own-Drinks Party!* Phil has a cash bar. Fuck Phil. I thought Phil promised he'd lend a helping hand to the poor. For I, like the State of California, am broke. Perhaps if Democrats had a winning season for once, it would be an open bar. I put my Phil sticker on a piece of baklava and get the hell out of there. I'm home in bed by 11:00 pm. Bah!

BRING ON THOSE CRAAAAAZY YOUNG REPUBLICANS!

MY CLICHÉ REPUBLICAN CATCHPHRASE: "STUPID DEMOCRATS!"

"REPUBLICANS! REPUBLICANS!" I chant with my arms in the air, entering the GOP Spring Convention at the Hyatt hotel by the airport. The concourse is a conservative's wet dream, splattered with Bush/Cheney signs and numerous pictures of Junior (without any irony), scattered amongst others trumpeting, for the newly elector governor, to *Join Arnold*. The crowd is white and very white, milked with big hair and fat cats resembling *Gilligan's Island's* Thurston Howell. Yes, Orange County is in da haus!

I've shaved my sideburns, took out my earrings, and stuffed my shoulder-length dreadlocks under a Kangol hat. Adopting a blue suit jacket, American flag tie, and khaki pants, I've made the uncanny transformation to Young Republican, fully infiltrating this faction by joining the Silicon Valley branch of the Young Republicans. Going by the conservative name Chet, I am now fit for Young Republican consumption. What could be more nauseating than to be a young, pumped-up and Republican?

I meet the YR club president in the lobby, a former U.S. Marine (I'm sure he knows several ways to disembowel the wimpy president o the Young Democrats). My reception is much warmer than at the Young Democrats.

"So you're from San Francisco," my new president exclaims. "You're deep in enemy territory."

"Yeah, I'm the lone Republican in San Francisco." I boast. "I have to live in that city full of liberal freaks whining about our troops."

We smile. The reason that the YR president fawns so much attention—I'm now one of the only six members of the Silicon Valley Young Republicans here at the convention.

"I got to look after my investment," expresses the chapter president, who introduces me to several political heavyweights who give firm handshakes.

"I won't let you down," I mutter several times. Showing I'm someone on the fast track, I add, "I'm thinking of starting a chapter of the Young Republicans in San Francisco!"

We smile. Then I'm told the Young Republicans "really like to party."

"You'll party like you never partied before!" the YR president professes.

I'm sure he's right. I've never partied YOUNG REPUBLICAN STYLE!

"Hi Daryl," my new club president says to a conservative man passing in the hall. I'm told that *Daryl* is "A congressman from San Diego, who borrowed one million dollars for the recent recall election."

"This floor's for all the governor's workers," I'm told as we slide past security, noting three large men with ear-pieces standing guard by one door in particular; Arnold's door. The Terminator is here to speak at this evening's dinner ($150 extra for a photo-op).

"Have you ever seen him before?" I'm asked.

"Yeah, at a Planet Hollywood opening," I reply. "It was wicked!"

THE YR CREW

"Do you want to buy a raffle ticket?" asks a tiny woman as we make our way to the upstairs bar.

"What do you win?" I ask with Republican curiosity.

"You win a chance for a dinner with George W. Bush," she

answers with a sales smile like that's just the greatest thing ever. At twenty bucks a pop, I tell her to reserve a few for me and I'll pay her later.

I meet two of my fellow clean-cut Young Republican brethren. One of my new, clean cut peers explains, "I joined the Young Republicans back when Gore was trying to steal the election."

I hit it off big time by mocking the contingent in front of the hotel here to protest our beloved Gov. Terminator's appearance. We take turns mocking the protesters.

"Waa! Waa! I want health care," mocks one of the Young Republicans.

"Waa! Waa! I want human dignity," I join in with the mocking, waving my hands in the air.

"Are you coming to the big protest tomorrow?" asks another Young Republican whose shirt is adorned with various "funny" political buttons (such as "Village Idiot" showing a picture of Hillary Clinton).

"You bet I am," I respond. Then a few seconds later. "What are we protesting again?"

"We're protesting illegal aliens getting drivers' licenses," he explains. "I've already got my sign ready."

"Stupid illegal aliens!" I then add. The event is put on by honorable US Senate Candidate Howard Kaloogian. In theory, if drivers' licenses were given to illegal aliens, that would mean more Democratic voters.

"Why don't we just say, hey if you want your licenses, here they are, you just have to go across the border to get them!" quips a rotund man with a red tie.

"Stupid illegal aliens," I once again declare. "What's your sign going to say?" I ask.

"I got a large driver's license with the word ILLEGAL written over it," he explains with a smile.

I share, "I'm going to have a sign that says *If you want to drive, then go back to Mexico!*" The rotund guy let's out a hearty laugh.

"Stupid illegal aliens," I restate with agreement from the others.

The Funny-buttons man exudes how thrilled he was in meeting various politicians. "I got to hang out and party with guys running for State senate," he exclaims with almost a girlish squeal. "It was cool!"

Me and *funny-buttons* hit if off. We take time to mingle on the convention floor. Funny-buttons gets star-struck, recognizing a Republican candidate running for congress. These are his rock-stars. A bit flustered he shyly introduces himself. The bulbous nosed politician, with obligatory firm handshake and strong eye-contact reserved for potential voters, shares a scandal story about his political opponent.

"She told such lewd sexual stories that a staffer had to excuse himself to go into he bathroom and vomit."

"Who does she think she is," interjects funny-buttons, "Bill Clinton?" We share a good laugh (Republican humor). "Yeah, Bill Clinton," I repeat. When the laughter dies down, I add, "Stupid Democrats!"

The big event for the evening is the hospitality suites where you can schmooze with your favorite Republican candidate, and, most importantly, drink all their free booze.

"There's some nice Republican women here," shares funny-buttons. I look around and see various women wearing conservative blue with big Orange county hair.

"Is that part of the hospitality suites?" I wink.

"Well," he says slyly. "I don't want to marry some Green Party chick!"

"Yeah," I agree. "Stupid liberals."

DAMN YOU PROTESTORS

Surprisingly, a contingent in front of the hotel is protesting our beloved Governor. Now I'll get to see a protest from the other side.

"ARNOLD SAYS CLOSE THE SCHOOLS. WE SAY SHAME ON YOU!" blares through a bullhorn.

The news' cameras arrive. I quickly grab a Bush/Cheney sign.

A group of eight adults in suits are taunting the protestors. Two Orange County ladies in sparkly dresses do snide dance moves, rubbing the protestor's noses in their decadence. I stand close to my new conservative peers, waving the Bush/Cheney sign, making a stern face as the TV cameras roll. From out of the hotel, suddenly comes rushing a group of pumped up teenaged kids with protruding foreheads, wearing blue suit jackets. They're smirking.

"We're the high school conservative club," the leader explains. These teenagers get confrontational, waving Join Arnold T-shirts in the protestor's faces. An adult in a blue suit rounds up the testosteroned group. With an air of authority, he presents the leader with his business card.

"I'm an attorney. I'm an election law specialist. If anyone gives you shit, call me!"

"Cool!"

Two of the conservative high school kids, from the world of privilege, high-five as one of them pulls out a bullhorn to further taunt the "lower classes" who have come here to protest the need for basic human rights.

"SHAME ON YOU! SHAME ON YOU!" chant the protestors, several who have brought small children.

"You don't deserve education," sneers a man who looks like a corporate leader. He then immediately turns to his conservative compatriots next to him and discusses where they should go for a good crab dinner later in the evening.

"SHAME ON YOU! SHAME ON YOU!"

I realize now, with my cunning disguise, they are pointed at me, ME! For I now look like a stereotypical Republican. I have no other choice but to chant back.

"I LOVE ARNOLD MORE THAN SCHOOLS! "I LOVE ARNOLD MORE THAN YOU!"

"We appreciate your efforts, but come inside," requests a large suited man to the high school youth.

"We're all for free speech as long as it's not us," cries the teenage leader who feels his civil rights have been violated. Before they go in, the large, suited Republican man takes a picture of the high school clan.

"Say GOP!" he requests as they confidently smile as a group of high school conservatives. Yes, these are our future chairmen of Enron and other corporations.

"SHAME ON YOU! SHAME ON YOU!"

A protestor wearing a tu-tu tries to get inside the hotel to use the bathroom. The security guard stops her.

"She tries to get in here to use the bathroom, then starts snooping around. You know they're very sneaky," confides the security guard with her take on liberals.

"Yes, they are very, very sneaky," I add. "Very sneaky!"

BUSH BOOTH

Before party time, I venture to the Bush for President booth and slap numerous Bush/Cheney stickers all over my blue suit jacket, introducing myself to Barbara (not George W's mom, but the county chairman for the re-elect Bush campaign) as a new esteemed member of the Silicon Valley Young Republicans.

"Why don't you start a Young Republican chapter in San Francisco?" Barbara asks, impressed by my giddy enthusiasm.

"You know I've been thinking about that," I say, slapping another Bush/Cheney sticker on my jacket, asking how I can help out with the Bush re-election cause.

"The first thing I'm going to ask you," Barbara says, "Do you want to be a Precinct Captain?"

Damn, I've only been a Young Republican for two hours and already I'm climbing the party ladder with a prestigious position that offers long hours, high responsibility, and no pay. Maybe she heard about my prestigious work with the Arrrrnold campaign? There's only one way to answer, "You bet I do!" I give Barbara the address and phone number of my Kerry-supporting ex-girlfriend and tell her to send as much campaign material as possible. "Just keep it coming!" I add.

Yes, I'm on the Republican Party's political fast track.

SIZZLER

Kicking back, we Young Republicans kill some time by sitting in a hotel suite, listening to a large man rant about what's wrong with the whole gay marriage issue.

"What's to say pedophiles can't now get married?" he argues, with Rush Limbaugh logic.

"Yeah," I interject. "God made Adam and Eve, not Adam and *Steve*." My comment generates a round of laughter.

"You know, I don't know why Nixon is so hated?" the large man rambles on, at which point I somehow bring everyone around to a discussion on how Bill Clinton caused 9/11.

"OK, we're going to dinner," announces the YR president. He points to people who will be among the inner circle at the Sizzler. A finger is directed at me. I am in the inner circle!

As I walk with my YR crew, I'm almost outed for the stinky liberal that I am. A female security guard comes up to me.

"Hey, you look familiar. Don't you do standup comedy?" she asks (most likely having seen one of my numerous "brilliant" comedy performances). The other YRs overhear what she's saying and come over. "Isn't your name something like, Harmon?" she blurts.

"No! No!" I correct. "My name is Chet! Chet! And I've never ever done any standup comedy before in my whole entire life. OK!"

"What did she say?" asks one of the YRs, who would surely kick my ass if he found out I was actually an undercover liberal.

"She's crazy," I explain. "She thinks I do standup comedy! Yeah, right!"

"Rent-a-cop," he scoffs, a minor dis to the working class.

We jaywalk across the street to the restaurant. "Apparently in California, you don't have to follow the law," someone quips, tying it all back to the gay marriage thing.

Gathering at a table in the back of Sizzler, I then proceed to have one of the most uncomfortable dinners I've ever had, cutting into my steak, all red and meaty.

"You know who has a good website? Gene Autry," shares a

large suited man at our Sizzler table, who earlier remarked that he once ran a gun shop. "They probably had some of my guns at Waco," he confided in us. "Or Wacko," he added.

REPUBLICAN PARTY TIME

Unlike their wussy liberal counterparts, the Young Republicans looooove to drink. Republicans have deep pockets, so there's plenty of free alcohol (remember, their beloved leader is the biggest party boy of them all—and just look at his daughters!).

In fact, *my club*, the Silicon Valley Young Republicans, is throwing a party in a hotel suite, for some reason called *The Bay Area House of Blues*. Now, the best part about this whole social gathering is that, I volunteered earlier to be on the party planning community! Earlier, I even handed out flyers for the event, with a guitar on it reading "Just Follow the Music!!!" There's no concern about getting a DWI; I'm sure everyone's father here could easily bail them out.

"Who wants a Silver Bullet?" cries the middle-aged suited fat man with a can in each hand, who earlier told me he owns a gun shop.

There's plenty of free beer donated, I'm told, by the ultra-conservative Coors brewing company. Imagine the worst party you've ever attended. Now imagine several of them going on at the same time, all in the same building. They're like mini-frat parties but with patriotic themes. To create a proper party atmosphere, some Republican decorating genius (with my urging) came up with the idea of putting the American flag on one wall, a large Silicon Valley Young Republican banner on the other, and a Bush/Cheney sign in the middle. LET'S PARTY!

Though appreciative of the free alcohol (in-your-face Young Democrats!), this has got to be the worst party I've ever attended. On many levels! It's a sad bunch. My conservative crew and I, comprised almost entirely of Young Republican males, stand stiffly in a corner waiting for other young conservatives to show up. The Eagles, *Life in the Fast Lane*, blares from the sound system, as funny-buttons does some mean air-guitar. We stand uncomfortably in the corner of the almost empty hotel suite, passing the time by bashing Democrats ("Stupid Democrats!").

"Kerry looks like Herman Munster!" remarks a man with a protruding forehead and smug superior laugh.

"Yeah, and Hillary Clinton looks like an ape," I inject to big laughs from funny-buttons.

"I go to UCLA," shares another Young Republican to an elder. "It's a pretty liberal campus, and I was one of seven people protesting *for* the war," he shares, recounting that his clever sign read, "Give War a Chance."

Others pass the party time by TV channel surfing to Fox News. Horny guys in ties salivate over the very few women in the room. To every new person I meet, I proclaim, "We're all family, we're all Republicans!" followed by a hearty slap on the back.

After taking a Jello shot, I have the uncanny desire to get busy with a random conservative Republican chick in a blue skirt and go to THE DARK SIDE! My fantasy is to dry hump one in the stairwell, hand under sweater, over bra. Then, as she orgasms proclaim "I'M A LIBERAL IN DISGUISE!"

"You know, I'm president of the San Francisco chapter of the Young Republicans," I boast, to a Bakersfield Young Republican, hoping she will want to use me, tonight, to climb up my political ladder. Like politicians have done through time, I use my political clout to help get a little conservative booty. After telling me she works at a non-profit in Bakersfield, I proclaim, "Wow that almost sounds like you're a Democrat." She looks at me as if I just called her a pedophile. She quickly walks away.

As the drinks pour the YR president starts intensely yelling at some poor random girl, accusing her of stealing a can of Coors Light. More Eagles music plays. Rigid dancing is attempted by the very white crowd in suits, who possess no rhythm what-so-ever. But I'm already rapidly climbing the Young Republican club ladder. The YR president passes off a potential recruit to tag along with me so I can introduce him to all the glorious benefits of being a Young Republican.

"We're all family. We're all Republicans!" I stress, followed by a slap on the back.

Meanwhile Republicans are taking turns singing patriotic karaoke while downing massive amounts of gin and tonics. We Republicans drink as, outside, Rome burns. A politician sings "California Girls" to cries of "Woo! Woo!" Things take a turn for the surreal as the next karaoke performer chooses to sing "Proud to Be an American" to the delighted crowd of revelers.

With the new recruit under my wing, I take time to make small talk.

"You got to join the Young Republicans," I express. "It's really a lot of fun."

"Yeah, it sounds great," he enthusiastically replies.

I move in closer.

"I'm also the president of another club if you're interested in joining. The new recruit shows interest. After all, since I'm an established member of the Young Republicans, he can trust me. He asks the nature of the club. I explain further. "Our club's purpose is to promote the advancement of white people." The new recruit's face turns white. "So what'd you say? Would you like to go to Applebee's?"

He declines. He quickly walks away. Oh well, as our beloved president Bush would say, "Mission Accomplished!"

10.
REPUBLICAN POLITICAL MERCHANDISE TIE-INS

The thing I like best about large political conventions is the tie-in political merchandise. Here are a few craaaaaazy items the Republicans had on sale at the State Republican Convention:

GEORGE W. BUSH DOLL

Goddamn it, they actually have a George W. Bush doll that you can buy for $29.99. The weird thing is, they are selling this item without even a tinge of irony. In a box, similar to the one which holds Barbie, is a miniature replica of one of the most hated men on the planet. It gets better. If you push a button in the back of miniature George W. Bush's back, the doll will say George W. Bush catchphrases. I'd want my George W. Bush doll to constantly repeat: "Mission accomplished!"

Funny Political Buttons

Republicans love funny political buttons that bash Democrats. Especially those that trumpet that Hillary Clinton is not very attractive in their eyes.

Here are a few of my favorites that were on hand to buy:

"The Good, the Bad, and the Ugly"

This "funny" button showed a picture of George W. Bush, John Kerry, and Hillary Clinton, in that exact order.

"Village Idiot"

Simple and to the point, this "funny" button had an image of Hillary Clinton, creating the impression that the wearer does not, I repeat, does not like Hillary Clinton.

"No RINOs"

RINO stands for "Republicans In Name Only." The only thing Republicans hate more than Democrats is a liberal-leaning Republican and this "funny" button with the word "RINO" and a line through it emphasizes that point.

"Loserman"

Hey, everyone, do you remember the 2000 election with that whole punch-card thing that went on in Florida? Apparently, the wearer of this "funny" button feels that the Democrats were a big bunch of crybabies when they complained how George W. Bush stole the election in the state where his brother was governor. Damn you stupid Democrat crybabies, damn you!

REPUBLICAN FUN WEAR

Besides your normal campaign hats and T-shirts, there was the most amazing jacket I've ever seen. It was so amazing, in fact, that I decided to "borrow" one. Retailing at $40, constructed of some incredibly cheap nylon/Gore-tex shell, this beauty is red, white, and blue, covered with stars and simply says with no subtlety in bold letters on the back, "Re-elect President Bush." If you want to check out a jacket like the one I "borrowed," simply go to www.LeslieJordan.com.

JOHN KERRY FOR PRESIDENT............OF FRANCE

(NOTE TO ART DEPARTMENT: CAN WE USE THE IMAGE OFF THE WEBSITE?) http://www.cafepress.com/kerryoffrance

This T-shirt is "funny," because it suggests that democratic candidate, John Kerry, would make a good president not to the United States of America—the greatest country on earth—but to France. As you already know the French is a big bunch of traitors and we hate them. Oh how we laugh, how we laugh, how we laugh!

11.
BAD JOBS THAT INVOLVE WEARING COSTUMES

Look at our sluggish economy. Bush hasn't created a single new job since he's been in office with a 2.4-trillion-dollar election-year budget that is bulging with military spending. Well maybe he has created a number of jobs, only most of them are in India.

My state, California, is living in the rubble of the now burst dotcom bubble, leaving it (California) on the verge of bankruptcy and borrowing billions—as unemployment rates continue to hold at near record highs. Not to mention, the great Governor Arrrrrrrnold has cut financial aid for college students.

So job-seekers, brace yourself: face your future. As you sift through the assorted crappy offerings in the want ads, the pickings are pretty bleak. What are the options?

Jobs involving wearing a uniform and waiting on customers are usually pretty bad. But jobs involving wearing a costume and doing bizarre things are even worse. If you're not working at Disneyland (or Disney World), soul searching is in order, particularly if you're an adult and your new vocation involves mandatory costume wearing.

But with the current economic situation, this might be the sorry state of choices for those looking for employment. That's why I went out and tried to land a few of the *worst* bad jobs that involve costume-wearing in order to hold a mirror up to your possible future.

COSTUME: DRESSING AS UNCLE SAM FOR A TAX SERVICE

The ad reads:

WEAR UNCLE SAM OR LADY LIBERTY COSTUME

PROMOTE OUR TAX BUSINESS IN THE NEIGHBOR-HOOD.

START ASAP...

I'm no rocket scientist, but I can safely say with authority, next to coal miner and working with hot tar, this has to be one of the worst jobs known to humanity. I drive to scenic North Sacramento. The office, decorated with red, white, and blue balloons, situated right next to *Planned Parenthood* and a place called *Options for Youth*, is *Liberty Tax Service*.

"I'm here to apply for the Uncle Sam position," I gleam with an award-winning smile to a man of foreign origin.

"Great!" he replies with thick accent, while perched under a framed *Proud to Be American* portrait. I'm given an Uncle Sam application. For special skills I put *Mime*, *Patriotic Clothes Wearing*, and *Sign Waving*. To secure the job, under education, I write *Harvard Law School*.

When I finish, the questions begin.

"Now, is it a really large Uncle Sam hat?" I ask, raising my hand toward the ceiling.

"No it's not."

I sit and wait for the boss to interview me. He holds the power of whether or not I become a complete jackass and wear the Uncle Sam costume in public. He finally emerges from an office and eyes my application.

"We want people who are really high-energy!" the thick-accented-boss explains. For some reason he raises his hands in the air (like he just don't care!).

I add for inside edge, "I've worked other jobs in costumes before."

"Oh really!"

"Yes, I worked as a giant human-sized Subway Sandwich. I also worked as a giant Liberty Bell."

"That sounds interesting."

I embellish, "Yes, a Liberty Bell with human features."

The job is explained.

"You will dress up like Uncle Sam and go around to businesses and drop off flyers for our tax service along with a box of donuts."

I nod my head vigorously, not knowing the whole donut connection. This will be done while paired with a Lady Liberty. More is explained.

"Then we'll have you out in front of the office on the street, waving a sign."

The boss gets animated. He role-plays the scenario. He puts his arms up like he's holding an imaginary sign.

"HEY! HEY! COME IN HERE! HEY! HEY!"

After his little skit, the boss explains how much I'll be compensated for degrading myself.

"We will pay you $7 per hour."

There's a deal breaker.

"Can you include some donuts with that?" I ask with big dreams. The boss assures a few donuts are no problem.

"Can you start tomorrow?"

"Yes!"

He asks if I know of anyone else who would like also to be Uncle Sam for $7 an hour.

"I do, but he's kind of short." I put my hand at Mini-Me size. "Would you have an Uncle Sam costume that would fit him?"

The boss thinks. He concludes the Uncle Sam costumes are a one-size-fits-all scenario.

GAME DAY

8:30 am my shift begins. 10:30 I arrive for work. They can wait. Why? THE JOB DOESN'T START UNTIL UNCLE SAM GETS THERE!

"Uncle Sam's here," I trumpet upon my return to the Liberty Tax office, that is now filled with people doing tax work.

My boss is giddy. He hands me a red, white, and blue Uncle Sam outfit, with striped pants, and a large Dr Seuss type hat. Other Uncle Sams are already stationed throughout the area.

"Did you bring along your friend," he asks, inquiring about my fictitious, midget amigo.

"He'll come tomorrow." Putting my hand at kneecap level, I add, "Just remember, he's very, very short."

I give a hard look into the mirror after making the transformation into Uncle Sam. Yes, I look like a complete idiot.

"Know what we need is beards," I state, miming a beard. "A beard would really drive home the Uncle Sam point."

"Oh, yes, yes!" replies my giddy boss. He likes the facial hair idea. "I will buy some fake beards tomorrow."

The boss and his second in command train me, both so giddy that they giggle like little girls; this is their mad vision come to life. Yes, these two foreign men are giddy for tax season. Before we leave, an army of multi-ethnic Uncle Sams comes marching in from the morning shift. There's also one Lady Liberty. She looks exactly like Lady Liberty if Lady Liberty was from India and weighed about 200 lbs.

I'm lead outside, directly in front of the office, standing on the side of busy main street.

"I want you to hold your sign and wave at cars as they drive past," the boss explains. "Try to get them to honk at you."

He demonstrates the type of waving he envisions (full over-the-head waving). According to him it says, "HEY, COME IN HERE!"

"Can I wave like this," I ask, doing a limp-handed effeminate wave. Once again I mention about the beards. I'm handed a large sign that says: "IT'S TAX TIME!" In very small print (too small for anyone to see), it says "Liberty Tax." To passing motorists I look like some fool, dressed as Uncle Sam, standing on the side of the road, maniacally waving, for the sole purpose of informing them in January, it's now "Tax Time."

Grabbing the sign, I start out by having extreme job pride. My sign waving begins at level 11. I quickly determine that this job will one day be replaced by a robot. This job is not unlike standing on the side of a road, holding a sign, while looking like a complete ass. A couple of people honk. A little kid in a car gives me the finger. A women yells, "I don't pay taxes." I keep waving with the dignity of a grown man dressed as Uncle Sam in the middle of January. "It's too early to think about taxes!" Others drive by and openly laugh as if to say, "I can't believe a person would degrade himself to that level." Oh, sure they laugh. But little do they know, each hour I'm $7 richer (before taxes are taken out). Those that honk, honk to say, "You're a big fucking idiot!"

Soon my waving gets replaced by simply pointing and coldly staring down motorists. My arm grows tired. I get a splinter (a job hazard). I feel like I've been out here for days. I look at the clock on my cell phone. Twelve minutes have gone by. I throw in some moonwalking to spice up the Uncle Sam routine. This would be the perfect job for a crack-head. I feel not unlike a homeless guy with a "Will Work For Food!" sign.

A bucktoothed kid and his little sister approach Uncle Sam on foot.

"Excuse me, here's a flyer for a church," the kid says, handing me a flyer for, well, a church.

Do I look that lost and pathetic that little kids feel I need the Lord's guidance?

"Uncle Sam doesn't go to church," I explain. "Uncle Sam is a fictional character."

"You can come on your own time," the bucktoothed kid insists, trying to be persuasive (if not slightly creepy). "Tomorrow?" he asks. "Promise."

The pair quickly scamper into a waiting white van, perhaps telling the driver, "We've saved that poor man dressed as Uncle

Sam!"

LUNCH

At lunchtime I sit in a small room with all the other multi-ethnic Uncle Sams. We have matching red and white striped pants. It's a grim bunch. One Uncle Sam has a look of pure insanity. We sit in stony silence. Where would I begin to make small talk? Oversized Lady Liberty leans over. She whispers with slight animosity, "You took my spot outside by the curb."

I approach the boss. He's mildly stressed, discussing something with a tax worker.

"I got a pair of stilts," I proclaim. "I could wear them and be a really tall Uncle Sam!"

"Go get them," the boss perks up. He hands me a stack of flyers.

"If anyone walks by, be sure to give them one of these." The flyers show a picture of the Statue of Liberty. The slogan: "If You Want To Save Money, Raise Your Hand."

"Maybe the flyers could say, 'If You Want To Save Money, Say Uncle,'" I suggest. "Then you could show a picture of Uncle Sam." I snort with laughter. "Get it, 'Say Uncle!'"

The boss barely acknowledges my suggestion.

"Yeah. Yeah."

I elaborate.

"You could even put a picture of me on the flyer."

"Yeah. Yeah."

There's an awkward silence. The boss goes back to his conversation with the tax worker. I break in, "You know, they're *really* great stilts!"

Oversized Lady Liberty reclaims her prized spot in front of the office. I get in a gray van with the rest of the Uncle Sams. The boss is going to drop us off at various locations along Watt Ave. I once again bring up the addition of beards. We're given a pep talk.

"I want to see who can wave the most. I want you to tell me

how many honks you can get!"

The van of Uncle Sams keeps driving farther and farther away from the office. We're no longer in walking distance. I'm dropped off at the sketchy intersection of in an industrial part of town right by a 7/11 and check-cashing place.

"I will come back at 4:30 to pick you up."

The boss speeds off, leaving me miles from the office, on my own, in an Uncle Sam costume. The flyers get immediately thrown out. Now what?! I can't just wander around in an Uncle Sam costume for hours without raising eyebrows. I'm trapped. Maybe my attitude needs adjusting. OK, I can handle 4 hours of standing here in an Uncle Sam outfit.

"Fuck you!" shouts a car full of teenagers whizzing by. It's the second time today I get the finger. My sign says "It's Tax Time!" with no discernable connection to any business. I feel cast down as an ominous presence like a Grim Reaper standing at an intersection with a sickle. Most drivers aren't mean, they just drive by looking at me as if to say "I'd hate to be that poor guy!" or "Mommy, who is that crazy man dressed like Uncle Sam?" Even if they can make a connection to the tax service, will people think," Honey, let's get our taxes done at the place where they make their employees look like utter buffoons!" ?

I put down my sign just to confuse people. Just a waving man dressed as Uncle Sam. Fifteen minutes into it, I take a self-appointed break and sit at a bus stop reading the paper. Someone honks. This time *I* flip them off. I actually get more honks without the sign, for people think I'm just being patriotic. A truck with an American Flag in the back slows down.

"That's cool! That's really cool!" proclaims the woman inside. She gives me the thumbs up.

"Uuuuuncle!" shouts some gangsta' types.

"Waazzzzup!" I yell back, glad they approve of me. More gangstas, on foot, look like they want to beat up Uncle Sam (it would be tragic if they found Uncle Sam dead in a trash dumpster). I'm working the same beat as a crackhead with an empty prop gas can asking people for change.

To greatly increase car honking, I work for a brief period

with my red and white striped Uncle Sam pants pulled down to knee-level. Time continues to go by slowly. OK, this isn't funny anymore. This is becoming like some weird David Blaine endurance stunt to see how long I can tolerate degrading myself in public. My sign droops pathetically on my shoulder. Soon motorists are treated to the sight of Uncle Sam sitting on the curb. Later, they are treated to the sight of the sign on its own.

I go into Rite Aid Drugstore. The checkout girl says sarcastically, "I can help you over here, Sam." The Rite Aid staff, though dressed in a Rite Aid uniforms, looks at me like I'm the Elephant Man. She rings me up and shares, "I always like to drive by and make fun of you guys."

I go back to my intersection. A gust of wind blows my sign into traffic and it gets run over. This adds another pathetic element. I've become a broken man, limply holding my sign, and wearing my red, white, and blue hat askew on my head.

"What do they pay you, a hundred bucks?" asks a homeless man. I tell him much, much more. I don't want to be mocked by a homeless man by saying it's $7 per hour.

"Do you want to hand the job down?" he asks.

"Sure!"

I give him my jacket, hat, sign, and $5. I let the homeless man take over the Uncle Sam duties for a half-hour so I can go to Long John Silvers. He doesn't seem broken hearted to relinquish his shift when I return.

At a few minutes before 4:30, I decide to put on a big show for the boss. He pulls up in his van full of Uncle Sams and I'm not only waving madly, but also jumping into the air, full of job enthusiasm. You would have to be completely insane to really keep up this waving-energy lunacy for all these hours. My hand is full of splinters.

"You're doing a great job," commends my boss. I once again bring up the necessity of beards and stilts. We drive down the main street to pick up the last remaining Uncle Sam.

"Brian is doing a great job," my boss announces. Brian's his favorite. Off in the distance, I see the last remaining Uncle Sam waving at cars with an even greater frenzy than my phony display.

"I must of gotten over three dozens waves and probably a hundred honks," he states with utter job pride. Brian gets into the van. We lock eyes. Thank you President Bush and a hearty thank you, as well, Governor Schwarzenegger!

UNEMPLOYMENT FUN FACT: Did you know California's recent (6.4 percent official unemployment rate approaches 1982's 10.8 percent record), at least for men?

JOB #2 HAUNTED HOUSE WORKER

COSTUME: Scary Clown
The ad reads: WORK IN A HAUNTED HOUSE. GREAT JOB FOR ACTORS!

PREPARATION FOR INTERVIEW..............OF TERROR!
1 Black Cape
1 Pair of Fangs
1 Scary Attitude
1 Pseudonym (Franklin Stein)

How can they deny hiring a guy with haunted house vocational aspirations who's already adorned in fangs and cape?! With costume in place I head towards a Marin County shopping mall and a huge white tent in the parking lot, the site of Nightmare University. Raising my cape in the air-Dracula style, I approach a group of men hammering various scary items into place.

"I'm here for the haunted house interview!" (Since my fangs are too big for my mouth, taking up the entire circumference, sadly sticking half in, half out, they hear, "Rmmm rmm rmm rmm.")

"What?" replies a large man with his belly hanging out the bottom of his shirt (I assume he is the leader).

"The haunted house interview!" ("Rmm rmm rmm!")

"You must be here for the haunted house interview," the

large man concludes (he IS the leader). "OK, you can take those fangs out now!" he adds, not smiling.

"OK." ("Rmmmm.")

Handing me an application, the one-who-is-the-leader says, "Give a scream when you're done."

"Should I make it a "scary" scream?" I exclaim with a sly wink, showing my scary spirit.

Since haunted house workers are going to be hired on the spot, I put down on the application anything I damn well please within the haunted house industry.

PAST JOB EXPERIENCE:

-The Teepee of Terror
-The Haunted Canoe
-Nightmare Traffic School

Upon completion, I once again raise my cape and give a heart-pounding, "WOOOOOOO!"

Looking over my application, the one-who-is-the- leader asks, "What was Halloween like when you were little?"

Replying like a 17-year-old girl in a black turtleneck and beret, I take a poetic approach. I sit back and reflect, pausing between thoughts.

"Much laughing. Costumes. Bags of candy. Running," I recite, twirling my hair, "Falling asleep with a smile."

The one-who-is-the-leader extends his large hand. "I'd like you to work for us."

I twirl my cape, put my fangs back in and proclaim, "I won't let you down!" ("Rmm rmm rmm!")

IT'S SHOWTIME...................OF TERROR!

I'm late for opening night at Nightmare University. My haunting coworkers are already milling about in costumes. Haunted house folks, not to be confused with "carnis," are primarily chubby men with a man/child delight for the Halloween holiday (I'm all for this, don't get me wrong).

"I'm here to scare the beejeebees out of people!" I proclaim to the second-in-command, adorned in a white lab coat and Janet Jackson headset. "What character should I be?"

"THE CLOWN!" he and those surrounding announce in unison.

It's an inside joke. Ha-ha, I'm the clown, very funny, haunted house co-workers.

Coulrophobia is the fear of clowns. I'm playing on some people's worst nightmares. Perhaps, for the younger in attendance, I'll cause major childhood traumas that will stem into adulthood! Right on! Hand me that clown outfit.

"Can I have a knife," I demand, adjusting the large bright polka-dot clown suit with enormous belly and frightening clown mask, with razor teeth, and ill-fitting eye-slits that smells like a cross between latex and sweat.

"Sure," exclaims the second-in-command. One is presented to me.

"Last year, someone punched the Dot-Room guy," the leader briefs us in the graveyard room. "I won't put up with any guests harassing you."

We learn other important tidbits such as, don't go outside to the Porta-Potty while in costume. No one likes to see a headless Frankenstein going to take a dump (it breaks the "fourth wall"). Also, stressed, never make fun of those with disabilities, and, most importantly, don't grope people in the dark.

"Actors take your positions!" booms the leader over a loud-speaker as the halls are filled with the background soundtrack of various screams, loud heartbeats, and creepy laughing that gets on my nerves within mere minutes. "We're about to open the doors."

There's an unusual sense of quiet before the haunted storm (perhaps a little "too" quiet!). In my scary clown room, lit with a creepy, swirling light, I'm situated in a large Jack-in-the-Box with a huge, ugly clown head and dangling arms sticking out the sides. When patrons enter, I push a button, which flips open a smaller box, revealing a scary clown lit by orange light. Caught off guard, I fling open my larger box with a loud thud, and jump out screaming, wielding a large knife. Yes, scary Clown!

SCARY ATTEMPT #1- THE WAY OVER THE TOP APPROACH

A rail separates me from those who might punch me (like last year's unfortunate Dot-Room guy). I take my position alone in my clown box. A surefire way of making people scream would be bursting out without wearing pants. ("I'M A BAD, BAD CLOWN!") An executive decision is made to keep on my pants. Instead, I'll test the numerous, different levels of *scary*. Let the haunting begin! WOOOOOO!

When I see a strobe light go on in the Scream Theater, I know a new group is approaching. The group enters. I storm out of my clown box.

"AAAAAAAARGH!"

I'm face-to-face with a bunch of bemused middle-aged adults. They stare at me, waiting for me to do a lot more, or perhaps, scare them. I'm given a look like "yeah, yeah, you're a big scary clown; so what else can you do?" After the initial shock, I have a lot of filler time until they'll leave the scary clown room.

"AAAAAAAARGH!"

So I decide to go mental. I take my knife and start maniacally stabbing the long, dangling arms of the fake clown and various other parts of the set, arms flying, knocking things over, doing something that resembles Riverdancing. No go. They lethargically saunter to the next room.

SCARY SCALE 1-10: 3. I need to turn my scaring to level 11.

SCARY ATTEMPT #2 – THE HIP-HOP APPROACH

The best people to scare are groups of teenage girls, because everything to them is soooooooo much more dramatic! They approach the scary clown room clutched together.

"Oh my god! Oh my god!"

"I hate clowns!"

"I'm not going in there! I'm not going in there!"

On this attempt, I decide I will give these teenage girls my haunted house mission statement, informing them exactly who I am and what I do. They creep along the rail. I burst from my box.

"I'M A BIG SCARY CLOWN!" I shout "LOOK AT ME DOING SCARY-THINGS!"

As expected, the teenage girls scream. Adding to the recipe-of-fright, I throw in some breakdancing maneuvers, spinning on the floor, concluding by dancing "the robot" (complete with scary robotic noises).

"BEEP-BOP-BOOP!"

I throw in a frightening, "GO '9ERS!" The clutching teenage girls run, screaming, from my clown-room-of-terror. Success! There's nothing like screaming teenage girls. I think a kitten and a bag of cookies would've scared them, but regardless, a scare is a scare!

SCARY SCALE 1-10: 8. Clown breakdancing has proved an effective weapon on the war against non-scaredness.

SCARY ATTEMPT #3 – THE SUBTLE APPROACH

Being a scary clown is lonely. Between groups I stand alone in my clown box, reflecting on moments of my life that have led up to this point. But it's short-lived. The haunted house rush begins; groups of people keep coming; one right after the other.

The worst patrons are groups of high school guys; they have a bit of an attitude, not wanting to seem like big scared wussies. So, I'll make a fright adjustment and scare them on a different level.

Some guys with baseball caps enter my domain.

"This place is trippy!"

They stand around waiting for something to happen. I hold off, letting anticipation build. Finally, I gently open my box a mere crack. Slightly sticking out my head, I use the affected accent of a Southern dandy.

"Booo!" I softly lisp, first clearing my throat, letting out a singsong voice. "Booo! I'm scary," followed by a wave.

I gently put my head back in the box and softly close the

door.

"This place is trippy!"

The tramp out. A dad and son combo is hot on their tail.

"You go first!"

"I'm not going first, you go first."

I dramatically switch gears. This time when my box opens, I make it look like they caught me off guard. My clown mask is pulled up and I'm talking on my cell phone. The dad and son stand there, waiting for something to happen. I keep talking, scratching myself with my fake knife. They're not sure if this is scary or not. When I finally look over, I act like I was caught off guard. Quickly, I close the door of my clown box for some privacy.

SCARY SCALE 1-10: 5. As it turned out, I was just as scared of them as they were of me!

SCARY ATTEMPT #4 – THE BREAKING THE FOURTH WALL APPROACH

As far as jobs involving actors go, this one has the least chance of being "discovered" by a big Hollywood agent. Witnessing my last haunting attempt, the second-in-command critiques my scaring ability.

"When you jump out of the box, come all the way up to the rail," he coaches and demonstrates.

"Is my energy good?" I ask from a method-acting point of view. "Do you think I'm using a strong enough motivation?" I inquire, using acting terms.

In that department he gives me the A-OK. Thus it's time to expand my portrayal of "the scary clown," and give him a little more theatrical depth. I decide to verbalize exactly why they should be scared. Adding to my character's movements, I abruptly come out of my box really low, like a duck waddling in fast motion. My knife is extended way over my head.

"I'M THE MOST FRIGHTENING THING YOU'VE EVER SEEN! I'M STEVEN THE SCARY CLOWN." I then add, "I LIKE DOING MATH PROBLEMS!"

I'm face-to-face with a mom who's brought in her way-too-young child. The small, petrified child clutches to her with the look of pure, unhappy terror.

"Mommy, help me!" shrills the poor small child.

"I LEFT THE IRON AT HOME! REMEMBER I'M STEVEN THE- SCARY-CLOWN!"

For added effect, I rapidly pull my clown mask on-and-off, revealing my real face.

"AAAAH! AAAAH! AAAAH!"

"Mommy!"

But do they applaud my thespian merits? No. Instead, the mom and her small child make a beeline for the emergency exit (the small child is scared shitless). Maybe the mention of excelling at math problems was too much for them?

SCARY SCALE 1-10: 11. Excellent, I've mentally scarred a child for life. Little do they realize, technically, what I've done here is broken the "imaginary fourth wall" in a display of Beck-ettian Absurdist Theater.

SCARY ATTEMPT #5- THE "I'M BORED" APPROACH

The main haunted house rush is over. The evening suddenly becomes very monotonous. My haunted coworkers keep checking their watches.

"When do we get out of here?" asks the Dot-Room guy. Bored haunted house workers mill about in the darkness trying to kill time. The Scream Girl is starting to get on my nerves, while the heartbeats and creepy laughter somehow seem louder.

"You can take a ten minute break," the-one-who-is-the-leader informs me.

"That's OK, I'll just stay in my box," I reply, tightly closing the clown box's door.

Moments later, someone screams, "Couple of people coming!" Everyone frantically goes back to their respective scary rooms.

A group of old people enter.

"I LIKE THE TV SHOW *FRIENDS*! CHANDLER IS MY FAVORITE! WOOOO!"

They are virtually unimpressed, but take a wrong turn and go through the door to the backstage area. I have to tell them to go the other way while staying in character.

"DON'T GO THROUGH THAT DOOR, IT'S FOR EMPLOYEES ONLY! WOOOO!"

I have to repeat myself twice. They're followed by a high school couple gripping each other like tropical panda monkeys.

"NO ONE LIKES ME! I SECRETLY WEAR LADIES CLOTHES. WOOOO!"

During mid-scare, a group of teenage girls from before, have taken the opportunity to walk backwards through the haunted house. This time they heckle me.

"Can I hold your knife?"

"Veeeery Scary."

I retort with, "I'M LAUGHING ON THE OUTSIDE, CRYING ON THE INSIDE!"

When my room clears, I leave my post and wander around the haunted house like a senile old uncle, passing customers in the hallway.

"Hi there."

I try to sneak up and scare my haunted house co-workers, who just seem annoyed.

I make my way to the graveyard room and hang out. There's the old people who were just in my clown room.

"Hi, you saw me earlier."

Bored, I take off my scary clown outfit, open my clown box, and leave it hanging inside like I suddenly just vaporized. I slip out the back. Clown time is over.

UNEMPLOYMENT FUN FACT: Did you know by the time Bush leaves the White House he will have earned his reputation as the President who bested Hoover in job losses?

STOP #3

COSTUME: A LARGE ELEPHANT OUTFIT

The ad reads:

MINOR LEAGUE BASEBALL TEAM MASCOT WANTED

$8 PER HOUR

I've decided to give in to the machine. If I'm going to have to work in a job that involves wearing a costume for low pay, it might as well be the best damn costume job there is—and that's THE minor league mascot for the beloved Modesto A's.

With a firm grasp on the long floppy trunk, I insert my head inside the elephant head. It's smells really bad; there's a very distinct funk to minor league mascot heads. It smells of sweat, fear, the chubby guy who wore it before me, and too many high-fives.

"Any words of wisdom?" I ask my mentor, the suit's previous inhabitant.

"Don't fall."

The costume weighs about 141 lbs. Not really. With head in place, I do my newly patented "PeaNUT walk" in the Modesto A's locker room. The players openly heckle me.

I'm off. Assuming my newly patented PeaNUT walk, I head toward the stands. Modesto A's fans are about to be treated by inspired team mascotting.

As soon as I hit the bleachers, a girl immediately runs up and gives me a shove – a big shove – almost knocking me down. She hates PeaNUT (or she senses I'm a new PeaNUT?)

Already, I'm sweating so much I can barely see, or breathe for that matter. But suddenly, I'm the most popular person in the whole damn half-empty stadium.

"PeaNUT rules!"

"PeaNUT! PeaNUT!"

THINGS YOU CAN DO AS PeaNUT!

- Go up behind old men and start massaging their backs

and have them smile.
- Randomly hug strange girls and have them hug back!
- Shake your big elephant butt in someone's face and have them laugh.

The fans scream as I crank up the spirit, madly waving my arms and moonwalking down the aisle. It's your standard, lovable mascot fare.

Then, I snap.

Or should I say *PeaNUT* snaps. As if possessed by the costume, I start running all over the place like a high-speed, high-fiving machine of tomorrow. I stop to shake my large elephant butt at entire sections as they, in turn, cheer. I don't want to brag, but I think the crowd likes my insane version of PeaNUT much better than that of the regular guy. I get down on one elephant knee and rotate my arms.

"PeaNUT, can you sign my cap?" asks a kid. He hands me a pen and I sign it, *"Best wishes, Gene Hackman."*

In the back of my mind, I imagine some major league mascot scout is sitting in the stands and is going to sign me up for the big leagues.

I run over to the middle-aged groupies who clearly love PeaNUT, grab one of their beers and pour it out. Then I do a "funny" dance. Yeah, how much do you love PeaNUT now, huh?

I lean in close to one of the guys. "Call the police! Help Me!" I plead from inside my giant head. "They're making me do this against my will! Help me."

Suddenly, I'm herded out onto the field for the "chicken dance." Everyone in the stadium stands up for the chicken dance. I'm supposed to lead them.

The chicken dance music starts. I put my arms at my side and jump up-and-down like a chicken, throwing in the robot and a few mime-trapped-in-a-box moves. I start running around like I'm caught in a swarm of bees. And then, PeaNUT goes down. Hard. I'd like to say the fall was on purpose. But I can't. I lay there on the ground motionless for what seems like an hour. I can see through one of my eyeholes that those who were dancing with PeaNUT have stopped and now look concerned. I lay there perfectly still, as if just plowed over by a semi. I hear someone say, "Get up PeaNUT!" But for some reason – I can't really explain why – I remain frozen.

"What's the matter with PeaNUT??" someone cries from the stands.

PeaNUT's handler rushes over. So do others. They now seem concerned as I lay perfectly still. There's talk of paramedics. Just when children's dreams of human-like elephant mascots are about to end, I spring to my feet and jump high into the air. The crowd goes completely ape shit. PeaNUT is back! And he's not dead! It's a sea of high-fives as I'm escorted from the stadium.

12.
MASTER OF CORPORATE MANNERS

They say comedy is the weak taking on the powerful. What better way to exemplify this by infiltrating a very uptight manners and etiquette class for insecure corporate CEO-wannabes? You know, that upper, top echelon that gets all the wealthy tax breaks. Fortunately, I came across a website showing pictures of people in business clothes eating expensive dinners, laughing, and looking self-assured.

"Present yourself with confidence and authority in any business or social situation!"

The upper-crust actually pays $245 for a class that teaches you how to behave, and take "power-lunches," so you can climb like a mannered monkey up the corporate ladder. According to these manner-maniacs, once I master a strict set of etiquette rules, a whole world of success will be magically unlocked. The bastards! So of course I sign up for their five-hour manners and etiquette class, to learn such earth-shattering topics as: dining etiquette, handshaking, eye contact, and how to be a perfect guest at a power-lunch. Yes, please sign my stinky, unmannered, dredlocked, white ass up!

I decide to attend the manners and etiquette class under the alias of Chas Lemon. Posing as Chas, I am in desperate need of this service. Who needs this class more, than a "manners breaking menace to society"? On the online enrollment form, I say that Chas works as *"An Eccentric Millionaire,"* further explaining that Chas is signing up because his "bitch said to get some manners!" As Chas, I wear a black Oakland Raiders stocking cap. To get into character I haven't bathed or shaved in two days. Yes, the world is Chas's oyster, he just happens to be using the wrong, motherfucking fork. It's time to get some manners!

The class is held in a posh downtown hotel.

"The rain in Spain falls mainly on the plain," I mutter, getting into the proper mood. Already committing my first manner's faux pas, I'm purposely forty-five minutes late. Inside a small ornate, private dining room are five of the most uptight people I've ever encountered, sitting rigidly at a large oak table. Everyone is on their best manners as they listen to a petite, immaculately groomed woman named Cheryl lecture on the proper use of the soupspoon. Entering, everyone looks at me like I just did a bad smell.

"Is this where that manners-thing is being held," I grunt, picking at my arm. I feel like an out-of-place character in one of those screwball Rob Schneider movies. My five classmates resemble middle-aged corporate types; two anal-retentive men and three anal retentive women; all adorned in business clothes. I have the sudden desire to loudly fart—just let one rip.

"You must be Chas," says Cheryl, who perhaps is the politest woman on earth. Her and her manner-prowess were even featured once on *Good Morning America*.

"What s'up," I mumble, wiping my hand before shaking. Cheryl makes her way clear across the room to greet me; utilizing both strong eye contact and a firm, but not too firm handshake. I assume this is the proper way to greet tardy people at an etiquette class, being she is the damned teacher.

This is the most adult function I've ever attended. You can almost feel the clenched buttocks at this anal-retentive gathering.

"I was just sharing a little trick on how to remember your place settings. BMW—'bread,' 'meal,' 'water.'" Cheryl states.

"Cool!"

I'm directed to a placard by a chair. Written on it are the words "Chas Lemon." In front of everyone is a place setting with about 20 different spoons and forks, and thirty different glasses. The deal is, we're going to be taught how to use the twenty different spoons and forks, while being served a three-course meal.

With the proper tact of one who teaches an etiquette class, Cheryl adds, "Chas, would you mind taking off your hat?"

I smile and nod. "Oh, sure, no problem."

The hat remains on. Yes, I've committed another faux pas! I slouch in my chair and take vigorous notes on soupspoon usage.

"Here's one way to remember it," says Cheryl "Like a little boat out to sea, I eat my soup away from me." Isn't that fucking cute?!"

"Now Cheryl," inquires of the uptight, businesswoman, who looks like she dreams of one day putting heads on the corporate chopping block and who sits to the right of me.

"With the soup bowl, the spoon goes in the bowl, but with a soup plate, it goes on the side, correct?"

To answer her question, Cheryl shows us a series of slides, circa 1989. Unhappy, well-dressed people use the wrong manners, while happy, well-dressed people use the correct manners. The gist I get from this: that you're doomed to a life of misery and ultimate failure if you display improper manners.

"The plate is not a rowboat," Cheryl adds. "A knife and fork should never be placed like a pair of oars in a rowboat."

Petite Cheryl goes on to show us other wrong ways to hold a knife and fork, such as "the pitch fork" and the dreaded "cello."

"Now Cheryl," interrupts the uptight businesswoman with the head-chopping cravings, "When it comes to bread is it Okay to break off a piece?"

The petite instructor poo-poos the notion, saying that the thumb should dig out a little piece. Then butter it, remembering of course to use the entire pallet, putting the remainder on the side of the bread plate. Of course, you need to fold up the butter foil and NEVER put it on the tablecloth.

"Cheryl, back to the bread for a moment. When passing it, does it go to the left or right?"

Oh my God; there's four and a half more hours of this crap to go. This is slow, inane torture. Put a bullet in my head now. Pretty please!

I raise my hand.

"Now what do you do if your host makes loud racist comments?"

Cheryl ponders this. Then she suggests politely excusing yourself.

Finally it's time for the food.

"Bring it on," I almost shout.

Before it comes out, Cheryl tells us about our proper eating posture.

"Both your feet should be planted on the floor. Never cross your legs. Your back should be straight, and your elbows should stay off the table."

Like robotic, Pavlovian idiots, we assume the position; all sitting identically.

"You never have a second chance to make a good impression!" she adds with a smile.

This is so unbelievably uncomfortable. This is how they rigidly eat in a Dickens-ian orphanage. Our server, a well-mannered French guy, brings out our leek consommé soup.

"Like a boat out to sea, I eat my soup away from me," Cheryl inanely repeats.

No one looks happy as we eat soup. In fact these CEO-wannabes look kind of sad. Yes, these poor people appear worried about their spoon usage, realizing that up to now they've had inferior usage. As if, in the past, they committed a tragic etiquette blunder, which must have cost them that promotion to executive vice-president, along with exclusive corporate privileges. Yes, they must have been so distraught that they actually enrolled in this goddamn class, so they can get a leg up in the business world for future POWER LUNCHES.

My fingers hurt from holding the spoon the proper way. My purpose now, is to act like a guy who just doesn't get it; who never has and never will fit in a "well-mannered" society.

"Like a boat out to sea, I eat my soup away from me," I say to the chopping-block businesswoman, dropping my spoon into my leek soup. I pick it up again, hold it for a few seconds, then drop it.

"It takes a bit of practice," coaches Cheryl.

"Like a boat out to sea, I eat my soup away from me," I repeat, overcompensating by doing the maneuver ten times larger than required. Disregarding the rule of only filling the spoon 3/4th full, I loudly slurp my soup.

"I like soup!" I state to the uptight woman next to me. I slurp, then drop my spoon. With one bowl of soup, I manage to commit several manner faux pas.

"Now ladies, here's how you avoid getting lipstick on your glass." Cheryl sticks out her tongue, places it over her lip, then drinks. She looks like a petting zoo llama consuming a feed pellet.

"You've got to be kidding," I say, stunned. "People actually do that?!" Cheryl confirms its validity, then goes on to share some other classic, anal-retentive tricks of etiquette.

"If you're worried about having a clammy handshake, you can try spraying your hand with antiperspirant."

"That blows my mind," I say, shocked that people actually do that in real life. What if they're allergic to their antiperspirant? Then what?!

I make sure I'm the last one to finish my soup.

"Are you done Chas?"

"Not yet."

I slurp again. Then I drop my spoon.

About five minutes later, "Yeah, I'm ready to 'ten/two,'" I say, making an inside etiquette joke about correct knife and fork placement upon finishing. The group lets out a low, uptight chuckle. Aah, manners-humor!

The French guy brings out the main course— chicken in a

red wine and mushroom sauce.

As we begin eating, Cheryl gives the moronic advice, "Under any circumstances, don't put the knife in your mouth."

"What do you do if you have to go to the bathroom during a power lunch?" I ask.

"You discreetly say to the person next to you, 'excuse me for a moment.'"

I turn to the uptight woman on my left. "Excuse me for a moment, I feel like I'm going to flippin burst."

I get up and waddle to the bathroom. Once there, I make sure I stay way too long. Let them play with their little forks and spoons without me. When I return, the manner-learning group is already on to dessert.

I discreetly turn to the uptight woman next to me, "I feel ten pounds lighter!" Bing! Another etiquette faux pas!

Cheryl is telling the group, "Always hold a wine glass in your left hand while networking, so your right hand is accessible for handshaking,"

In the end, Cheryl gives each of us a little manner's class diploma. Mine reads,

"Chas Lemon is hereby awarded this Key to Confidence." Well fuck me sideways!

We go around the table and each of us shares one thing we've learned in class.

"For me, it was the knife and fork and what to do with it while dining," states the decapitational businesswoman.

"I never knew that a nametag should be worn on the left side for 'the power stance,'" states an uptight businessman.

It's my turn. "Like a little boat out to sea, I eat my soup away from me!" I say and, in leaving immediately insert my finger directly in my nose.

TEST YOUR ETIQUETTE AWARENESS

By Chas Lemon

QUESTION #1
After a sloppy one-night with a one-toothed crack whore named "Flo," a thank you note should be sent within 24 hours.
TRUE   FALSE

QUESTION #2
When making a first impression, it's best to stare at the other person and say, "I can see the inside of your brain, monkey-boy"
TRUE   FALSE

QUESTION #3
At the completion of a meal, it's best to place your knife and fork in your jacket pocket, but first cause a diversion by tripping the busboy.
TRUE   FALSE

QUESTION #4
When walking on the street downtown that smells like pee, you and your date come across a puddle of junky vomit, you should lay down your jacket and let her walk over it.
TRUE   FALSE

QUESTION #5
The following is an example of a proper introduction: "Mr. Smith (CEO), I'd like you to meet my bitch, Rita."
TRUE   FALSE

QUESTION #6
If you drop your crack pipe accidentally on the floor during a meal, it's best to pretend it didn't happen.
TRUE   FALSE

QUESTION #7
It's appropriate to place your dentures on the table when there is no food in front of you.
TRUE   FALSE

QUESTION #8
The proper way to smoke hash is to break the block into little pieces and then smoke it one piece at a time.
TRUE   FALSE

QUESITON #9
In a restaurant, you may use the palm of your hand to get the voices out of your head.
TRUE   FALSE

QUESTION #10
Name tags should be worn at all times, 24 hours a day.
TRUE   FALSE

QUESTION #11
In a business introduction, you should always extend a one-dollar bill in your hand.
TRUE   FALSE

QUESTION #13
You should refer to people by their employee number rather than their name.
TRUE   FALSE

CONGRATULATIONS! WELCOME TO THE WONDERFUL WORLD OF MANNERS!

13.

ACTION ALERT!
A MESSAGE FROM THE
AMERICAN FAMILY ASSOCIATION

From time to time, I am delighted to get informative emails from the American Family Association, that directs me to their website, providing useful information in regard to how America can be a much better place:

TELL HARDEE'S TO STOP DISGUSTING BULL RIDING AD!

Offended by Hardee's new "mechanical bull" ad? Take action here!

Hardee's is airing an offensive commercial featuring a scantly clad woman riding a mechanical bull while eating a Hardee's hamburger.

As one member put it, "They have a young women suggestively riding a mechanical bull eating one of their thickburgers in a rather pornographic way."

Another member said, "[The] woman is moaning and simulating sexual arousal."

Sadly, Hardee's and a few franchise owners have chosen to disregard the collective voices of thousands of concerned parents.

Now contact your local Hardee's store manager or owner. Firmly, but politely, let your local Hardee's store representative know that you are offended that the Hardee's corporate office has shown absolutely no regard for your concerns.

Ask him or her to speak to Hardee's corporate office on your behalf to pull the "mechanical bull" commercial. Please take action today!

14.
NEW URBANISM MON AMOUR!

Picture paradise. A new planned community with Fourth of July parades and school bake sales, spaghetti dinners, and fireflies caught in jars. You sit back on your front-porch swing, viewing your hopscotch-and-tag neighborhood, as pies cool on open windowsills. Why, it's a special place for goddamn families, situated in a time of motherfucking innocence. It's small town living, conveniently located right outside of the heart of the city, where lemonade stands are set up on every corner and your new smiling neighbor brings over a freshly baked beef stroganoff to welcome you to the neighborhood ("Hi Neighbor! Welcome to the neighborhood!").

Ok, are you done vomiting? Then wipe your chin and grab your camera (for a Kodak moment) because this conservative utopia has come to San Jose in the guise of Timberline Village, where *The Truman Show* has now come to life to enshrine us in a Starbucks of residential living. Welcome, my friends, to the world of *new urbanism*.

WHAT THE HELL IS NEW URBANISM?

New Urbanism! The term sounds like something lifted out of Aldous Huxley's *Brave New World* (note my literary reference), a futuristic hybrid of communal life, where jetpacks of tomorrow scoot people from one place to another. On the contraire mon frere, this concept refers to an architectural movement which spawns pre-planned communities: they are nostalgic yet functional, directly in reaction to the post World War II suburban sprawl that's produced a lifestyle dependent on the automobile (yeah, like I knew that right off the top of my head). Briefly, the principle of new urbanism is to erect fabricated "small towns" with an increased density of friendly residential neighborhoods, schools right down the block, and happy residents harmoniously living, working, and playing, all within walking (or skipping) distance of their home. Again, that's in theory. Like the comforts of returning to the womb, new urbanites find themselves seeking a simpler, isolated place within the alienated suburban growth and erosion of inner-cities. This residential utopia sounds like it should produce an *ah-shucks*, neighborly interaction amongst town-folk, achieving a desired effect of restoration of the lost feeling of "community." Or better yet, it conjures up the image of an isolated yuppie bio-dome devoid of "bad elements," crime, and, of course, the pesky poor.

HOW THE HELL DID NEW URBANISM BEGIN?

Baby new urbanism was given birth to by Miami-based architects Andres Duany and Elizabeth Plater-Zyberk, who won recognition in the early '80's for their Florida coastal development, that was knighted *Seaside*. This husband and wife architect team (that has zany sit-com possibilities) attempted to recreate the scale, form, and nostalgic feel of a 19th century rural Southern town. You might be familiar with Seaside; it was the artificially surreal setting for the movie *The Truman Show*, parodied as *Seahaven*; the brightly lit suburbia whose daily toothy-white grinning routine imprisoned protagonist Truman. *The Truman Show* reflects the utopian ideals of new urbanism: there is no crime, no bad weather, (probably no swearing), everyone has money, the homes all feel the same, people chat over picket fences and neighbors are cut from the identical cookie cutter mold. Where as one side sees this as a community that encourages conviviality, *The Truman Show* portrays it as menacing (and kinda creepy). Tragically, it was discovered that Seaside's local housewives were actually being replaced by robots; murderous robots!!! No wait, that would be the plot of the movie *The Stepford Wives*. My apologies.

I WILL NOW SHOP FOR A GODDAMN NEW URBANISM HOME

I, Mister "Big and Clever," will travel into the heart of the beast that is the *new urbanism*. In order to come to my subjective "conclusion," I will practice something called having an "open-mind." With my newly found "open-mindedness," I drive down the 101 and head towards the foothills, passing the aforementioned suburban sprawl with its sterile strip malls, onward to Timberline Village.

"Nestled along the foothills with the prestige of a San Jose address is the Classics at Timberline Hills; a master plan community with old fashion charm."

Yes, isolated from the "sprawl," there stands—Timberline Village Square. By damn, if it doesn't look, not unlike, the town square right out of the movie *Back to the Future*. Except it seems like it was built last week. The place could be described as "cute." Unfortunately, I'm too cynical and jaded; "cute" just doesn't fly with me. Wait, that's not being very "open-minded." I take that back. A large fountain sits directly in the Center Square ("a self-contained small town atmosphere with a central hub to encourage strolling, people watching and neighborhood interaction"), surrounded by a park that looks like the perfect location for the Timberline Village 4th of July bake sale. Surrounding the square are a bunch of quaint businesses with minimal practical appeal, along with the large, upscale Lunardi's Market. This leaves pedestrian Timberline Village residents with the shopping and dining options of Quizno Subs, a haircutting place, health club, coffee shop, and ice cream store; all which are almost entirely empty. Now, if new urbanism's point is to react against the suburban automobile culture, then most of the Timberline Village citizens must work at Lunadi's Market and dine on Quizno subs. Those with "jobs" at "other places" or fancy to eat something that isn't a Quizno sub, will find themselves having to use their "automobile" to drive there.

In my "open-minded" mode, I'm beginning to be hyp-no-tized by the appeal of the new urbanism. Why I imagine living here, letting the days drift by, sitting at an outdoor table at Peet's Coffee, sipping mochas in a valium-induced haze pondering what new exciting meatloaf recipe I'll prepare for dinner for my adoring family (the little ones are a handful!). There are no *weir-does* or *bad people* here. Surely, you won't run across Stinky McNasty sitting in a hovel on a park bench with his belly hanging out, drinking a 40 ounce next to his shopping cart filled with baby doll heads. New urbanism wants to restore the lost feeling of community, and I can "open-mindedly" say I think that's great to do with mostly white people and the rest of all races and nationalities with money.

Taking an outdoor table at Quizno Subs (a quick shout out to their delicious toasted sub sandwiches!), I nudge up to an older couple who would look perfectly cast in an antacid commercial. After biting into my delicious toasted sub sandwich (another big shout out) I turn to them and point to the central square and spout propaganda.

"You know, I enjoy this small town atmosphere with a central hub to encourage strolling, people watching, and neighborhood interaction!" I state with a piece of luncheon meat dangling between my teeth. Oh, I forgot to mention earlier, I came dressed to Timberline Village wearing a black T-shirt that reads "KILL 'EM ALL, LET GOD SORT 'EM OUT!"

The antacid couple looks up at me, my stocking cap, and

dark shades, as I tap my fingers that have fake tattoos scrawled in marker across the knuckles that says H-A-T-E and H-A-T-E. The antacid couple acts like they don't hear me, so I repeat myself again, but louder.

"I SURE DO ENJOY THIS SMALL TOWN ATMOSPHERE WITH A CENTRAL HUB TO ENCOURAGE STROLLING, PEOPLE WATCHING, AND NEIGHBORHOOD INTERAC-TION!"

They look at me again like I'm speaking a foreign language. I get right to my point.

"I'm your new neighbor," I proudly proclaim, extending my onion-dripping hand. "I'm moving into the neighborhood, neighbor!" Even though they don't appear to have finished lunch, they seem to depart in a hurry. Bah, they surely won't be invited to any of my potluck dinners, goddamn it. To hell with our future chats over a picket fence!

I am in a foreign land. The streets here are clean and safe for upper middle-class consumption. There's no graffiti. The thought of skateboarders doing Ollie Backside Grabs off the fountain ledge would be laughable (skateboarding, most likely *is* a crime!). Not to mention panhandlers, who, I imagine, would be dramatically run out of our new urbanism town (right before given a beauty makeover, a pat on the back, with a hearty wish of "Good Luck!").

Though the activity of "strolling" is stressed as a new urbanism selling point, there is a large void of "strollers" around the designated central square magnet for strolling. People simply drive up in their cars, do what they need to do, then drive off. Perhaps all the great "strolling" is to take place later at the big community stroll-off. For right now (2:00, Saturday afternoon), all potential strollers must be off doing other community-building activities. Thus, if appointed emperor of Timberline Village (besides going "mad with power"), I'd hire actors to portray elderly, but wise, citizens, who would always be on hand to fix a kite, or give wise, elderly advice from a park bench, adding to the self-induced small town charm that their promotion advertises.

Since no one is "strolling," I've decided to "stroll" through

the numerous, identical neighborhoods that feel sterile and arti-
ficial in their own unique way.

"Can you spare some change?" I confront a man, whose eyes
glaze over at the mere mention of these words within the small
town charm of Timberline Village community limits. "Any
penny will help!" I add, sticking out my hand. The man makes
some excuse about not having any change, so I throw in the sarcastic, "Well, have a *nice* day!"

I stroll on, noticing how the houses scream, "Hello, we are
the upper middle class!" The whole place looks like it was put
up overnight. It's like a new car, with that new car smell, even
though the development has been around for four years. Everything seems to be immaculately in its right place. In abidance
with the architectural rules of new urbanism, neighborhoods are
within walking distance to the Town Square, with narrow streets
to reduce the influx of cars. It's like walking on the *Flintstones*
where the background repeats itself after every three houses and
a tree. This would just tickle the pink little ass of many Americans who would go apeshit over this cleansed, sterile habitat.

Passing the houses on Bouquet Park Lane, situated right on
top of each other (starting at the $700,000 range and up), I take
in the similar socialist quality of the homesteads; all different,
but yet exactly the same. I bet residents often make the mistake
of coming home late at night and accidentally walking into the
wrong house, for no house is bigger than the other, and all are
equally spaced apart, with small, but yet well groomed yards.
Still, weirdly void of people, I can imagine this place when it's
really kicking. Bathrobed Timberline Village residents coming to
their doors to pick up the morning paper symmetrically placed
on their doorsteps by Jimmy-the-local-paperboy, who greets
them with a smile and a friendly ring from the bell on his new
ten-speed bike. But where is the big small town community
interaction as boasted? One would be led to believe that a big
block party limbo contest would be taking place with hotdogs
being cooked on the grill by a guy in a clean, white chef's hat,
with his neighbors breaking into spontaneous laughter.

In order to continue my anthropological romp (to proportions of Jane Goodall and that stuff she did with the apes), I venture into an Timberline Village real-estate office. My trusty girlfriend is by my side (she was also with me at Quizno subs, but I forgot to mention it). The best way to describe how she is dressed, is that of being ultra-slutty. Her belly shirt and thick clown-painted makeup are also for anthropological-study-purposes (Jane Goodall-style). Now, I want to test the new urbanism's philosophy of welcoming diversity to their harmonious community.

The real-estate office, like the ice cream store and coffee shop, is also empty. I see the back of someone's head on the phone. I yell out using hip-hop lingo of my own creation.

"Yo dawg!"

A well-groomed woman, swings her chair around and comes over and stands by a small, miniature model of the entire Timberline Village community. She could be described as "snippy." I put out my knuckles with H-A-T-E, so we can touch fists, gesturing even more wildly than white-boy rapper Eminem, as I point to the small houses in the miniature Timberline Village.

"I want to use my bling-bling to move into a crib in your 'hood!" I state.

"You can take a look at the model next door," she sneers, looking at my T-shirt that says *Kill Em All, Let God Sort Them Out*, clearly not wanting to speak to me any further. She gives me the big chill cold treatment and hands me a price list as if it were a stinky turd.

"Ain't cha gonna give me a sales schizzel?" I question, wanting her to elaborate on the joys of new urbanism living.

"No! Just look at the models and let me know if you have any questions." She abruptly ends our interaction and goes back into her office.

"Come on baby, let's go eyeball the place," I tell my fauxslutty girlfriend as I give her a loud slurping French kiss in the middle of the sales office.

Not everyone looks kindly to new urbanism and its brethren. *The New York Times* (10/28/01) architecture critic, Herbert Muschamp, used such words as "controversial" when describing these communities.

"*Should we be optimistic that a solution will be found in the compact communities of the so-called New Urbanists? Appealing to what are essentially non-urban ideas of harmony and conflict avoidance they are as likely to increase social isolation as to overcome it,*" observes Muschamp.

My man Muschamp ironically envisions problems with these ideal Disney-like utopias, isolated from surrounding areas and motivated by the naive belief that a good development design can suddenly create a fabricated, forced community.

"Imagine being stuck in some suburban community planned by the New Urbanism. Talk about isolation: the buildings are close together but disconnected from anything large than market research," continues Muschamp.

With a philosophy that partly plays on inner-city fears, residents might be more concerned about their safety rather than partaking in the weekly community three-legged race. Also pointed out is the reality of not sharing your cramped new urbanism block with low-income families. In these largely white, very condensed communities, the prospect for some of rubbing elbows with the lower classes is "scary." The idyllic cultural diversity that new urbanism strives for is also undercut by the fact that these houses aren't cheap, and thus the price range protects them against "bad people," thus enabling the "strolling" and "neighborhood interaction" (if there really happened to be any) to go unhindered. And that's why, much to the horror of the real-estate agent, I'm French kissing my faux-slutty girlfriend to hold a mirror up to this prejudice. Or something like that.

We go next door and enter the model house. Inside, for display purposes, it's decorated in a style that they assume is the way the average new urbanism residents would want to decorate their home. This involves a great deal of wicker and what appears to be a long stopover at the Pottery Barn. Another couple, who look not unlike, those in the high-tech industries, are also going from room-to-room, discussing the merits of the house.

"Hey you could be our new neighbor," I offer with a snort of laughter. "Huh neighbor?"

The woman part of the high-tech couple makes an unhappy face.

"Yup, neighbors from the neighborhood," I once again stress. The man part of the high-tech couple sort of half-smiles. I pull my faux-slutty girlfriend closer, once again planting her with a loud slurping French kiss. By the time we finish, the high-tech couple has left the room. Noticing that we're now alone in the new urbanism house, we enter one of the wicker-filled bedrooms and contemplate engaging in a new urbanism sex act on the new urbanism model bed. Things come to a grinding halt when I suddenly spot a sign by the light switch that reads *"Premises Under Video Surveillance."* CAUGHT ON TAPE! Articles of clothing are quickly adjusted back into place. As we run for the door, Muschamp is once again brought to mind from an article he wrote in *Architecture Review (5/96)*. Idealistic new urbanites overestimate their plans since these more compact cities lead to a new set of problems. The new urbanist design theory relies "too much on esthetic solutions to the social problems created by urban sprawl." People looking for the simpler, purer, good old days, will be naïve to the fact that the progression of society creates a new set of social ills. I can see the appeal of this place for raising small children, but once the child was old enough to know he was living in a sterile cultural void, then what? It would be like the 70's Matt Dillon movie *Over the Edge* (nice obscure reference!) where a middle-class family moves into this quiet, idyllic preplanned, suburban community that's a virtual, isolated, cultural wasteland. There's nothing to do. There's no where to go in their bland little preplanned community designed with conformity in mind. In the end, the alienated teenagers rebel by locking all the parents and grownups in the high school and setting it ablaze. (Sure I'm not advocating that, but that's one hell of a great movie ending!)

Strolling (very quickly) to the central core of Timberline Village, we run across another house for sale. It doesn't look much different from the last place, but they too are having an open house. This time, there's a perky real-estate agent in a tie, on hand to answer enthusiastically any and every question about new urbanism living, boasting that this is the new, hot, up-and-coming area in the South Bay.

"Almost of the people living here are young professionals," he babbles.

"That's good," I grunt in reply. "Right now I live in Oakland. I just want to make sure I won't be living next to any of......THEM!" I slur. "You know who I mean? THEEEEEM!"

The guy in the tie is not sure which ambiguous minority group I'm referring to, so I repeat once again.

"You know....THEM.......THE CANADIANS," I stress and nod before moving on to the backyard that is almost the size of a carpet sample and about one inch away from the next, identical yard-sized house on either side. It feels very claustrophobic, devoid of privacy, like someone will always be sticking their nose into your business. The only thing separating the properties, is the legendary aforementioned picket fence, low enough to see the going's-on in the next yard.

Since this might be my new home, I poke my head over the fence and take on the role of the fabled wacky next-door-neighbor as seen on many a sitcom, including the Tim Allen vehicle, *Home Improvement*.

"Hi neighbor!" I bark to a man next door doing yard work. I point to one of his gardening tools. "Hey, I might want to borrow some of those when I move in," I exclaim with a cheesy grin. "See ya, neighbor!"

The man doing yard work gives me an I-won't-partake-in-your-potluck-dinners look. I turn to the enthusiastic agent.

"How is this area for noise?" I ask.

"You'll find it's very quiet here," he confirms in a perky sort-of-way.

"Yeah, but what about MY noise? I like to mix a lot of hip-hop music late at night."

The man in the tie explains that the walls are very sound-proof. He adds that there's also an apartment in back I can rent out. I tell him I'd like to use it as a crash pad for my hommies visiting from the hood. I also tell him how I'm going to decorate my front lawn with old furniture, and how, being a political activist, I'm going to picket Peet's Coffee due to their inhuman animal testing of coffee on monkeys. He doesn't have a problem with any of this. Maybe I was all wrong about new urbanism? Maybe it is an ideal, harmonious utopia for all walks of life; yes all walks of life who can come up with his asking price of $838,000. Realistically, that would keep out such riff-raff as myself. But since all the residents here don't all work and dine at Quizno's, the allusive dream of a self-contained, self-sufficient, walking utopia is shattered with the fact that anyone who lives here has to drive a distance to dine on something that isn't a sub. In my "open-minded" summary, I'd say that new urbanism isn't really changing how people live, it's merely another suburban subdivision masquerading as a small town. I came here looking for something *weird*, but all I found so far is a sterile, manufactured sense of beyond *normal*. The normal we grew accustomed to from our favorite family TV shows. It's an American dream. It's sheltered. It's something that would make you go mad.

15.

ACTION ALERT!
A MESSAGE FROM THE
AMERICAN FAMILY ASSOCIATION

Once again, I am delighted to pass on another informative email from the American Family Association in regard to how America can be a much better place:

HOLLYWOOD MAY LIKE OFFENSIVE CONTENT, BUT YOU DON'T HAVE TO WATCH IT!

I'm sure you agree that Hollywood is producing movies as though morals and family values are a thing of the past. Movies are being made with a shocking amount of offensive content, making it nearly impossible for a family to watch a movie together. While we are unable to control what is in the movie theatres, we can control what is viewed in our homes.

Let me introduce you to CleanFilms, a company who takes popular Hollywood movies titles and professionally edits out the offensive content. You no longer need to worry about unpleasant surprises while watching movies together as a family. CleanFilms has a large selection of DVDs to choose from and the entire inventory is free of profanity, nudity, graphic violence, and sexual situations. Thanks to CleanFilms there is no longer an excuse to subject yourself or your children to such vulgarity.

CUSTOMER PRAISE FOR CLEANFILMS

Just wanted to say thanx again for cleaning up movies and making them available! As a rule, my husband and I don't see R rated movies because we don't want to be "entertained" by obscenities, crude sexual humor and gore even though there have always been some that we really wanted to see. Thanx for eliminating that for us and letting us be able to watch a movie worry free—for our daughter's sake too. We are enjoying it so much, we went out and bought a DVD player for our bedroom too! Thanks so much!!! LOVE IT!!!!!!!!!!!! -Heidi

It is such a pleasure to be able to sit down and watch a good movie without the offensive language, nudity and gore that dominates the movies being released today. The quality of your work is unbelievable! If one didn't know that they had been edited, one would think that the movie was originally produced that way. Your editing is done in such as way as to maintain the integrity of the story and isn't at all distracting. Your movies aren't edited movies, they are good movies that have been enhanced to be great productions! Thank you so much for what you do! -D. W.

I received my rental of 'The Matrix Reloaded' from you yesterday. After watching [it], all I can say is: "Wow." The movie was edited with professional quality. Although there was no profanity, no sexual situations, no nudity and extreme gore, the film felt like nothing was hardly removed at all. Even my girlfriend was highly impressed with the quality of your work. It's nice to be able to sit down and watch a movie without having to worry about objectionable content coming across the screen. A greatly satisfied customer, Michael

I and my family LOVE CleanFilms! We are moving to Italy and the only reason we are not ecstatic is because there is no CleanFilms there! I cannot express how excited my family, and especially my children. Finally they can watch the movies all their friends are watching, but mom and dad (and honestly they too) are happy they're not getting all the unnecessary language, violence and sexuality they'd otherwise be exposed to! -Dia

I'd have to say that I don't feel I'm missing anything except the stuff I don't want to see or hear in the first place! Thank you for establishing such a great service that allows me to enjoy one of my favorite past times without all the filth that Hollywood interjects! -Scott

"There are people like me out there rooting for you. I'm a 35-year old who is tired of all the graceless and gratuitous "adult content" . . . I'm glad that people [like me] have another option. Freedom of choice shouldn't just extend to the more liberal among us." - Karen

"Enemy at the Gates is our first rental . . . and I want to thank you for providing such quality editing. With teenage boys who love war and adventure I have found it difficult to accommodate their desires and not violate my biblical standards. Keep up the good work." - Doug

"Our family is so happy to have your service that we just can't even believe it. The world is filled with so much that is evil, and to be able to enjoy movies without the bad things has been worth more than we can express" - Donna

Yes, Hats off to you CleanFilms, for taking liberties to edit directors movies and artistic vision, but most importantly, keeping America terrorist free!

16.
MY PART IN HOMELAND SECURITY!

We live in a security conscious age. People are paranoid. Look around, frickin' security guards are everywhere. Their purpose: keeping things in our country............ SECURE! With security guards in such demand, perhaps a good majority aren't of the upper echelon. Maybe the crème de-la-security-crème have already been scooped by such elite enter-prises as Taco Bell and WalMart.

That's why I set out to answer security guard want ads to see how undesirable one can be and still be hired for security work! What is the criteria for becoming a rent-a-cop? Can a rejected high school hall monitor be hired-even if he's really "creepy"?

FIRST STOP: Midrange security company

LOCATION: Downtown

PERSONA: The Questionable Background Guy

I'm dressed like a sniper wearing all black, stocking cap, and dark shades. After running up the stairwell of a building right out of a 1940's Sam Spade movie, I enter the office on the 6th floor. It's completely empty. Ironic, yes, for the security office......HAS NO SECURITY! I wander around from room-to-room, trying to find another human, with no results. Waiting, I take a position in the corner of the reception area under a sign that says "The Commitment to Integrity and Service." My legs are shoulder width apart, my hands around the belt-buckle area, as I do the security guard stance demonstrating how I could easily fit into the security scheme of things.

"I ran up the stairs!" I enthusiastically remark to a man of a nondescript foreign ethnicity in a blue suit, providing him with this information as he enters his own office. "I'm here to apply for the security guard job!"

"Is it for armed security guard?" he asks with a thick accent.

"Yes, armed!" I cry with conviction.

The guy in the blue suit distracts me while filling out the application, by arguing with his assistant over paying people overtime.

"Done!" I scream, holding up my completed application like an Olympic figure skating scorecard.

"Yes, I want to be an armed security guard!" I stress once again. I lay my Ernest Hemingway work of fiction on the man's desk. "I'm also a professional kickboxer," I throw in, striking a pose.

The man makes an excited face. Application in hand, he starts dialing his phone.

"Have you worked in security before?" he asks, momentarily stopping the dialing process.

"Yes! I did security for a place called " Club Valencia Street."

I fail to mention this exclusive "club" is my apartment address. Providing my cell phone number, I tell him to call my fictional boss Chas Lemon.

"Did you work for a security company at this club?"

"No, but I was the man in charge of the whole operation." (This really isn't a lie.)

He keeps reading my application. I stare straight ahead, like I'm harboring a terrible, terrible secret.

"What does it say here?" he asks pointing to the education portion of my application under Jefferson Hancock Military Academy. "You studied, is it 'American and.......Muslim

Studies?!'"

"Yes, I studied both!" Quickly, I gloss over this fact and change the subject. "I also went to Bounty Hunter school," I gleefully add. "They taught us how to hog-tie people'!"

In great detail, I elaborate. Once again, he reaches for the phone, almost dials, then doesn't. He looks again at my application.

"Your name is different here!"

The man points to a page that has both my name and the name *Osama Bin Leon.*

"Oh, yeah, I sometimes go by that name." Again, I quickly change the subject.

"Now what kind of places do you do security for?"

"Everywhere. Office buildings, residential, parking facilities......"

"Do you do airports?"

"No."

"How about *Payless Shoes?*"

No."

The man asks if I want to work full or part time. I answer like Travis Bickle in *Taxi Driver.*

"I'll work full time. I'll work part time. I'll work days. I'll work nights."

The man once again reaches for the phone, almost dials, then doesn't (who is he dialing anyway?!). I'm informed that he'll call me in a few weeks when the job is available.

"Remember, I want to be armed!" I run back down the stairs.

SECOND STOP: Large Corporate Security Company
LOCATION: Business District
PERSONA: The Overly Nice Guy

This is the Starbucks of security guard companies, with a chain of identical offices scattered about the city. I give the lobby security guard a respectful nod as if to say: "I support your plight fellow security brethren!"

Entering a nondescript office with several varieties of

authoritative plaques on the wall, I use my superior wit.

"Can I *'secure'* a job application" I say to a woman who opens a sliding glass window to interact with me.

"Did you see the ad in the paper?" she asks.

"Yes! I'd like to do my part in keeping our city 'secure.'"

"Do you have experience?" she adds

"No. But I think I would really look good in a security uniform," I say, pointing to parts of my body where the uniform would be worn.

I settle into the application, putting for past experience, elementary school crossing guard and high school hall monitor.

"They'll give you a call if they think you're qualified," says the woman behind the glass.

"Great, cuz I really want to protect people from 'THEM!" I state in a low raspy voice.

She looks up from my application expecting me to elaborate.

"You know 'THEM'......The Canadians!"

Again, my loathing of Canadians gets blank stares.

THIRD STOP: I'm Not Sure If It's A Security Company or a Knickknack Shop!
LOCATION: The part of town that smells like pee.
PERSONA: Guy who's really into cheese processing

I'm wearing a full tracksuit. I look like a Swedish tourist or a Romanian landlord. My final security guard interview is on the corner of Crack Ho Street and Pee Stench Boulevard.

I've dropped several levels on the security guard food chain. Inside, piles of junk seem to be randomly thrown everywhere, as a large man in a security uniform goes behind a rack of bikes and searches for my prized application.

Standing under a sign that reads *Assertiveness—The Key to Resolving* Conflict! Groping for an application, I elaborate on my years as an elementary school crossing guard as he continues. I don't know where the hell the uniformed man has gone.

"Do you know where those applications are," he yells to an

unseen person behind some bikes.

The uniformed man reemerges. He's empty-handed.

"Just come to the orientation meeting on Tuesday," he grunts. Hired! Bingo! It's that easy.

"I won't let you down," I say as I skip off like an excited schoolgirl.

TRAINING DAY

Tuesday, I ring the bell. I wait. I ring the bell again. Finally, a large chubby man answers, leading me past piles of junk to a backroom where two guys sit on a beat-up couch seeming to watch a TV with bad reception. One is sleeping to the point of snoring; the other, an old guy in a military hat, wears, for some reason two pairs of glasses simultaneously. I guess that these two guys could be propped up like human scarecrows.

The bell rings again. Who's next to join our elite security force? A lovable talking robot named Marty? The rest of the crew files in. They look like the kind of people you'd find working a telemarketing job. This is like Scooby Doo and the Mystery Machine gang, as we're led by a large African American man in a security uniform who goes by the rank of "lieutenant."

"If you come to work high, how can I trust you?!" is his first order of business—apparently an issue for someone in the room.

"I told all of you to wear a uniform for training," barks the lieutenant. "Do you know what 'S-T-O-P' stands for?"

"Stop," yells the guy wearing two pairs of glasses simultaneously.

"No, Standard Training Operation Procedure."

"I don't care what you say, it's 'stop,'" retorts the guy with two simultaneous pairs of glasses.

"If you're ready to work, look like it," stresses the Lieutenant.

The floor is open for inane questions.

"Do we get paid an hour extra because it is daylight savings time?"

Afterwards, everyone is scolded for not bringing their time sheets. I hand in my heavily- laden-cheese-processing-work-experience application. The Lieutenant glances at it for about a second, then pulls out his schedule.

"Your 'tour of duty' will be at the Oakland Denny's Friday night from 10 to 5 in the morning."

He wants me to be a white security guard for the graveyard shift at Denny's smack in middle of "the hood"?! The Lieutenant says this like he's shipping me off to battle. He's trying to call this white boy's bluff. Does he call it a "tour of duty," because it's a lot like war?

Glancing at the security report from last Friday night, I note the part where the police had to be called.

"I don't want to surprise you, but they'll be a lot of hostile, disrespectful people at the Oakland Denny's," stresses the Lieutenant. "If you don't look serious, they will walk right through you!"

Obviously the Lieutenant has figured out what I'm up to otherwise, why would he assign me to one of the least desirable security gigs known to humanity.

"When I work, I don't even laugh or smile," pipes a security peer about the size of a child. Great, I always wanted a job totally devoid of both laughing and smiling—all for $7.50 an hour!

"The guy who trained me stayed in his car the whole time," someone else adds.

"You may not see me, but I can see you!" the Lieutenant stresses before we depart.

He's testing me. I'll show him; I'll play chicken. I'll call *his* bluff by taking the graveyard security shift in the hood.

TOUR OF DUTY—DENNY'S

Friends of mine tell me not to do it because they think I'm going to get killed on the graveyard shift in *the hood*. The afternoon of my big security gig, I get a message on my answering machine from the Lieutenant.

"You don't need to come in tonight. Come in next week instead."

What?! My world's crumbling. I need to be a security guard NOW! This is a mere technicality I'll show him; I'll just show up anyway. Venturing to a thrift store, I buy a makeshift security guard uniform, consisting of a blue jacket and hat that says "Security," then I attach an overabundance of keys to my belt. I just upped the ante.

I get to the *Oak-town* Denny's a half-hour early, enabling me to begin my self-appointed shift before the scheduled security guards arrive.

"I was told to work security tonight," I say to a mildly disinterested woman behind the register. "What should I do?"

"Uh, I guess you can stand by the door," she answers, making me feel at ease that any clown in a makeshift security uniform can walk into Denny's and be knighted with an authority position. Making a "mean" face, I stand by the entrance, glaring at people as they enter. My philosophy—every customer is a potential troublemaker.

Then in walks the Lieutenant and three other scheduled security guards in much superior uniforms.

"I'm here for my 'tour of duty,'" I excitedly tell the Lieutenant who looks confused.

"Didn't you get my message?"

"No."

(Awkward pause) "OK."

Since I'm already here and wearing a uniform of sorts, the Lieutenant puts me to work, quickly briefing me, and referring to me and the other security guards as "officers." I'm an officer!

Denny's is pretty empty. But with the presence of four security guards, or *The Fantastic Four*, the place is very "secure."

As it turns out, our security overkill presence makes every customer very uncomfortable. It's like too many National Guardsmen at the airport.

"Why do you have so many security guards?" asks an elderly woman.

"It will get real crazy in here around 2 am," retorts my cosecurity peer who is the size of a child (he's my favorite).

"Then what?" she asks.

"We're going to hold it down!" explains the child-sized security guard. The elderly woman and her two elderly friends openly laugh their heads off.

"Are you guys having a convention?" mocks a hungry man wanting a table. "I've never seen a Denny's like this!"

'What's your job, just standing around," adds his date. This is a Catch-22. If no one causes trouble, all the customers mercilessly heckle you.

"When did Denny's start having security?" a pesky woman inquires.

"Since that one thing happened," I inform her.

"When?" she asks with concern.

"Earlier tonight!"

"What happened?"

"A guy tried to steal a Grand Slam Breakfast. He got away with the two strips of bacon, but we apprehended him before he got the two eggs and bacon."

The second in command, noting my excellent prowess in dealing with the general public, comes over.

"Why don't you patrol the parking lot," he orders.

"I'm on it!"

Minutes later, I return, frantic.

"We have a situation!"

"What?"

"SUV parked in driveway!"

"Go tell Aaron."

"I'm on it!"

Aaron situates me outside, with the important task of watching the driveway.

"Don't let anyone park here."

"I'm on it!"

I write in my hourly security report, "It's quiet, perhaps a little *too* quiet."

Moments later, someone parks in the driveway. I can't be bothered to tell them not to, since I don't really care. Instead, I

wander off Denny's premises. It's time for some "freelancing."
Going into the Food Mart, I approach the man behind the
counter.

"Do you need a security guard? I can start right away!"

He gives me a stern "no." I stand by the potato chips for several minutes, showing him what he's missing out on.

Moving on I go across the street to the competitor, *Lyon's
Family Restaurant*.

"Are you waiting for a table?" asks the overworked hostess.

"No. I do security at Denny's and was wondering if you were
interested in having me switch teams," I state. "I could start right
way."

She laughs. I don't.

Returning from my sojourn, I write in my hourly security
report, "There's hungry people here, perhaps a little *too* hungry."
I find that I'm being ostracized by the other Denny's security
guards. They occasionally laugh and joke, but for the safety of
the Denny's customers, I take no part. Instead, I use my position
to go MAD-WITH-POWER!

"You can't stand there, " I tell a girl wearing a UC Berkeley
sweatshirt, pointing to an ambiguous area.

"What?"

"We can't have people standing in this area!" I point again
to a square of carpet.

I move on to a table of diners. "Sir, do you know that man
just stole a fry off your plate," referring to his dinner companion.
"I just thought I'd let you know."

I turn to the thief, indicating my eyes with two of my fingers.

"I'll be watching you!"

Two people playfully push each other by the counter.

"We have a situation!" I scream to the second in command.
He doesn't find it as serious as I do. Instead he sends me out to
patrol the parking lot.

I nod my head, and instead go into the kitchen and make
myself a large cocoa. Mmmm cocoa.

At roughly 2 am things drastically change. It's the "rude" and
"disrespectful" part as mentioned in training. Drunks, aggressive

people are let out of bars, and they are HUNGRY! Hoards of angry, drunk and mainly males with little patience for waiting for a table, hit Denny's. It's our job as security officers to keep order.

I write in my hourly security report, "I'M FREAKING OUT MAN! I'M REALLY FREAKING OUT!"

"Can you stand by the door and not let people in; we're full," directs the second in command.

"I'm on it!"

My purpose it to be an intimidating force. But instead I take a laissez-faire approach. A group of eight ADHs (Angry, Drunk, and Hungry) demand that they get in NOW!

"Sure go right ahead," I say, holding open the door for them. I also hold the door open for the group behind them.

"How come you're letting people in?" questions an irritated second in command, relinquishing my command.

"Oh, that's what you meant," I sigh, like I just don't get it.

"How long do we have to wait for a table," whines a drunken woman.

"Normally it would be at least a half hour, but for you it's going to an hour or more!" I say, penalizing her by, tacking on more time.

"Can't we take that table," she insists, pointing to an empty booth.

"No!"

"Why not?"

"Security reasons!" I stress. "And if you ask me again, I'll add another ten minutes to your wait!" I have to stand firm on my policy or risk losing my authority.

I spend the rest of the peak rush going into the kitchen and making myself a large cocoa with extra whipped cream. Mmmm cocoa.

In the end, I survived my graveyard shift at Denny's in the hood. At 5 am I bid farewell to my fellow security guards. But don't be disappointed at my early retirement. Next time you venture to Walmart, Payless shoes, or the airport, just remember, there will be guys like me, keeping things SECURE!

17.
Do Your Part— Help Fight the War on Terrorism !

I often consult the Do Your Part website (www.doyourpart.us) in order to know exactly how I can do my part, here in America, to fight the war on terror:

DO YOUR PART-FIGHT TERROR-BOYCOTT THE ENEMY!

Join Our Boycott - Protest Forum
Does it matter what others say and do?

Yes it matters. By giving aid and support to terrorist They are putting the world, our troops and our children at risk.

How can everyone help?

By boycotting and contacting any person, company or country that supports, aids, or harbors terrorists. We can't stand by and let them think they can aid, support, or harbor terrorists without paying a price. As President Bush said " Freedom is a two-way street". Don't wait for another 9 - 11, do your part now.

PROTEST THE DIXIE CHICKS AT NEW YORK'S MADISON SQUARE GARDEN

When the Dixie Chicks get to Madison Square Garden in New York (6/20/03 - 6/21/03), I'll be there. I'm going to let the Dixie Chicks and the World know I have not forgotten 9-11. We can't let anyone talk crap about the President when he is trying to make the world a safer place. I hope all New Yorkers help me protest the Dixie Chicks. They may not have received many BOOS in other cities but when they get to New York they will find they are not in DIXIE !!

BOYCOTT MCI

I think MCI should terminate the sponsorship contract it has with Danny Glover because of his recent comments condemning the war with Iraq, and his comments about Cuba being better than the US. I think MCI should not let Danny Glover do their commercials because MCI will lose money if Danny Glover is on the air on MCI commercials. It might not be the correct thing to do, but still, MCI will lose money if they don't take Glover off the air. The majority of the USA agreed with the war, so the majority of people will be turned off by MCI commercials with Danny Glover sponsoring them, resulting in less $ gained by MCI for airing the commercial. If MCI keeps airing Glover in commercials, I will never buy MCI again (not that I did in the first place).

Boycott Danny Glover, and even MCI if they keep airing ads with Danny Glover on them!!!!

18. WHAT PART OF *ILLEGAL* DON'T THEY UNDERSTAND?

With a whistle on my lips, a song in my heart (not to mention a skip in my step), I saunter past a sign that reads "No Loaded

Guns Past This Point." It gets better. I've arrived at the Cow Palace for the *Crossroads of the West Gun Show*. I'm here to infiltrate a group called FAIR—*Federation for American Immigrant Reform*. In order to go fully undercover, I'm going by the patriotic name *Franklin Washington*, adopting an American flag bandana and a T-shirt that reads *I Support Desert Storm*.

Why?

Recently, I saw this frightfully disturbing documentary called *Farmingville*. 1,500 Mexican workers immigrated to this small suburban Long Island town of 15,000. The locals' reaction was not unlike, say, Southern rednecks during the civil rights movement of the '60's. Suspicion of those who were different created fear, racism, and violence. For some, the immigration policies gave an arena to vent embedded racist opinions of those of color (no one vents on the Canadian invasion from the north). Such notorious hate groups as the *National Alliance* and the *World Church of the Creator* began recruiting in the Farmingville area once the story hit the national news. FAIR was the group spearheading the local racist protestors' plight to remove the immigrants. FAIR flocked to Farmingville to throw fuel on the xenophobic fire.

At the Cow Palace, FAIR has arranged to have a booth where it can solicit signatures for a petition that would put Proposition 187 on the ballot. Prop. 187 would *Save Our Licenses*. I had learned about the measure in an earlier telephone conversation with Carol, a kindly sounding grandmotherly type.

"Since it's a gun show there shouldn't be a problem getting people to sign," Carol briefed me over the phone, adding about a recent protest. "Some people said it was racist."

"It's not racist," I gleefully injected to gain brownie points. "It's just American!"

As Carol explained: "The main issues are, we're against drivers licenses for illegal aliens, no public benefits for illegal aliens, no welfare, and no college tuition."

I responded by uttering my new, soon to be overused, catchphrase, "What part of illegal don't they understand?"

A classic infiltration is actually becoming the face of an organization you extremely hate. That's why I've volunteered to man FAIR's *Save Our License* booth and solicited hardened Americans to sign their inane petition.

Studying FAIR's website, Glen Spencer's American Patrol, and uber-conservative treasures of the hyper-white Barbara Coe's California Coalition for Immigration Reform, which sees a Mexican conspiracy to seize control of the US, I'm now ready to throw a skewed version of their twisted moon-man logic right back in their faces. I'm now ready to hold a sad mirror up to their spouting asinine rhetoric.

Big bellies abound. The overweight really relish gun shows for they seem to have come in abundance. Directly next to a row of assault weapons, rifles, and for some reason, samurai swords (only a few rows down from a booth selling Nazi flags and pictures of Hitler), is our table with a huge sign reading, NO DRIVERS LICENSES FOR ILLEGAL ALIENS!

"What part of *illegal* don't they understand!" I state to the other volunteers, shaking my head and pointing to the sign.

How surprising, FAIR's entire crew is comprised entirely of retirees. Go figure that those behind this drive are people with way too much free time on their hands. We're now a ragamuffin bunch; kind of like a moronic crime fighting team from another dimension or world of tomorrow, set upon this earth to rid America of those pesky illegal aliens with their funny music and crazy hats. Why there's Carol, Roy, Tom, Kay, and me. Pointing to the sign, making a good first impression with the organization, I proclaim, "What part of illegal don't they understand?"

I can tell Roy is clearly the leader. Taking me on board, he explains, "We need 600,000 signatures to get Proposition 187 on the ballot." Roy then gets real animated and intense about why illegal aliens shouldn't have drivers' licenses. "It sends a message. It says, *you got to go home, I don't want you HERE!*"

Kay, wearing an American flag pendent, seeming like the type who'd bake pies and let them cool on a window sill, adds with seething bitterness under her grandmotherly demeanor, "I can hardly pay for healthcare, now I have to pay for THEIRS too?!"

"What part of *illegal* don't they understand!"

"You now have to be bilingual to work at Radio Shack," comments elderly Tom, as I pick at my elbow. "My son can only speak one language and he can't even get hired there."

"What part of *illegal* don't they understand!" I say again for effect, absorbed that Tom is the father of a Radio Shack reject.

"What do you do for a living?" asks Tom.

"I'm a puppeteer!" I answer with pride, moving my hands like I'm operating a marionette. The group nods in approval. "They're taking our jobs too!" I add, as the group heads' nod again in agreement, interrupted only by Roy spewing with disgust over why 187 is not on the ballot.

"Ever since the feminist movement, the legislation has been all wrapped up in women's issues!"

"Where I live, all these day laborers line the street looking for work. It's just not safe. You know, like for women," I spout, leaning in close to Carol to instill Bush-era fear of those who are different, for they might eat your babies. "You know what I mean?"

"This is true," she solemnly comments. "This is true."

"One of our members in Mountain View takes photos of license plates of people picking up day laborers," she offers as one of their strategies. Carol makes my thoughts drift back to the documentary on Farmingville:

The residents of conservative and staid Farmingville began to take to the streets in protest with such signs as "Use the Military To Deport Illegal Aliens!" They began hassling contractors who swept into town looking for workers, harassing landlords who rented homes to illegal aliens, confronted politicians, and formed activist groups to face the problem that had come to their suburb. Inevitably passions would rise and the issue at hand would become clouded in accusations and charges, as xenophobia and racism reared their ugly heads. They imagined the immigrants coming to re-conquer and take over the country, and together they sang "God Bless America."

My task today is to approach some of the scariest people known to humanity and ask them to sign our petition. With clipboard in hand, Roy shows me the ropes.

"Just say to people, 'If this is an issue that concerns you, please sign our petition.'"

With that, he swarms down on a man in a black wife-beater T-shirt who looks like, yet, another guy who runs his own country in the woods.

"Come on! Let's get you signed up!"

"Hell ya! Hell ya!" exclaims the scary man. As an aside, he adds, "I wish they'd tighten up the borders!"

Giving it a try, I have the option of also handing out informative flyers that read *"HAD ENOUGH? By definition, ILLEGAL ALIENS are CRIMINALS in violation of Federal immigration law.* Tired of "rewarding" criminals with *YOUR* hard-earned tax dollars?" Emphasizing this point is an illustration showing a check written out to *Illegal Aliens.* The check, belonging to *California Citizens,* is made out to the amount of 5 billion dollars. Subtlety is our friend!

"You're letting them get away!" criticizes Roy on my early attempts at petitioning people, the kind of people you might see profiled on A&E's *City Confidential.*

"Will you sign our petition to prevent illegal aliens from getting drivers' licenses?" I ask a sweaty, paranoid man with shifty eyes.

"I don't put my signature on ANYTHING!" he barks, then disappears into the crowd of gun lovers.

For the most part, though, the gun crowd loves our cause.

"It's fucking bullshit. Those liberal bastards," rants a crusty old man, shaking his head in disgust.

"Wake up America!" I contribute, throwing in my two-cents.

"Tell me about it. I worked for the INS for 20 years. Big dummies," he repeats then adds, "I'm going to get my friend to sign this."

"If I were in charge," fanaticizes a guy with a big belly and bulbous nose and rifle strapped to his back, "nobody would be getting through, NOBODY!" He hands me back my clipboard.

"Save our jobs!" I proclaim.

"Save our country!" he adds.

"Enough is enough!" (I top him.)

"It's a fight for America!" (He tops me.)

"If Mexico wants a fight, all I can say is COME AND GET IT!" (I am back on top.)

Then the big belly man adds, "Yeah, we'll bomb them back to the Stone Age!" (I guess he won that round.)

I approach a Hispanic guy to sign my petition.

"I don't speak English," he responds with difficulty.

I continue. "The petition's against illegal aliens getting drivers' licenses."

"I don't speak English," he repeats again.

I try to further explain using mime. He yells something in Spanish to a group of friends, who yell back and then shoot me a look like they want to kill me (they're in the proximity of guns, mind you.)

"They probably have illegal drivers' licenses," Carol sneers as they walk away.

I shake my head with disgust. "What part of illegal don't they understand?"

When the immigrants wanted to organize a soccer tournament in Farmingville, in an attempt to build a bond with the community, concerned citizens actually wrote the mayor and said 'I can't believe you are going to let them use OUR soccer fields and play amongst our children! We don't know who these people are. They're undocumented and could have criminal records!'

"Do you like Lugars?" a crusty, large man randomly asks me. "They're cool," he adds.

"I'm more of a Glock man myself," I respond.

"You should join the California Rifle Pistol Association," he explains, saying the organization protects guns from being banned in our state.

Bringing the focus back to the cause, I hand him a petition and state, "Guns don't kill, illegal aliens with guns kill!"

Oh how we laugh.

After the initial rush, my group is stuck sitting at our *Save Our License* table, which has all the atmospheric pleasantry of, well, a gun show.

"You know, I wouldn't mind buying a bayonet," I offer as my

part in making small talk.

Tom starts rattling on about how he likes to tinker around with Model T Fords in his spare time. Tom's completely lost sight of our group's plight. Trying to bring the focus back, I shake my head and abruptly blurt, "What part of illegal don't they understand?!"

This seems to wake up Tom, putting him back on track.

"Eisenhower got it right with *Operation Wetback*. The police lined the borders and removed illegal aliens," he recounts with a hint of nostalgia about a simpler time. "We should've got Pat Buchanan in here 4 years ago. He would've cracked down on it!" Tom tells me how he voted for the Constitutional Party for President since they have the toughest policy on illegal aliens. "This is the big issue for me," he shares. Amazing. God-fearing George W. Bush is not conservative enough for this group. "I'd like to give Bush a big kick in the behind!"

"You mean you're mad at Bush for letting them come across the border?" Roy retorts.

"What about the Northern border? What about the influx of Canadians?" I inquire to see if their wrath extends to white immigrants as well. "You know, they come over here with their funny accents, taking our jobs." I rant.

"I don't think there's too much of a problem of that," Kay replies, looking though she's never really pondered that notion before.

"Sure there is," I elaborate (wondering why Kay doesn't have a problem with illegal Canadians). "If Canada wants a war, all I can say is *COME AND GET IT!*"

The conflict in Farmingville escalated with a hate-based attempted murder of two Mexican day laborers. Two white supremacists picked up the day laborers and took them to an abandoned building. Once there they brutally beat and stabbed the young men, leaving them for dead. Before picking up the day laborers, one of the white supremacists was quoted to have said, "Let's go find us some Mexicans!"

Adding to my sales pitch, I digress on the issues!

"Prop 187 means no cable TV and health club memberships

for illegal aliens," I explain to a concerned hefty woman who's eating nachos.

My goal now is to have no one sign the petition. I shall get subtly more racist in my sales pitch to see if I can creep people out, while acting really indignant towards those who don't sign.

"Fine!" I shriek to a man from Contra Costa County as I roll my eyes. "See what I care when THEY are running rampant in your neighborhood, spreading diseases, and playing that Cucaracha music."

"I agree with you in principal but not in legislation," a man with glasses responds to my request for petition signing. "I have to think about it."

"You can't argue successfully against the fact!" I lean in real close and whisper, "Come on, do you really want THEM dating your sister?" Locking eyes, I shake my head with a concerned look.

"I came here twenty years ago," comments a large Russian, who, for some reason, is wearing army fatigues, and is signing Carol's petition. "We're a country of immigrants."

"Yes, but the other immigrants came here legally!" Carol responds.

"Yeah, especially the good ones. You know the white ones from Europe," I add with a wink and a nudge. "You know what I mean?"

I decide to lighten the mood of the gun show by interjecting something I call, a little "humor." After roaming to some of the dealer's tables, I've returned with my purchases—"funny" bumper stickers.

"Look what I got," I smirk to Kay, ready to share a laugh, laying a bumper sticker on the table that reads *Welcome to America—Either Learn the Language or LEAVE!*

"Isn't that great?!" I add.

Kay laughs. Laugh Kay, laugh! Just a little humor among two like-minded people.

"I like those bumper stickers that say, *Vote Democrat—For Those Who Don't Like to Think!*" she injects with delight. "I'm thinking of getting some of those printed."

We laugh. We're really getting along. I lay another bumper sticker on the table.

"Look what else I got!" I proudly tell Kay. This bumper sticker has a Confederate flag. It reads *The South Was Right!*

I nudge Kay and let out a high-pitched squeal.

Carol and Kay share how they picketed outside several large Silicon Valley companies that hired employees that must have a great deal of education training, and require very complicated technical expertise. Yes, my group also has a bad taste for immigrants who come over here to work even high-tech jobs with an H1B visa! Kay even closed her Wells Fargo banking account to protest the company's support of MALDEF (Mexican American Legal Defense and Education Fund); an organization clearly not to her liking.

"I actually went undercover and infiltrated their meeting. I wore a wig so they wouldn't recognize me and tape recorded the meeting," she shares with a devilish smile.

"Let me get this straight," I inquire. "You put on a disguise and went undercover in order to infiltrate their group?"

"Exactly!"

"That is *so* clever," I add, adjusting my American flag bandana and fidgeting with *my* tape recorder. "I could never do anything like that."

A large man with baseball cap doesn't sign hardcore Roy's petition!

"Well, if you made all the illegal aliens in the country, legal," the man offers as a solution to their argument, "then they would be documented and have to pay taxes."

This stumps Tom and Roy; they really don't know how to respond and momentarily grow quiet, staring at their shoes.

I break the silence by offering, "What part of illegal don't they understand?"

Argument won! When the man in the baseball cap leaves, Roy whispers with a smug smile, "Something tells me he hires illegal aliens."

The hate-filled, attacks in Farmingville shifted sympathy in the community as the anti-racism sentiment moved to the forefront. Omi-

nously, however, the shock of the incident served to polarize and harden feelings rather than bring the community together.

The gun show winds down! With skewed rhetoric reverberating in my head and the image of large Americans waving guns, I'm so glad I never have to come back here and hang out with these people ever again. Gun dealers start covering their assault weapons and rifles for the day. Roy begins counting the number of signed petitions. Earlier, I had the uneasy feeling that the day was going to end with a little blanket party in the parking lot with the retirees, Kay, Carol, Roy and Tom hitting me with large sticks. But instead it seems Roy likes my gung-ho attitude and feels confident there will be a future generation that will carry on his leadership torch.

Carol suggests we leave our petitions here until tomorrow, remarking with a warm-hearted chuckle, "This is the safest place in the world because everyone here knows how to use a gun!" A real chuckle.

Roy vetoes the idea.

"You don't know who's around," he remarks.

"Some people don't like what we stand for," Kay comments.

I shake my head in disbelief, then add, "What part of illegal don't they understand?"

"We got 360 signatures today," Roy proudly proclaims. "I'm going to look these over tonight to make sure everything is in order."

"You know, if you want, I could take some of those home and look them over for you and bring them back tomorrow," I suggest with mock job-pride.

Roy smiles. I'm pegged as a new go-getter. As the stack of petitions are handed to me, I smile madly at Roy. Wake up America!

19.

WHAT WILL YOU DO WHEN THE ILLEGAL ALIENS COME?

The Citizens Against Illegal Immigration (CAII) have outlined on a website what will happen if there were an influx of illegal aliens in YOUR neighborhood. When reading this, remember, the term "illegal alien" as referring to Canadians.

DO YOU WANT TO PREVENT THESE EFFECTS OF ILLEGAL ALIEN IMMIGRATION IN YOUR NEIGHBORHOOD?

1. Increase in crime. (WAKE UP AMERICA!)

The destruction of our language and our culture. (WAKE UP AMERICA!)

Increased litter and other environmental issues, as well as more animal welfare problems. (WAKE UP AMERICA!)

Breakdown of law and order. (WAKE UP AMERICA!)

Unresponsive government officials who literally couldn't care less about the 2/3 of Americans who say in every poll that they want immigration laws enforced NOW. (WAKE UP AMERICA!)

AND LAST, BUT SURE NOT LEAST—

Voter registration and election fraud by non-citizens. (WAKE UP AMERICA!)

Don't wait for "someone" else to solve these problems, because that "someone" is YOU!

If we are to persuade our elected officials to listen to us, restore trust in government, and rid us of these curable problems, we must act together and act now.

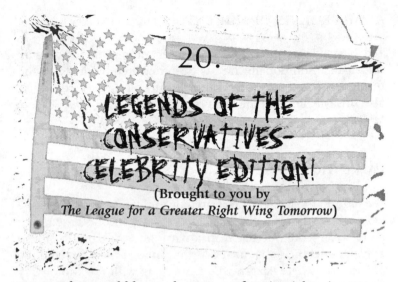

20.

LEGENDS OF THE CONSERVATIVES— CELEBRITY EDITION!

(Brought to you by
The League for a Greater Right Wing Tomorrow)

What would be a salute to our favorite right-wing entertainers be without a nod to the Motor City Madman himself, Ted Nugent. Yes, who would have thought the rock guitarist who would play on stage in a loincloth and sing about *poontang*, would also be almost as conservative as Jerry Falwell? Ted Nugent, we salute you for being one conservative mofo, and we're damn glad to have ya, buddy!

BIRTH: December 13, 1948

BIRTHPLACE: Detroit, Michigan

OCCUPATION: Motor City Madman, bow hunter, beef jerky manufacturer.

TED NUGENT FUN FACT

Did you know that Ted Nugent's nickname is The Nuge?

ACHIEVEMENTS OF NUGENT

Ted Nugent was named 1999 Conservationist of the Year in Michigan. Additionally, he has been honored by the NRA and firmly respects the four F's, Faith, Family, Flag, & Freedom. He also firmly believes in the two G's and two R's, *God, Guns, & Rock 'n' Roll*.

PATRIOTIC HEAVY METAL

Ted Nugent took a new direction in his musical career in the late '80's when he formed *Damn Yankees*—a patriotic based rock band. What could be better in a patriotic rock band than also enlisting the forces that included the guitarist from *Styx* and the bassist from *Night Ranger*, who teamed up with the 'Motor City Madman' to create some flag-waving rock!

TED NUGENT FUN FACT

Did you know that Ted Nugent is straight-edge? He doesn't drink or smoke.

NUGENT SPEAKS HIS MIND

Yes, Ted Nugent, The Motor City Madman, is not afraid to speak his mind. And if liberal pansies out there can't take it, then they can KISS HIS ASS!!! Such was the case when Nugent was barred from a Houston concert venue after he did what they claimed was some Immigrant bashing against Latinos, which the liberals couldn't take because the Nuge wasn't afraid to speak the truth and come out and say exactly what's on all our minds!

Opening for KISS at the Cynthia Woods Mitchell Pavilion, those who came to hear Nuge crank out such classics as *Cat Scratch Fever* and *Wang Dang Sweet Poontang*, were pleasantly treated to an informative diatribe on stage concerning *the truth* about Latino immigrants. "If you're not gonna speak English, get the Fuck out of America," he told the crowd. Also, weighing as a factor in his being barred was the Nuge's continual use of the word "faggot" throughout the show.

Way to go Ted Nugent! Way to represent what we conservatives are thinking by speaking the truth!

NUGE SPEAKS HIS MIND SOME MORE

Following the concert, Nuge reiterated his position some more on immigrants when he spoke to the *Houston Chronicle*. "If you're going to be an asset to America," Nugent said, "it would only be logical to speak the language. How can you be a benefit to your family, neighborhood or country if you can't speak to your fellow citizens? C'mon, if you can't speak English, get out of America."

Hats off again to Ted Nugent; one who doesn't shy away from the truth!

NUGGETS OF NUGENT

Ted Nugent's appearance on a Denver morning radio show was cut short after he used derogatory racial terms for Asians and blacks. The Nuge defended the remarks, "I made the comment that you can't play real, authentic, soulful, tuneful blues on a Jap guitar. My use of the word 'Jap' has obviously upset some people. Get over it."

To legitimize his argument, aren't *British* called *Brits* for short and isn't *country* called *cunt*?

Yes, America, get over it; especially all you angry Japs out there!

HUNTING NUGE-STYLE!

An avid hunter, Ted Nugent was a frequent visitor to Canada until the government of Ontario cancelled the spring black bear hunt in 1999. Upset that he could no participate in the hunt, Nugent vowed to never set foot again in what he described as "an idiotic country." (I warned you about those Canadians!)

TED NUGENT FUN FACT!

Ted Nugent manufactures his own brand of beef jerky!

DID YOU KNOW?

Did you know Ted Nugent is one of the most notable bow hunters in America today? This causes controversy amongst crybaby liberals who find bow hunting to be one of the cruelest forms of hunting known to humanity, just because archery equipment ends up wounding more animals than it kills. For every animal dragged from the woods, at least one animal is left wounded to suffer - either to bleed to death or to become infested with parasites and diseases. Boo-hoo-hoo!

What does Nuge have to say about this?

"Our honorable hunting heritage remains a vital drive in our modern culture today because of the force of our families to demand this connection with the inner soul of man, and all life giving elements that provide us sustenance," says Nuge. "Natural resources for the body and the spirit. We thrive on independence and that spirit of community. We wallow in her beauty. The stimuli. The contest. The hunt. The touch. Clear days and dangerous storms. Mother Nature can bitch, but we still love the hell outta the ol' gal."

Wow, that's profound, man!

NUGENT ON NUGENT

"My life is an adventure. For example, when I go hunting, I don't go to get meat. If I wanna get meat, it's a lot easier to go to the fuckin' store. You know what I'm after? Adventure."

Way to go Ted Nugent! We're right behind you, whether you're in a loin cloth swinging across a concert stage, manufacturing beef jerky, hunting a deer with a bow and arrow, or keeping those wetbacks in their place. Rock on Nuge, rock on!

21.
I SPY ON THE FBI

Hey everyone, it's the first annual FBI Media Day—a public relations stunt put on by the Sacramento Federal Bureau of Investigation for the esteemed mainstream conservative press. With an open invitation to the FBI headquarters, what better way to find out how they are spying on citizens? Even though it's always been nearly impossible to get any information from the FBI, especially stories regarding people detained under the Patriot Act, their goal, through Media Day, is to now convince us they're indeed human and accessible. Could it be a result of the backlash from those concerned about civil liberties violated through the Patriot Act?

My goal then will be to act like a counterspy, infiltrate their hardened walls and find out what they're really doing in these investigations. They, on the other hand, will most likely be watching me. Yes, step forth with me into the world of *Spy vs. the FBI*.

Now, since I'm an aforementioned esteemed journalist, I, of course, should be attending conservative Media Day. For the sake of irony, I'm wearing a white shirt and tie, trying to create my impression of *Special Agent Leon*. The fellow attendees will be a collection of mainstream conservative media at their mainstream conservative media best. Yes, a fun-filled day as the FBI lets the press inside to fire neat gun simulators and take wicked polygraph tests, making us forget that in reality they, in all circumstances, refuse to give out information on current cases because they deem it as *classified*.

A word of wisdom, never get mildly baked right before spending a day at the FBI headquarters. Not to say I did, but you'd really find yourself feeling paranoid pulling up to the gates of the nondescript brick building, across from a fabric store whose sign reads in bold font *Federal Bureau of Investigation*.

Once inside, I collect a FBI all-access building clearance pass, get questioned on whether I have a picture phone, then saunter through the metal detector. It goes off.

"Face the *10 Most Wanted*," informs the uniformed security guard, waving a wand which initiates buzzing. I stare straight ahead, focused on a picture of Hopeton Eric Brown within the *10 Most* framed picture. A conservatively dressed woman escorts me down the FBI hallways as we pass men with guns and framed pictures of guys in suits looking very serious.

"Nice place you have here," I say, making small talk.

A very serious looking man in a suit tells me, "Help yourself to some bagels and coffee," as I enter the sterile conference room filled with people in *Ross Dress For Less* bad suits and mandatory ties. Blue is a primary color. This is the mainstream conservative press. But, apparently, the esteemed journalists are on holiday. The B-team has been sent with badges trumpeting such media suave hotbeds as towns with names like Redding, Vacaville and Fairfield. But they're prepared. Some have special notebooks that say *Reporter Notebook* and their name written on the front. Even with the addition of my ironic tie, with my still scruffy appearance, amongst the conservative press B-team, I stand out like a sore thumb with herpes.

FBI FUN FACT: Did you know that Sacramento boasts the largest FBI division in square miles in California? Established in 1967, out of the 56 FBI divisions in the United States, Sacramento is the newest with 118 agents.

Things are kicked off by an introduction from the special agent in charge of the Sacramento field office. He gives us the lowdown on media day, which he says will provide an inside look into the structure and operations of the FBI. On one side of the room, in a row of chairs, sit various agent Mulders (no Skullys) under a somber wall dedicated to pictures of FBI Martyrs. The FBI is primarily a boy's club. Their suits are far superior to the media's. Sitting along the wall, they look like stern father types.

The guy sitting next to me, who writes for a newspaper on legal issues, whispers to me about his prior FBI media experience of not getting much of anything from them, even when he's spotted FBI agents conducting business at a crime scene.

"It's hard to get information, to confirm or deny, even though I just drove by and saw them."

"We're going to have some fun," the FBI head proclaims before introducing the FBI agents—a varied mix of good cop/bad cop types, that head each department. They will give a brief presentation at a podium that reads Sacramento Division, on their specialty with topics ranging from white-collar and cyber crime, to drugs and terrorism.

"If it's Bubba and Cooter, I'd be investigating them," explains the FBI dry special agent, with really droopy puppy dog eyes, in charge of domestic terrorism who keeps referring to his boss as "the boss." He adds, "If it's Mohammed then that would be International terrorism."

His international terrorism counterpart, the most *no nonsense* man I've ever seen, explains why in the past they haven't been able to give the press information concerning citizens held under the Patriot Act.

"We've heard that the FBI doesn't share information. We can't by law. It's classified," he asserts sharply.

It makes me wonder about all those Muslim immigrants who disappeared in the night—don't they have rights that supercede the FBI's need to classify everything about them as a secret? And what about the esteemed media's right to ask the detainees how they feel about getting no right to a fair trial? So much for getting information on those citizens.

By far, this FBI agent is the worst public speaker of the bunch.

"We have to learn about cultures and language," he continues stiffly. "We're always looking for those who can engage us in those cultures." I see, they want snitches to rat on their fellow immigrants.

The speeches go on and on from agents with various degrees of public speaking skills. Bank robberies, wiretapping ("It's not just flipping a switch."), surveillance ("We can install devices on vehicles to see where they go."), online wiretaps, agents posing as teenagers attracting pedophiles on the Internet, health care frauds, and, of course, counter-intelligence.

"It's your traditional Spy vs Spy scenario," explains the last dry FBI special agent. "If I tell you more, I probably can't let you leave the building."

Everyone chuckles. Ah, FBI humor!

I can firmly say that I marvel at the fact that any of these men could be breaking down my door, putting their boot on my throat, and pointing their gun at my head. And then I'd get a free trip to Guantanamo Bay, all because I happened to surf the wrong Internet site that sets off an in-house red flag.

But if that scenario was to play out, it would be, or course, classified.

FBI FUN FACT: Did you know that 57 years old is the mandatory retirement age for a FBI agent?

After the lengthy FBI presentation, we take a break. The majority of the room needs to use the restroom. Since it's the FBI headquarters, we're escorted to the facilities. You know that phenomenon that happens when you're at football games and even though you have to pee, you can't because there's a large line behind you? (I call it *stage fright.*) Try peeing with roughly eight FBI agents in suits waiting behind you. (I'm wondering if it's because they're waiting to take a sample for a drug test?!) Going to the urinal, I merely *fake it,* hoping I don't arouse suspicion.

THE POLYGRAPH TEST

The bad-suited media is divided up. My media group of journalists in bad suits goes to the FBI interrogation room that's designed with a two-way mirror, for a polygraph demonstration. Little do they know, in a mere half-hour, I will leave the FBI agent in charge of the polygraph test with egg on his face.

"Has anyone here taken a polygraph test?" asks the agent in a gray pinstriped suit (who looks vaguely like Robert De Niro in *Meet the Parents*, and the *hilarious* sequel, *Meet the Fockers*). I think he should ask us while we're hooked up to the damned machine. I get the feeling that this man would really be able to screw with your head in an interrogation scenario; his steely demeanor playing both roles of good cop/bad cop.

"The goal of the polygraph test is to obtain a confession," he explains matter-of-factly. "Our bread-and-butter is the terrorist test." He goes on to explain the purpose of which is to get those that disappear in the middle of the night, to sign for their ticket straight to Guantanamo Bay.

The other purposes are for job applicants in the wake of the notorious Hanssen affair, who was the most treacherous man in FBI history and was arrested by fellow agents for working as a Russian mole for 15-years. Yes, the organization tests its own to see if members of the rank and file are DOUBLE-SPIES!

"I look at the polygraph as a substitute for evidence," he relays dryly. "Anyone who takes a polygraph does so voluntarily. There's no reason to take it. 95% agree at the spur of the moment. At any time they can say, 'I don't want to talk to this agent anymore.'"

The focus then moves on to us.

"Does anyone want to volunteer to take a polygraph test?"

Wanting to further infiltrate their methods, I immediately shoot up my hand. "I'll do it!" I bark before he can even finish the word *volunteer*. I follow at his heel as we parade to the interrogation room on the other side of the two-way mirror. I'm face to face with the standard FBI "polygraph multi-component system" used since 1978, which is sitting on a table.

"You're not going to keep a file on me, are you?" I ask jokingly (but with actual mild concern). He deadpans "no." Maybe I haven't thought this through, hoping they don't ask any questions about history of drug use, strange sexual encounters, or, most importantly, what's in my sock.

"The test reads three ways, pass, fail, and inconclusive," he states, telling me the machine is 85%-95% accurate.

I sit down in the interrogation chair in the small room. The two-way mirror now shows my reflection. I'm already nervous and I haven't even done anything wrong. (I prepare a "I WAS FRAMED!") Fingerplates are hooked onto my left hand to read sweat glands. A chord is strapped around my chest to detect changes in breathing. My blood pressure is monitored for changes in heart rate. Four pens on the polygraph machine will relay sudden changes when questions are asked and the incorrect response is given. Having that background information, I think I can beat them and their little interrogation toy. BRING IT ON FBI BITCH!

"Does it make any difference if the person is of sub-par intelligence or mentally delusional?" I ask, making FBI small talk. Dryly, he tells me that mental competency is tested beforehand, once again reassuring me of the machine's accuracy.

"You do come across cases like John and Patsy Ramsey who passed the polygraph test," he states, giving insight into his impression of guilt or innocence in that case. "It's more of an art than a science. If I see someone trying to deceive the test, that's pretty much a fail."

I ponder this as the rules are explained. I'm told to pick a number between 2 and 8. I tell him my number is 5. He then writes the numbers between 2 and 8 vertically on a piece of paper and tapes it to the wall in front of me, as I stare straight ahead.

"I'm going to go down the list and you tell me if it's your number."

He starts with 2.

"Yes!" I exclaim, wanting to test out the polygraph ASAP.

"We got a smart aleck," he remarks dryly, once again

explaining the rules.

This time he reads the numbers and I'm supposed to say 'no' to each of them. The polygraph will clearly show I'm lying at "5."

Relaxing, I go into my own personal cave. It's warm and safe in my own personal cave, filled with big, lush pillows. I do breathing exercises I learned once in a yoga class. The interrogator reads each number, then pauses ten seconds to let the anxiety sink in and my body to register.

"Is 5 your number?" he interrogates.

"No!"

I hear giggling from behind the two-way mirror in the other room. If a FBI interrogation agent could blush, then he would be blushing. He shows me the results. The FBI agent seems embarrassed.

"You're a good liar," he proclaims, showing me that the polygraph couldn't register that I was lying, putting me in the same class as the best of liars.

"Nooooo I'm not" I once again lie.

The rest of my media group comes bursting through the door.

"You must be really good at lying," confirms a woman from a newspaper in Redding.

"No," I again declare. I just beat the FBI polygraph test!

FBI FUN FACT

Did you know in his book *Official and Confidential: The Secret Life of J. Edgar Hoover*, Anthony Summers claims that Hoover did not pursue organized crime because the Mafia had blackmail material on him for being a cross-dresser? The longtime director of FBI was said to like wearing a fluffy black dress, very fluffy, with flounces and lace stockings and high heels, and a black curly wig. He also liked to be introduced as "Mary."

EVIDENCE RESPONSE TEAM

Throughout the morning, I get this paranoid feeling that when the day is over, an agent is going to approach me and say, "Mr. Leon, please step into this the room. We'd like to have a word with you!"

In a demonstration from the FBI Evidence Response Team on the use of their tools, they "claim" they want to get an impression of my boot print in sand. They "claim" they want to demonstrate how they recover footprints at crime scenes with the assistance a cast imprint that can even collect footprints in water and snow.

Then, the fingerprint specialist (who I'm told is "the best finger printer this side of the Mississippi) "claims" he wants my thumbprint on a piece of magnetic paper.

"If I'm not mistaken, I've seen these at the post office," he says with a sinister chuckle (more FBI humor).

As we put on special glasses and dust the print under black light, he "claims" that we'll be able to determine if my print is the rare *plain arch* or the more common *loop*; all which can be fed into the computer to potentially garner an immediate match.

It's not a coincidence. These FBI agents are singling me out. Hell yes! They're doing this because I beat their damn polygraph test. They now have my boot and fingerprint on file. Soon my email will be monitored. Some higher up (watching from a third, two-way mirror) now thinks I fit some sort of potential master-criminal profile and should be monitored under the Patriot Act. Soon a laser sight rifle will be beamed right at my aorta, as I'm told to "GET DOWN ON THE GROUND! NOW!"

They got me now! That's too bad because I do take a shine to the Evidence Response Crew (ERC). This would be the department I'd be in, if I enlisted in the FBI (don't hold your breath America). They're just plain goofy with a nerdy quality of astonishment, as compared to the other hard-ass agents. They work with gruesome homicides, crime scenes, and plane crashes trying to find evidence among luggage and body parts, taking everything from the scene that could pertain to the case.

"It's nothing like you see on TV," states the ERC leader with glasses, khaki pants, and blue tucked in short sleeved shirt. "A lot of what we do is tedious and time consuming. There's a lot of paperwork. It's not glamorous; you're there because it's important. The person's dead and you are their only hope."

They use such fun tools as Electrostatic Dust Lifters that have a silver electromagnetic sheet that can be placed on a door, and through a charge of electromagnetic energy, they are able to take any prints right off. There's also the Superglue chamber that spins around and attracts the molecules to show fingerprints on an object. These guys know such keen facts as a fingerprint can be taken off a piece of paper for up to 40 years, while the hardest thing to fingerprint is human skin.

"We go out to these really grizzly crime scenes where people are mutilated. We want to get as much evidence as possible to use in court," he explains further.

I'd like to go drinking with these guys. They have the stories to tell.

I'm handed a large tennis shoe that has a much smaller ladies tennis show bolted to the bottom of it. I'm told it's a replica of Ted Kozinski's (aka The Unabomber's) shoe.

"He put a woman's shoe to the bottom so when the shoe left prints at a crime scene, people would be looking for someone who wears a size 6 woman's shoe."

What an insane genius, just like the Riddler. Mr. 27-Year-Fingerprint-Expert tells a similar story while perched under a framed photo of cross-dresser J. Edgar Hoover (or Mary!) sans dress.

"When they searched Ted Kozinski's cabin in Montana they find a copy of the FBI's *Science of Fingerprinting* manual," he says. "He knew how to handle bombs without leaving fingerprints."

This guy has great stories about such criminals as Roscoe Pitts, who surgically had skin attached to his fingers for the purpose of not leaving prints (this resulted in hair growing on his fingers). One of his very first cases was that of mysterious parachuting highjacker D.B. Cooper.

"He probably didn't make it," he confirms. "A little boy later found a case of money on a beach with the same serial numbers."

FBI FUN FACT: Did you know that Blimpies subs are the official lunch at the FBI headquarters for Media Day?

At one of two long tables under the FBI Martyrs wall, I eat my lunch among the various Mulders, as well as the conservative mainstream reporters in bad suits from obscure small town papers.

"I want to throw out a general question about the Patriot Act," asks a reporter in a bad suit as we start biting into our Blimpies. There's a collective sigh of "here we go again."

"Before we answer, can we get your last name?!" replies the head honcho.

Mild chuckles. That FBI humor.

This is the hot-topic being that the Patriot Act, itself, is very un-Patriotic. As you know, the Patriot Act allows the FBI to monitor everything from your e-mail to medical records to library accounts, providing frightening access to once private information. They can now more easily wiretap phones, break into homes and offices, and access financial records without "probable cause." Also, it broadens the meaning of terrorism to include domestic terrorism that could potentially be used to target activist groups speaking out against President Bush. Let's not forget immigrants who can be detained indefinitely based on suspicion alone, and on whom, according to the morning FBI speeches, the media can't get information by law. It's classified! Here we are, eating our Blimpies inside the very institution that administers investigations under the Patriot Act, which conjures up nightmares reminiscent of George Orwell's *1984*.

"There was many facets to the Patriot Act," he explains. "How much does it affect what we do? I'd say it has minimal effect. One area we utilize it is our ability to access records. We do that infrequently. I've seen every request that comes in through the field and there wasn't that many."

The head honcho claims that it's mainly used to get into people's bank records, to see if money was being filtered into it for terrorist purposes.

"We use it to find out if Mohammed [who's this Mohammed, or is the name of a prophet being used as a racial slur?] has a bank account then follow it up with the normal subpoena process. Up front, it assists us to get the process started," he states, telling us it's only used to confirm suspicions and let the floodgates open up to the rest of their investigation (then the wiretapping and email interception will take place).

The atmosphere quickly changes back to the earlier warmer give and take. Media Day is made to feel like a chummy slumber party, like somehow all has changed and the media and the FBI are now dating, and we can call them at all hours for an all night bull-session. Except of course on matters deemed classified, or things they don't want to tell us. The irony is, the FBI needs the media for *our* information.

"We scan papers to see what's happening and if it looks like something we should check into," the head guy explains. "We've opened cases on stories we've read. I'm more than happy to talk with any of you. Our switchboard will get in touch with us on the weekend if you call."

I'm sure they really want the guy in the bad suit from the Fairfield news calling at all hours. To test the love of our new relationship, a bad suited reporter asks about a recent cross-burning incident.

"It is an open case," explains the agent involved. "It is a priority for the bureau and we're moving forward with it."

So what he's saying is they can't comment on current cases, which are deemed "newsworthy," but they're more than happy to talk any of their past cases.

"Didn't they smell gasoline on a suspect's clothing?" the bad-suited reporter persists.

"I can't comment on that part," he remarks. "But we are taking the case seriously and moving forward. We don't want to be so overt with this because we don't want to damage anyone's reputation."

The honeymoon ended before it began.

FBI FUN FACT: Did you know the most common FBI handgun is, you guessed it, the Glock, which has the same trigger pull every time, all the time. While the most popular machine gun is, yes, the MP5 A-2!

Next, two large men are going to lead us journalists through *Deadly Force Decision Making Training* with the Firearm Training Simulator System. That's right. We'll learn to make split-second decisions "that will affect you the rest of your life," on whether to shoot or not shoot.

"We're going to give you tactical scenarios that could be encountered on the street," explains the larger of the two large FBI men. All I can think to myself is "All right, BRING IT ON!"

The tiny woman from a newspaper in Redding is the first to test her ability to apply deadly force. She approaches the large video simulator with a gun attached, personally having to live, again as we're told, with the consequences. In the back of the room, the head of the FBI legal department stands ready to fill us in on whether our shooting was legally justified. The larger of the large men chooses the tactical scenario of *"Bad Guy in Living Room."* Not only are we supposed to shoot at the appropriate time, but we're also supposed to yell commands at both the suspect and our onscreen video FBI partner. Bad generic rock music plays. The screen shows a realistic video POV shot, as the video FBI partner enters the suspect's house.

"What the hell you want! What are you doing in my damn house!" shouts the bad guy in the living room.

"Drop the weapon sir," the reporter says very politely. The Bad-Guy-In-Living-Room ends up graphically blowing away her onscreen FBI partner. Game over.

"I'm going to stick to writing," she remarks glumly.

"Continue to address the threat until the threat is eliminated," deadpans the FBI legal advisor in the back of the room.

It's my turn.

I get a scenario where a bad guy grabs my FBI partner. They both start rolling around on the ground. "Shoot him! Shoot him!" shouts my onscreen FBI partner. I shoot both of them. But I did address the threat until eliminated, for my fictitious FBI partner had been cheating on me with my fictitious wife. Next time I'd rather have the scenario where zombies start attacking the FBI agents.

FBI FUN FACT: Did you know that in the wake of the incident, the FBI admitted to firing flammable canisters at the Branch Davidian compound in Waco, Texas?

Before we leave, as we're walking out, I try to think of a good question to ask the head of the FBI, that really piques my curiosity. Something along the lines if the FBI thinks the media are annoying in the way they sensationalize crime stories, such as the Scott Peterson case—where the story is constantly shoved down our throats, and the media sometimes play both judge and jury.

I put on my serious reporter face and ask, "Do you find when the media sensationalizes stories it sometimes hinders an investigation?"

"That's a loaded question," interrupts a reporter in a bad suit from Fairfield.

The head honcho takes time to ponder this. For some reason the question appears to make him seem uncomfortable. I'm simply curious.

"It doesn't hinder a case, but it does sometimes make it frustrating." He brings up Waco and goes off on that tangent, saying they were trying to take a professional view in terms of dealing with the media and maybe didn't provide them with needed information, which in retrospect, perhaps should've been dealt with differently. Despite not understanding, I keep nodding vigorously.

On the way out, I once again go (unescorted) into the FBI restroom. Since I couldn't pee before, now I really have to pee. I enter the men's room. At the other urinal is a FBI agent who just witnessed the deadly tactical training (is he stationed in here?). He starts talking to me about gun tactics at the urinal, praising my shooting. I look down. Again, for the life of me, I can't pee next to a FBI agent.

Ironically, I depart the FBI headquarters feeling like they've learned a lot more about me than I've learned about them, leaving behind my polygraph test, finger and boot prints, and two near urine samples. Well, I can be sure this story is definitely going to end up going in their files.

POSTSCRIPT

The days pass slowly now in anticipation of my open invitation for an all-night bull session with the FBI, after they promised to provide information for my news stories. I finally find the opportunity to have them lavish upon me information when I spot: "Programmer's home in S.F. raided by FBI." This story in the daily paper prompts me to find out more and also test my new-found relationship with the FBI stressed on Media Day. With broad enthusiasm, I phone the FBI representative. But my enthusiasm is quickly squelched.

"We do not make comments on cases that are ongoing and really are not going to be able to assist you in this in any matter actually. We just don't comment."

What?! Huh?! It's me, Harmon, from Media Day! It's not even late Saturday night; why it's early Thursday afternoon.

"I don't know where else you might go, but it certainly won't come from us."

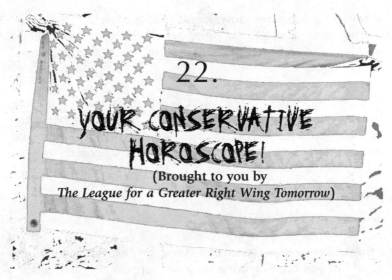

22.

YOUR CONSERVATIVE HOROSCOPE!

(Brought to you by
The League for a Greater Right Wing Tomorrow)

Scorpio: (Oct. 24 — Nov. 21)

Out in front. You may channel some of your feelings into creative or artistic work, something that evokes and expresses your deepest self. This should involve boycotting corporations that donate money to support the homosexual agenda. Sing opera while doing so.

Sagittarius: (Nov. 22 — Dec. 21)

People power. Emotional outbursts and impatience are likely. You're in a combative, energetic mood. Release these combative, energetic moods by trying to put prayer back into the school and classrooms where it belongs. Ridicule the French.

Capricorn: (Dec. 22 — Jan. 19)

Do the right thing. Steer clear of the office gossip mill; whether you're telling or agreeing. It could damage your rep on the job or at least be a distraction. Instead, fill your time writing down the license plate numbers of those who pick up illegal aliens working as day laborers. Treat yourself to a chocolate sundae.

Aquarius: (Jan. 20 —Feb. 18)

Make up your mind! You are motivated to work at resolving any ongoing problems you may be dealing with, but apt to be rather irritable and edgy. Scream at co-workers for looking at you wrong. Buy a gun and nickname it "Sharon." Let Sharon show people who's the boss! Blue is your favorite color.

Pisces: (Feb. 19 — March 20)

Shiny happy people. Over the next few days expect close friends or relatives to ask for your emotional support. Key issues may involve failed relationships or complex workplace struggles, and putting the Middle-Eastern fellow named Greg who works in accounts on your personal watchdog list of potential threats to homeland security. Pray for the day when computer chips can be planted into people's heads.

Aries: (March 21 — April 19)

Laughter is the best medicine. Social discussions and short-term dealings with friends may become emotional over the next few days. Expect others to passionately defend the poor and lower classes as useful members of society who shouldn't be exploited and openly laughed at. Show them they are wrong by openly laughing. Shred all documents that may incriminate you for any wrongdoing.

Taurus: (April 20 — May 20)

A brush of genius. A close friend's enthusiasm and creativity are invigorating. This will rub off on you as the two of you plot to picket a local art show you find obscene that features confusing ideas that are highly different than your own. Later, weep and cower.

Gemini: (May 21 — June 21)

Adventurous day. Public comments and social criticism may be mildly annoying this week. Monday/Tuesday expect workmates to boldly offer uniformed guards to escort you from the building, as they confiscate your computer and personal belongings. Just because you won't stop talking about your proof concerning the Jewish conspiracy to take over the media and what you plan to do about it. Plastics are your friend.

Cancer: (June 22 —July 22)

The language of love. Long distance messages or announcements from old friends may be on the agenda this week. Early Monday afternoon watch for unexpected invitations from a secret admirer who suggests you get together and write letters to major television networks on removing certain programs that you find both offensive and obscene. This could lead to true romance. Dream one day RoboCops will be real.

Leo: (July 23 — August 22)

Different strokes for different folks. Today, more people around you will differ in their beliefs from yours. Rather than clash with all of them, listen respectfully to their opinions. Then, only if absolutely necessary, label all those who oppose the president as "un-American" and "pinko-Commies." See what a paper cut on your tongue feels like.

Virgo: (Aug. 23 — Sept. 22)

Relationship elevator going up. Romantic communications will deepen over the next few days. Ask loved ones to actively participate in family events, including erecting a Ten Commandments monument on public property. When completed, drape it with your collection of numerous Confederate flags. Take up knitting.

Libra: (Sept. 23 — Oct. 23)

Today you'll have dual duties. But multitasking has never been your problem. You'll want to take part in social activities, but also you'll need some time alone to reflect on how best to close down all abortion clinics in your area. Fortunately, you can and should do both! Wear a power-tie and a smile.

23.
ANGRY TALK RADIO CALLERS—UNITE!

R ead with me:

PATRIOT DEFENDERS NETWORK

Supporting our Veterans, Troops, and Families

Respecting God, Country, our Flag and President

I'm intrigued. I must infiltrate. The ultraconservative civilian think tank known as the Patriot Defenders Network sponsors sit down meetings every month under the banner of Town Hall (www.townhall.com), in cities around the country. The purpose: to discuss how to make America a better place, free from wacko liberals. Yes, it's time to get inside this little tea party and hear the Mad Hatter rally the pissed-off citizens—the ones who call right-wing talk radio shows.

My Persona: Drake Sutherland — American!

Disguise: American flag tie. Patriotic stars and stripes jacket (stolen while infiltrating the state Republican convention) that reads "Re-elect President Bush."

Accessory: A tiny, hand-held American flag.

My Overused Catchphrase: "America for Americans!"

"We're a little bit different than some of the other Town Hall groups," an enthusiastic man named Dave explains over the phone. He seems overjoyed to have fellow conservative Drake Sutherland on board. "We tend to be a little more proactive. Our liberal friends on *the other side* would call that anal-retentive."

"Well, I have a few nasty names for them as well," I spout. *"Tea-baggers."*

We both laugh. We're really getting along.

"We have our own sentiments for them," Dave says, laughing. "We just tend to be a little more polite about it. But we got some *great* people in our group. Great people."

"You're preaching to the choir," I say.

"Drake, I think you found a home in the belly of the beast otherwise known as *the Socialist Republic of California.* [Laughs] Anyway, you'll like who you see and who you'll meet."

"Wicked!"

"Drake, you'll hear our members all the time calling in on one issue or another," enthusiastic Dave says, referring to his favorite local right-wing talk radio station. "We use a lot of time on the airwaves and that platform to recruit people. It helps."

"That's how you got me," I confess.

"We need more young Republicans coming out of our colleges and universities who have been fighting for their very existence in those institutes of quote 'higher learning' end quote. [Pause] I tend to call them terrorist training camps in California."

"Colleges?" I ask, caught off guard; I hadn't heard higher education equated to terrorist training camps before.

"Yeah, colleges and universities," Dave confirms.

"I like that," I tell him. "I call it the same thing. [Pause] Sometimes I even call them the *University of bin Laden Lovin'!* It just teaches anti-American ideals!"

Dave now likes my attitude. "Oh, but it's happening all over the country. We Californians just happen to be leading the way."

"Uh-huh!"

"They want to indict and put conservatives in prison for hate-speech if we denounce one thing or another as supposedly being contrary to the values established in this country," enthusiastic Dave explains. "They're working rather hard to convince liberal judges who also graduated from places like UC Berkeley that we should go to jail because we are engaging in 'hate-speech.'"

"Yeah, the media doesn't help either," I note, throwing fuel on the fire.

"Oh, yeah, thank God for Fox News, you know!" Dave proclaims.

"Yup, thank God for Fox News," I agree.

This is beginning to sound good to me. There's plenty of room to grow within the Town Hall organization.

"If I have ideas for the counter-terrorism team, can I bring them to the table?" I ask.

"Absolutely. There are all kinds of ways you can get involved," Dave elatedly replies.

"Is there any way I can help track down terrorists in our country?" I inquire. "Like, can I set up a hotline where people can call in if they suspect cabdrivers and stuff of being terrorists?"

"At this point, hey, that homeland security project is looking for someone who's interested in taking it on," Dave says, seeming to grow even more animated.

"Great, 'cause I want to start reporting suspects and rounding them up."

[Pause]

"We can talk more about it," Dave thoughtfully answers.

"How about if we pose as a terrorist group on the Internet and lure people to interact in a chat room and boom, we nab them?" I ask.

[Another pause]

"You know, as I say," Dave says finally, "we don't put limits on people. People rise to their own levels of interest and dedication and commitment."

Hot damn!

IHOP is where all the great conservative minds converge. Yes, great conservative minds, filled with extreme right-wing views, converge best over flapjacks at budget prices, with a multitude of delicious syrup selections.

About thirty-five extremely white Americans have gathered. It's composed mostly of concerned retirees, crusty men with red puffy faces, most of them sporting mustaches. Their arms are folded. The ladies are hardened; they tend toward round, with curly poodle hair.

"Are the French *really* our allies?" I ask the man at the door.

"Be sure to sign the toastmaster sign-up sheet," I'm told, so I jot down Drake Sutherland and my proposed topic: "The French: Traitors who love Jerry Lewis!" I settle in as an elderly toastmaster with a bad complexion and a blue Christmas sweater opens the festivities with some jokes about the Democratic Party's displeasure with the last election.

Elbowing my way into the center of a table, I take a seat next to a guy with a red puffy face who looks generally pissed off about everything. I direct my attention to the speaker's podium and try to look pissed off as well. The toastmaster reads off a piece of paper, in the monotone persona of George W. Bush doing a monologue that recaps the events of 2004. His bit draws huge smug laughter from the crowd as the primarily Latino wait-staff brings out plates of pancakes. (I haven't decided between the chocolate and the new caramel-apple fruit pocket pancakes.)

With his confusing George W. imitation, he shouts, "Michael Moore. You big idiot. I made that movie for you, and you still blew it! [Ha-ha-ha] Teresa Heinz Kerry. You big dummy. My first cousin wouldn't have screwed up like that. [Ha-ha-ha] Maybe give up using that stupid hyphenated last name and go back to using Heinz. [Ha-ha-ha]"

A man resembling an evil schoolmaster — he has a mustache and is wearing a blue sports jacket with an American flag pin — is brought to the lectern to huge applause. This man is on the board of the Pacific Legal Foundation. He presents tonight's

Town Hall topic: "America's 21st Century Challenge—Preserving Individual and Economic Freedoms in the Increasingly Collectivist World."

"I think it's very important what you're doing," he tells the IHOP gathering, then launches into a joke, apparently to show off his conservative "funny" side.

"Eventually an American bomb catches up with Osama bin Laden and propels his fiery soul to the pearly gates," he reads from a piece of paper, gripping the podium. A red-faced, bulbous-stomached man starts shaking his head and convulsing with laughter, apparently having heard the joke before.

The joke progresses with George Washington, James Madison, and James Monroe kicking the shit out of bin Laden at the entrance to heaven.

"Wait till they get his ass in Abu Ghraib prison," I tell the red-faced man, giving the thumbs up and pointing at imaginary genitals Private Lyndee England-style. He convulses with laughter once again.

The evil schoolmaster continues: "Osama bin Laden screams, 'But this was not what I was promised!' An angel replies, 'I told you there would be 72 *Virginians* waiting for you.'"

Huge laughs are followed by claps and sighs. I slap the table, shaking my head, repeating, "Seventy-two *Virginians*!"

Our sojourn into humor is only momentary. The evil schoolmaster's dry demeanor turns drier. He no longer smiles. Neither do the conservative pancake eaters. "PLF is the leading public interest organization of its kind in the country," the schoolmaster says. "PLF has its own approach to some of the problems we have in the country."

Everyone responds:

"Amen,"

."Yeah!"

"You got that right!"

"America for Americans!" I yell.

The evil schoolmaster offers a definition of the term "collectivist" that links it to liberals, socialists, and leftists; he punctuates each of these terms with a sneer. "Let me give you an example you may appreciate."

The schoolmaster spins a tale about Hillary Clinton, who supposedly told a group of well-heeled Democratic contributors how well off they were with Bush's tax reduction for the rich. According to him, she then remarked, "The tax cuts may have helped you. We're saying for America to get back on track we're probably going to cut that short and not give it to you!"

The crowd gasps.

"'We're going to take things away from you on behalf of the common good,'" he sneers with disgust. "Well that pretty well tells it."

There is disbelief. Audible grumbling rolls through the crowd. I raise some maple syrup to the cause.

"America for Americans!"

Collectively, this IHOP crowd is angry, and that's strange. Their president is in the White House. The state has a Republican governor. Congress is run by the Republicans. Yet these folks are one bunch of pissed-off pancake-eating conservatives! The world doesn't conform to their rules—how they see the Constitution— and that pisses the hell out of them. I guess.

"Some years ago, collectivist social engineers created a government program called *affirmative action*," the schoolmaster continues.

There are gasps; heads are shaken; those with folded arms fold them tighter; red faces turn redder. The schoolmaster proudly declares that the PLF is the only entity working the courts to enforce Proposition 209, a law, passed by initiative, that prohibits racial preferences by state and local agencies in admissions, hiring, and contracting.

"Recognizing that the Constitution grants rights to individuals. The Constitution says 'every person'; the Constitution doesn't say 'every black person' or whatever. It says 'every person.'"

"Here-here!"

"Amen!"

"Yup! And no one seems to care if they are illegal or not," grunts a man who looks like the creepy uncle who'd offer candy and insist you bounce on his knee.

"America for Americans!" I cry.

The creepy uncle shoots me a look.

"A case going against the City and County of San Francisco is an uphill battle," the evil schoolmaster says. "Finally we got an honest judge, a strong, courageous judge who nailed it and saw what the city of San Francisco was doing in granting race-based preferences in public works contracts in San Francisco, and he nailed it."

Huge clapping. Shouts of "All RIGHT!" I pull out my hand-held American flag and wave it around.

"Go Niners!" I cry for no reason.

"I got two questions," asks one of the many large red-faced men with arms folded. "How do we fight this when we see it happening in our town? My second question: Can we really stop it or are they doing things now under the table?"

"That's what collectivists and the government do," the evil schoolmaster says. "I mean, they aren't going to give up. One thing you can do is if you have information that suggests that that is going on, that race-based preferences are being used, I'll give you my card."

These uber-conservatives have a love/hate relationship with Affirmative Action. There's hate for the program, but looooooove for its existence since they use it as an excuse when minorities get ahead of their white pimply asses in business. They then can claim race preference, rather than have a self-realization that they might not be the sharpest of tools in the shed. It allows them to be racist without being *blatantly* racist.

Finally my caramel-apple fruit pocket pancakes arrive, and they're absolutely delicious! As I pour on the boysenberry syrup, the evil schoolmaster moves to other serious matters.

"The collectivist state and local government have sought to deny to the Boy Scouts of America their constitutional right to practice their long-held philosophical beliefs and values," which alludes to the Boy Scouts' opposition to gay membership in wearing the gayish looking Boy Scout uniform.

As others gasp, I attempt a shocked spit-take with vanilla

shake in my mouth. The creepy uncle shoots me another stern look.

"It is important to say that this is not a gay rights issue that the collectivists categorize it; but a freedom of speech and association issue."

"Here-here!"

"Amen!"

The schoolmaster dives into the problems that collectivist wackos have created by enforcing environmental laws. He tells a story about a Michigan businessman who was, supposedly, sentenced to 10 months in a federal prison camp and fined $185,000 just for "moving sand around on his property and filling in a *scientifically questionable* wetland on his property."

"What?!" someone says.

"No way!" another outraged Town Haller blurts.

"Boycott France!" I yell.

Now the sarcasm comes thick as the whipped cream on my neighbor's pancakes as the topic turns to endangered species. The schoolmaster smiles with thin lips. "So you have a person who owns a piece of property," he says. "The federal government comes in and says, 'I'm sorry, we have noticed that this little critter lives on this property, so we're going to list it as an endangered species under the Endangered Species Act.'"

"America for Americans!" I say, waving my tiny flag. I stop when the creepy uncle starts whispering to his neighbor.

"As a result of that, anything you do that harms, even psychologically," he continues, "I kid you not, even psychologically harms the species, will cause legal action.

"What the collectivists and what the environmental movement and what the Sierra Club is trying to do is return 50 percent of this country to the wild. You say that can't be. Yes, that is their agenda."

Amid appalled gasps, a concerned, mustachioed man, wearing suspenders, screeches, "Basically put the people on reservations."

"Boycott Germany!" I suggest.

"In effect that's what they are doing," the schoolmaster confirms, then speaks very slowly and distinctly. "So ... animals ... can ... migrate ... all ... the ... way ... across ... the ... western ... United ... States ... up ... into ... Canada."

"Is there a Mexican migration?" bellows a plump, red-faced man with crossed arms, who enjoys an enormous swell of laughter from a roomful of IHOP patriots, who are, to all appearances, absolutely oblivious to the Latino waiters clearing away their pancake plates.

I got to admire the dedicated commitment that these Town Hall conservatives have in their plight against liberal whackos. On the way out I bump into *creepy uncle,* who, as it turns out, was actually admiring my youthful conservative spirit that I displayed against the collectivist machine.

"I've been in this town raising hell for ten years and nobody has taken me out yet!" creepy uncle shares to inspire me.

(Pause) "Ok."

He goes on to speak his conservative mantra.

"Yeah, we get a lot of hate mail but I pay no attention to it. Cuz I figure it's some prick who has no time on his hands other than being a keyboard warrior, then screw it." Creepy uncle then adds solemnly, "The bullet that takes me out I'm never going to hear or see anyway!"

(Pause) "Ok."

JOKES ABOUT THOSE TRAITORS
WHO LOVE JERRY LEWIS—THE FRENCH

The French are traitors. How dare they not want to take part in our very expensive, needlessly instigated war?! To show our American displeasure to the French, and their ungrateful, cowardly actions, I went to several websites to see what true Americans think of our frog-loving friends, using something they like to call, "humor."

JOKE: The makers of French's Mustard made the following recent statement: "We at the French's Company wish to put an end to statements that our product is manufactured in France. There is no relationship, nor has there ever been a relationship, between our mustard and the country of France. Indeed, our mustard is manufactured in Rochester, NY. The only thing we have in common is that we are both yellow."

JOKE:
Q: What do you call a Frenchman advancing on Baghdad?
A: A salesman.

JOKE:
Q: Why do zee French have zee onion and zee Arabs has zee oil?
A: Because zee French had zee first pick.

JOKE:
Q: How many generations does it take to learn ingratitude?
A: Trois.

JOKE:
Q: Why do the French call their fighter the "Mirage"?
A: Because it's never seen in a combat zone.

JOKE:
The only way the French are going in to help us is if we tell them we found truffles in Iraq.

JOKE:
The French are always reticent to surrender to the wishes of their friends and always more than willing to surrender to the wishes of their enemies.

JOKE:
Q: Why do the French use a lot of bleach on their sheets?
A: So you can see their white flags better.

JOKE:

Going to war without the French is like going hunting without an accordion.

JOKE:
Donald Rumsfeld was being heckled by a French anti-war weenie when he suddenly turned and asked the Frenchman:
"Excuse me. Do you speak German?" The Frenchman replied "No." Rumsfeld looked him in the eyes and said "You're welcome."

JOKE:
Q: What is the other way to spell the name of the French president?
A: Jacques ChIraq.

JOKE:
A man asks his companion, "What's the most common French expression"? His friend scratches his head, shrugs his shoulders and replies, "I give up!"

JOKE:
Q: Why is it good to be French?
A: You can surrender at the beginning of the war, and the U.S. will win it for you.

JOKE:
Q: How many French soldiers does it take to change a light bulb?
A: Five: one to sit on his butt and watch and do nothing.
One to turn tail and run.
One to roll over.
One to surrender to the light bulb and snitch out occupied sockets.
And one to pick up a phone and cry to the United States.

JOKE:
Q: Why do we need France on our side against Saddam and

Osama?

    A: So the French can show them how to surrender.

JOKE:
Q: What color is the American flag?
A: Red, White, and Blue.
Q: What color is the British flag?
A: Red, White, and Blue.
Q: What color is the French flag?
A: White.

JOKE:
Q: What do you call 100,000 Frenchmen with their hands up?
A: The Army.
Q: What did France used to be called?
A: Germany, and then we saved them.

JOKE:
Q: What are they calling the Germans, French and Belgians at the Pentagon.
A: The Axis of Weasels.

JOKE:
Q: Why did the French celebrate their World Cup championship so wildly?
A: It was the first time they won anything without the help of the U.S.

REPLACEMENTS FOR THE FRENCH NATIONAL ANTHEM:

"Runaway" by Del Shannon,
"Running Scared" by Roy Orbison,
"I Really Don't Want to Know" by Tommy Edwards,
"Surrender" by Elvis Presley,
"Live and Let Die" by Wings,
"I'm Leaving It All Up to You" by Donny and Marie

Osmond,
   "What a Fool Believes" by the Doobie Brothers,
   "Raise Your Hands" by Jon Bon Jovi

I'M A LITTLE ANGEL WITH THE GUARDIAN ANGELS!

In my ongoing effort to be an active part of homeland security—in order to keep America safe—I've decided to join up with the Venice Beach Guardian Angel Chapter. Some people think the Guardian Angels are the hall monitors of society. A vigilante group in red berets without "real" legal power. A club for people who want to join a gang legally—a gang of good! Some feel annoyed by their presence. Sure, I, myself, have never liked authority figures, let alone volunteer authority figures. But, I decided to cast aside past prejudices in order to find out what makes the Guardian Angels tick? What are they all about? What are their likes and dislikes? Do they like soup? Are they nice?!?

I am sold by the recruitment flyer. A multi-cultural mix of Angels are on the front with the emblazoned words, "You CAN make a Difference!" It's time to wash the scum off the streets. Yes, I, Harmon Leon will make a difference!

MY PREPARATION:

   -1 Gung Ho attitude
   -6 Cups of coffee for a shaky effect
   -1 T-shirt of popular boy band of the moment
   -1 Catch-Phrase ("Gotta Get My Shit Together!")

TIME TO JOIN!

The Venice Beach Guardian Angels have hit on hard times. It just restarted three months ago after some of the original members were booted out for purportedly taking some of the group's petty cash. The headquarters is located on the beach in a row of apartments on the beach that resembles a string of crack-pads. It's situated among shops selling bad T-shirts, surrounded by amputee dwarf rap-singers, fat German tourists, naked women sculpted in sand, all of which are set against the backdrop of *Baywatch*-style lifeguard stands.

"*Everyone Entering HQ Will Be Searched!*" reads the sign outside. I enter. The place is pumping with testosterone. Immediately I'm searched, manhandled, and inquired about the possession of knives.

"We treat members like brothers, but watch them like hawks!" explains the manhandler at the door. Inside, there're three Angels, one of which is overweight, wearing soiled purple sweatpants, an rocking back-and-forth in a chair.

"......I used to smoke pot three times a day...."

He's the obligatory misfit chubby guy, like in a bad '80's sitcom. I go up to the Angel behind the desk.

"I'd like to join!"

We shake hands in the "cool-guy" fashion. He looks almost surprised.

"Why do you want to be a Guardian Angel?"

"Gotta' get my shit together!"

I'm then given the spiel.

"We are peace-keepers. Even when there's trouble, our job is to keep the peace. We want to build up and train this chapter so eventually we can go into other neighborhoods and patrol."

During the spiel, Tubby is wandering around.

"When do I get a red jacket? I'd really like a red jacket," exclaims concerned Tubby. I fill out the GA application. To become a Guardian Angel, it mostly involves not having previously stabbed anyone. Also fitting into the red beret. On the application, not only do you get to fill in your name, but also a "code-name." For my code-name, I put "Cha-Chi." This is fun. It's like having a CB handle. I hand my application back to the Angel behind the desk.

"Any questions?'

"Yeah, why the red berets?"

"It's a symbol people use to identify with us," says the

solemn-face Angel behind the desk.

"I've been here a week, and I'd really like a red jacket, " repeats Tubby.

"Welcome to the Guardian Angels, Cha-Chi!"

GLOSSARY OF GUARDIAN ANGEL TERMS

POST UP: Stand side by side in a single file line. This shouldn't be done in front of glass windows. GAs can be pushed through.

HAVE A SQUAT: To sit down and rest while on patrol.

MAD DOGGING: To give a dirty look.

NIGHT PATROL

Our patrol leader goes by the code-name "Street Hawk." He looks like he could do a person much harm. Five of us leave GA HQ. "I'm going to have to search all of you," demands Street Hawk. Didn't that just happen?! Again, I'm manhandled.

"We do this in front of the public to let them know we don't carry weapons."

Street Hawk is an eight-year veteran. He confesses that he doesn't have a girlfriend because he's married to the Guardian Angels. (I bet you get a lot more sex the other way.)

My "team" goes into what is called a "diamond formation": two in front, two in back, and one in the middle. Our job is to look for no-good-niks. This is like dressing-up and playing army. Collectively we must look like a pathetic, diamond-shaped crew. There's me (dred-locked buffoon), two seventeen year-olds, and Tubby. We will incite fear into the heart of no one. But I do enjoy walking in a group of similarly dressed people! I haven't done this since my days playing organized sports.

GUARDIAN ANGEL EQUIPMENT NEEDED:

1) A red beret
2) 1 Guardian Angel T-shirt ("Safety Patrol" written on patrol leader's shirt)
3) Walkie talkie/cell phone (patrol leader only)

Suggested additional items:

*a good, comfortable pair of shoes for walking patrol.
*a desire to make a difference!

HOW TO MAKE A CRACK BUST

Street Hawk tells us that smoking crack on Venice Boardwalk is a minor misdemeanor. The police usually don't want to get involved because it requires holding the crack-enthusiast for two hours after which they receive only a small fine. So what you do is:

1) Tell the crack enthusiast to "destroy the crack pipe." This involves his stepping on it.
2) If they refuse, tell them again "destroy the crack pipe."
3) If they still refuse, get on the cell phone, and "pretend" to call the police. This is called a "Code Blue." Then, using the Second City art of improv, enact a conversation with a police officer, until they give up the crack pipe.
4) If this still doesn't work, tell them once again "destroy the crack pipe."

Then what?
Marijuana is almost a laughable offense. There's pretty much nothing to do about it. I forgot to ask about heroin.
It's very quiet on the dark, deserted beachfront. That's fine with me. I hope we don't come across real gangsters. What the hell would I do?! Street Hawk gives a few pointers.

"If you see a guy with a gun, dog-pile on top of him!"

Shit, I get the image of a pile of dead Guardian Angels with a gun-toter on the bottom shooting his way out.

"You first try to talk your way out of situations. If that doesn't work, do what you have to do!"

Being on patrol is not unlike something that is actually very boring. It's much like walking in silence—in a group. I oddly get the feeling there's going to be some sort of hazing. My red beret will be pulled over my eyes. Then my pants will be pulled down, after which I'll have officially passed the initiation.

That doesn't happen. Instead, the two seventeen year-olds pull the gag where they stop and see how far we will walk before noticing they haven't moved. This is very funny to them. Just then the Guardian Angel bike patrol leader from NY passes us. The NY Angels have come out to this chapter to help whip it into shape. I note a mild rivalry between the bike and walking Guardian Angels. Kind of like a east coast/west coast rap rivalry. The bike leader mad-dogs Street Hawk.

"Why are your men laughing on patrol! And smoking!"

Street Hawk looks back.

This touches a nerve.

"Tuck in your shirt Cha-Chi!" Street Hawk commands. Hey, I didn't do anything.

"Gotta get my shit together!" I say. Apparently I'm a disgrace to the Guardian Angels. As soon as the bikes are out of sight: "Post up!" Street Hawk paces back and forth in silence as we silently watch him. After five minutes we march on.

"People look more toward the Guardian Angels than the cops. If a Guardian Angel fucks up, it's like a hero fucking up. Like OJ or Mike Tyson," explains Street Hawk before we go back into walking in stony silence.

We make it to the 3rd Street Promenade in Santa Monica; an affluent area of LA that resembles an outdoor shopping mall. I give a security guard a respectful nod. We are in the same law-enforcement game, except he gets paid.

"Tourists are sometimes scared of us. They think we're 'The Bloods' because of our red berets, " explains Street Hawk to his men.

I do feel part of a gang; a gang of good! I know getting laid is out of the question. If you want to avoid getting laid again, this would be the outfit to wear. I thought women loved a man in uniform, but this uniform seems to be a female repellant.

"Hi ladies!" They look at me like I'm a big floppy-shoed clown with a red-nose.

As we continue walking diamond formation through the crowd of well-dressed people, I hear various comments.

"Ha! Look at the Guardian Angels!"

"Here comes the Boy Scouts!"

and

"It's Charlie's Angels!"

My training has taught me to ignore these comments. Police Officers give us dirty looks (mad-dogging). They hate us! Is it because we're taking away some of their action? The bike leader rides up, momentarily stopping. Out of the blue, he says, "My girlfriend is better looking than 90% of the women here!" He rides off again.

A large crowd is gathered around a loud, annoying street juggler.

"I think we have a situation!" I say, alarmed, ready to make a citizen's arrest.

Street Hawk doesn't agree.

"You got to do what you got to do!" I confirm.

He still doesn't agree, but I firmly believe bad street performing should be a crime!

GUARDIAN ANGELS FUN FACTS

1) The Guardian Angels started twenty years ago in New York City by Curtis Sliwa.

2) Curits Sliwa has been stabbed about 5 times, been hit with a baseball bat, and shot about 8 times. Once even through the penis! *Ouch!!*

3) There used to be roughly 80 chapters around the country,

now there's about 20. There're chapters in Japan, Germany, Australia, and a few other countries that I can't remember.

4) A community has to invite them in before they can set up a chapter.

5) Chuck Norris is a Guardian Angel. He also once starred in the TV show, *Walker, Texas Ranger*, which was about a Texas Ranger named Walker.

6) Guardian Angels are an all-volunteer group that relies on donations for operation.

7) The Guardian Angels claim they are coming out with their own line of cologne that will be available at such fine stores as Bloomingdales. Now everyone can smell like a Guardian Angel!

DAY PATROL

I'm dying to bust someone. Being a Guardian Angel and not busting someone is like being a butcher and not cutting meat. I return the next day to headquarters. I expect to see everyone, like a scene from *Platoon*, bloody and bandaged from "the action" of the previous night. Instead, everyone looks the same. Some old-timers are sitting around swapping Curtis Sliwa stories.

"When did you enlist?"

"My regiment was from '85 to '90."

Tubby is still walking around in soiled purple sweat pants with food stuck to his face.

"I know you'd come today Cha-Chi!" says Street Hawk.

I think he's secretly aware that I'm not one of them. It's like *Reservoir Dogs*. I'm the inside informer, and soon I'll be tied up in an abandoned warehouse while getting my ear cut-off.

Street Hawk adds, "You know, we had to strip two members today!"

"What do you mean?! You strip searched them?" I thought they had raised the traditional search standards.

"No, stripped them of their ranks!"

Hold on there. We barely have enough for a softball team,

and you stripped the few remaining volunteers of their "ranks."
Now there's only about seven of us.

My duty today is handing out recruitment flyers. I feel like a
physical pain in the ass standing in the middle of Venice Beach,
handing out Guardian Angel recruitment flyers. Nobody really
wants them. Most are thrown immediately on the ground. A
Japanese tourist gladly takes one, thinking it's for a reggae dance
club.

Some people say "Hey Guardian Angels keep up the good
work." Other's just mock us. Another Guardian Angel with a
stutter is trying to solicit donations.

A kid with a skateboard comes by.

"Hey, do you know where I can buy some skunk-weed?"

Apparently he doesn't know who he's dealing with.

"Sir! I am a Guardian Angel! I don't want to hear another
word about this 'skunk-weed' or else your ass is mine!"

I point to my eyes to signify that I'll be watching him, after
which, I go back to handing out flyers. Tubby saunters over. In
an amazing string of non-sequiturs, he says, "Fuck the cops! You
see that," he points to his chin. "A cop smashed my head into
the hood of a cop car!"

"Why is that?"

"Because I hit someone over the head with a garbage can!'

He saunters away. I go back to handing out flyers.

"Cha-Chi, come here!"

It's one of my seventeen year-old patrol buddies. I swiftly
walk over with quick strides.

"What is it? Do we have a situation!!"

"No, just help me carry in these groceries."

Finally some Guardian Angel ac-tion!

BIKE PATROL

As noted before, the Guardian Angels with bikes seem to be on
a higher echelon than those who merely "walk." Kind of like
Teddy Roosevelt's elite Rough Riders. My innate leadership skills

must have shone through, because I'm asked to go on "Bike Patrol." I want to be the best I can. I give a strong confident nod to my commander.

"Yes sir!"

Hot Damn! I'm ready for ac-tion! I will keep the peace on two wheels instead of two feet. Perhaps I'll apprehend a ring of bike riding camera thieves. I'll probably get the Medal of Honor from the mayor. Or a key to the city!

Two of my fellow Guardian Angel brothers and myself take to the bike path. We get about ten feet.

"My tire's kinda flat," yells one of my brethren.

We spend the next twenty minutes trying to find a place to pump-up the tire, after which the patrol leader says, "Let's get back. I have to give everyone a demonstration on how to defend against a knife attack." On returning, we never hear again about the fending off a knife attack demonstration.

I'm back to handing out flyers.

Tubby's discovered a new sense of leadership. He walks over disapprovingly.

"Try smiling."

"I *am* smiling," I scowl.

"You should try saying something like "Hello sir, how are you today."

I absorb this knowledge and nod.

"I *should* know, I've been here a week you know!" he adds, pulling rank.

I also absorb this knowledge. Here one week and already razzing the new guy. I hope I don't get "stripped" of my rank.

"Gotta get my shit together!"

"OK, right now, see that guy, say 'Hello sir' and give him a flyer!"

Whoa! You're going too fast. Who does Tubby think I am? He's been here one week and already he's "mad with power." Some huge guy walks past, cracking-up, "Ha! The Guardian Angels! I can't believe these guys are still around. Ha!"

TRAINING DAY

Sunday is set aside for martial arts training. Street Hawk herds us inside. Finally we'll learn some real-life Guardian Angel combat maneuvers. Probably the ripping-out of hearts, the tearing-out of aortas, the pulling of spleens: all done with the skill of one finger.

A quick inventory of the room shows that the only remaining members of my Guardian Angel freshman class are myself (undercover journalist), a fat guy, an old guy, and a tiny woman. We are the future elite fighting force known as the Venice Chapter of the Guardian Angels. All we need now is a mime, a guy in a wheelchair, and a chimpanzee.

"Cha-Chi come here!" says Street Hawk. "I'm going to demonstrate a few moves and you're going to be the practice dummy."

In various scenarios we role play that I'm a bad man. During these scenarios my fingers are bent back, my arm's twisted, and various nerve points are pressed.

"They're going to call you Boy Scouts. They're going to call you Charlie's Angels (wow, they did!). Names are not going to hurt you. If someone calls me the n-word, I won't do anything! It's just names." explains Street Hawk.

"What if they call me '*frog*,'" pipes-in Tubby.

"What?!?"

"I'm French and that's a bad term for the French."

For at least four seconds the room is silent.

SUMMARY OF MY GUARDIAN ANGEL EXPERIENCE

If the Guardian Angels are going to have a new TV show, from my experience, here's what a sample episode would be like:

New Guardian angel recruit (Cha-Chi Leon) has trouble handing out Guardian Angel recruitment flyers. A young, recruitment flyer-recipient refuses his literature and throws it back in Cha-Chi's face. So Cha-Chi chases him down the boardwalk, corners him down an alley, and finally makes the young non-flyer-taking hooligan take the flyer. And once again the Venice boardwalk is safe!

Of course my few days of experience with the Guardian Angels is not a microcosm of all experiences, but it's still my experience. Here's is my final scorecard of action:

TOTAL ARRESTS: 0
TOTAL CRIMES PREVENTED: 0
TOTAL NUMBER OF FLYERS HANDED OUT: 275
TOTAL DRUG BUSTS: 0
TOTAL MOCKING COMMENTS:27
TOTAL POSITIVE COMMENTS: 24

For now, I'm going to retire my red beret. Both the streets, and America, will have to be kept safe and patrolled without me. But look at the bright side, at least I didn't get shot through the penis.

25.

MY RIGHT TO BEAR!

People have strong feelings about guns. As a card-carrying member of the NRA, I think it's my duty to educate ignorant liberals; every proud American should own a gun. In most states it's illegal to carry a concealed gun in public. I say "Ha!" In 1984, an unemployed security guard named James Huberty entered a McDonald's in San Ysidro, California, armed with three guns, killing 20 people and wounding 16 others, including children. Let's look at this logically. If these victims were allowed to carry guns (like the Constitution intended), then Huberty would have been blown away quicker than you can say "Happy Meal!" Maybe only four or five people would have died, sparing dozens of others. **WAKE UP AMERICA!**

There's a wonderful world of guns out there and the time is now for more people to get off their lazy asses and become a part of it. As Americans we need guns. Owning a gun is a blessed Constitutional right, right up there with the Patriot Act. Buying a gun is easier than you think. There's nothing to be scared of; chances are you won't be turned down. As an inspiration for you to become a new gun owner I'm going to go out and show you exactly how easy it is in America to put a gun in your fat little paws, and fire away to your Charlton Heston-loving-heart's content.

Gun Myths Disproved: Eight children a day die in deaths involving guns. Unintentional shootings commonly occur when children find an adult's loadedhandgun in a drawer or closet, and, while playing with it, shoot themselves, a sibling, or a friend. Let's be logical; we need to take our nation's children to shooting ranges as soon as they are able to hold a gun so they know how to handle them properly. **WAKE UP AMERICA!**

"Welcome Machine Gun Shooters!" blazes a sign outside a local liquor store as I speed on past. Yes, I'm about to spend a fun-filled weekend with 5,000 assault weapon enthusiasts at the Knob Creek bi-annual machine gun shoot and military gun show, held in—I shit you not—Bullitt county Kentucky. Aah irony!

Passing a parking lot full of pick-ups, following big-bellied men in plaid, I parade towards the entrance. Most wear guns as fashion accessories. Many look like they're harboring a terrible secret. Several could pass as the guys in ZZ Top.

A sign tacked to the entrance gate reads "Stop All Abortion!" Classic! This event is sponsored by the extreme Christian right! Someone should inform these clowns that "pro-life" should begin with people currently living.

"Are there going to be helicopters this year?" inquires a man in a "No Trigger Locks" T-shirt with a mullet-haircut, while gunfire, like giant crashing waves fills the air. As I enter, a hardened Christian woman hands me a pamphlets for "Camp America: Where God's Truth And Patriotism Go Hand In Hand."

"It teaches people about the Constitution," she explains, as I'm, at the same time, given literature from a man who fears social security numbers.

This will be the whitest event I've ever attended (including all the others mentioned in this book). In fact, some alternative names for the machine gun shoot could be:

*The We Live In The Woods And Have Our Own Country Convention

*The Big Belly Gathering
*The We Hate Blacks And Jews Jamboree

The little kid factor is endearing. For many, this is a family event. All pre-pubescent boys look like Bobby from *King of the Hill*. Entire families are dressed in camouflage fatigues. Some paint their faces to be less conspicuous. I didn't know costumes were a part of this. I would've dressed as a pirate (Aaargh!). Tell me again which war was fought in purple fatigues.

"Mustache Bob, your gun's ready at the firing range!" blasts the loudspeaker as heartily fed Americans sit on bleachers, waiting for the shooting spree to begin.

"Know, what I want to try is a jetpack!" says a man with the mind of a child, gleefully watching a flame-thrower demonstration. A Halloween-orange fire sprays from a gun shot by a helmeted man in a silver moon-man suit. He blasts an apocalyptic flame at a burnt-out car. He removes his helmet and insightfully adds, "It was hot; really hot!"

"Girl Scout bake sale!" shouts a table of little girls selling crumbled cakes, inside a tent showroom next to row after row of assault weapons. There's more assault weapons than in a Bin Laden playroom. If I ever wanted to start my own country in the woods, this is where I'd begin.

"How much for this gun?" I ask, putting the dealer's crusty head in the sight of his very own AK47.

"$5,000," he barks.

The gun's price tag is little too steep for me, so I move on to something I can afford—the crusty dealer's array of racist bumper stickers. An old Southern geezer with a glazed look of pure, engraved bigotry is transfixed. Which one will he choose?

*"The Original Boys In the Hood," featuring a picture of three hooded Klansmen.

*A Confederate flag with "It's A White Thing!"

*Christian America!

Or simply "AIDs Cures Fags!"

How maliciously subtle. I got a great idea for their bumper stickers. How about one that reads, "We Hate Anyone Who Isn't Us!"

"Don't take my picture!" snaps a guy, holding a rifle on edge, while wearing a T-shirt that says:

CHRISTIAN
AMERICAN
PRO-GUY
HETEROSEXUAL
ANY QUESTIONS?

"I don't want you taking my picture," he barks at my camera. "Hey, I'm not going to argue with a guy with a gun," I retort. "Whatever!" grunts the Christian, American, Pro-Guy Heterosexual. That's how it starts; a few more exchanges, then Blam-Blam-Blam, argument over!

Gun Myths Disproved: 70 million Americans own guns. 48 percent of all households have at least one firearm. A gun in the home is 43 times more likely to be used to kill its owner, a relative, or a friend than an intruder. Oh yeah? What a bunch of tree-hugging propaganda! Well look at these annual stats: US Highway Deaths: 42,815. US Flu Deaths: 36,000. US Gun Deaths (homicide, suicide, accidental): 28,163. Not to mention, one-sixth, of all deaths in the US are caused by lung cancer! We should be less concerned about taking away people's guns, and be more concerned with putting the emphasis where it belongs—making our nation's highways safer and providing more effective flu shots! **WAKE UP AMERICA!**

TIME TO SHOOT!

I'm snapped back to reality by a large blast of bullets. It's LOUD: real fucking loud! It's so loud, it actually makes sweat run down my back. It's so loud, everyone has to scream at each other like a complete fuck-wit. My point: LOUD!

The nearest provider of ear protection is my first priority, as I almost bump into a burly skinhead with a pit bull. Like a giant video game, the shooting range is scattered with shot-up cars, large wooden spools, and, for some reason, ovens.

"Whatever's cookin' in there is done!" screams a Grizzly Adams look-alike. The only thing missing is "bad men" dodging between obstacles to achieve a Play Station high score.

Large American flags flap proudly over the shooting area. Safety standards are an afterthought. A spray-painted red line designates where the large, surging crowd should stand as numerous assault weapons spray bullets. One guy fires too soon, spraying bullets just feet in front of him. A loaded clip falls out of the magazine of another. Shells fly everywhere. The orange-shirted security personnel are the only people without guns.

Three large, gruff, arms-vendors rent a multitude of assault weapons and machine guns—everything from M16s to AK47s. It's time to blow some shit up!

ASSAULT WEAPON #1: THE FIRE MONSTER

HK 51
.308 Caliber
I wait in line behind a pimply-faced kid with braces in a "Skynyrd Kicks Ass" T-shirt.

"Come on! It's a once in a lifetime thing," he begs, trying to convince his pimply-faced friend to shoot.

"Which gun is the most fun?" I scream at guy with a long beard handing out loaded clips. He recommends the Fire Monster.

"God damn!" screams a man who just finished with the Fire Monster. "God damn!"

"I know what you'll be dreaming about!" shouts the bearded guy taking his weapon. A proud father leads his son, again resembling Bobby from King of the Hill, to the Fire Monster.

"It's his first time," boasts the father. Like other "first times," Bobby is nervous, then fires away like an old pro. The kid is all smiles when finished.

"You won't forget that," shouts the bearded man.

"That's a little different than a video game," adds his dad.

"I got to get me one of those!" says delighted Bobby.

Now it's my turn to experience the thrills of the Fire Monster. I lean hard into the weapon.

"Put the flipper on 20, and you're ready to rock-and-roll!"

Blam! Holy shit! I feel like Chow Yun Fat in *Hard Boiled*. It's like having a flippin' tank on your shoulder. Dirt flies from the ground like mini landmines. The firepower thrusts me back. The bearded man puts his hand on my back. I feel downright giddy after the Fire Monster. I don't know if that's necessarily a good thing.

"God bless you," I say, handing the man back his Fire Monster.

ASSAULT WEAPON #2: UZI

9mm

30 rounds

You're back!"

I'm spotted as a repeat customer. Compared to the Fire Monster, the Uzi is like shooting through butter. There's very little kick as I spray around the targets with a sea of bullets.

"Take that, bitch!" I scream blasting bullet-riddled cars and ovens.

The Uzi jams. A guy in a white Panama hat comes over, adjusts the weapon, and it's back to rapid-fire shooting. The whole thing is over in 20 seconds. I hand the Uzi back to the guy with the beard.

"I got to get one of these for school," I mumble. "Fucking teachers." I feel like such a sportsman.

ASSAULT WEAPON #3: THE JUNGLE WALK

With the Jungle Walk, you run through the woods on a muddy

path, with a fully loaded assault weapon, trying to shoot 18 different stationed targets while being timed with a stopwatch. I think this event was organized by the genius who invented "running through the house with scissors."

Approaching a handwritten banner reading "Kill Charlie," with a drawing of a Vietnamese man, I sign up with an old guy wearing glasses, named Bob. He sits next to a skull propped on a stick with the words "Yank You Die." The Jungle Walk is Bob's weird 'Nam war flashback?

"We came all the way from Austria for this, " boasts a pair of Austrians, with eyes popping out of their heads with excitement, behind me.

"You know, I was impressed by the Austrian army when I was over there in '68," says the Jungle Walk commando in full army fatigues. He hands the popped-eyed Austrians a flyer for WWII battle reenactments.

"I read about this," admits one of the excited Austrians.

"See, we don't have a problem with this in the States," the commando states with pure American pride.

The commando gives us a quick briefing, screaming due to the blasts of gunfire. Everyone strains to listen.

"If you want to be John Wayne, that's up to you. Lean into it, across your body," he advises, pointing the Uzi directly at my face. Just then a gun goes off in the woods behind him.

"SHIT!!!"

It scares the living fuck out of me! Momentarily I see my life pass before my eyes.

"This is for you guys!" the commando screams again.

I'm up after 3 yahoos from Cleveland. We'll each get 50 rounds to fire. I put the second clip in my back pocket. Bob stands behind me with a stopwatch.

"Ready... Go!"

I take off running with my loaded Uzi. Bob runs behind me with his ticking stopwatch. I forgot to mention, Bob has horrible scars all over his arms

"Look through the sight," coaches horribly arm-scarred Bob. I fire at a metal plate attached to a tree. Sprinting to the next station, I blast some cans on top of poles. A hot shell flies out of the Uzi, hitting me in the neck. I'm hit! I'm actually wounded by flying shrapnel! Being a brave soldier, I run to the final station with a bloody neck. Arm-scarred Bob close behind; just me and Bob, alone in the woods! How would they react if shots were fired and Bob didn't come out of the woods?!

At 1700 hours the upper shooting range looks like downtown Beirut. Cars are on fire. Pillars of black smoke fill the sky. Enough artillery is being fired to fight off several armies. The range is nothing but a sea of bullets, all at various speeds, volumes, and rhythms. The only thing missing is people running and screaming. Fires break out everywhere. This is pure insanity. It's the love of mass destruction, the love of America; the thrill and high of violence. Am I Don Quixote, screaming at the midday sun?

In the end, I treat myself to a sno-cone (who doesn't like sno-cones?). My hearing hurts. I have a huge, dry bloody welt from being struck by the Uzi shell in the neck. Another kid who looks like Bobby from *King of the Hill* scoops ice with his bare, dirty hands, forming it into a snowball, He hands me my ice treat. Disgusted, upon paying, I immediately throw it in the trash.

26.
THE GUN SAFETY TEST

In most states, anyone wishing to buy a gun must first pass a Gun Safety Test, which begs the question: exactly how stupid can you be and still buy a gun in America? What the Bar Exam is to lawyers, the Gun Safety Test is to the shooting enthusiast. A mind-twisting 30-question quiz so incredibly difficult, that if you fail, they let you take the exact same exam the very next day. It's a good thing that the test is so tough, because it weeds out really stupid people (which I think that might be unconstitutional) who will surely have zany gun mishaps. You must get twenty-three of these brain-stumping, big boys correct in order to buy a gun. Here's a few examples taken from the Basic Firearms Safety Certificate Workbook:

1. Having a positive attitude is the first step in becoming a safe and responsible gun owner?
   TRUE
   FALSE
   (True, I guess if that's what those assholes want you to have.)

2. Handgun accidents can happen even when a person knows the safety rules?

TRUE

FALSE

(I say if they don't know the rules, the hell with them, they deserve to be shot.)

3. To prevent handgun accidents, safety rules must be applied:

Only when you have children around.

All the time.

Most of the time.

Only when you are firing a gun.

(I say b) Most of the time. Why put rules on your fun-it ruins spontaneity.)

4. Guns shouldn't be worn as fashion accessories.

TRUE

FALSE

(True? How can they possibly mean this? This is such bullshit. And especially you ladies should feel insulted.)

5. To ensure safety, you should store your gun:

Safely and securely when not in use.

Loaded in a locked container.

With your ammunition.

With your valuables such as jewelry or money.

All of the above.

(I chose c) With your ammunition. It only makes sense. I mean if you're home and get in some quarrel, there's no hassle with unlocking annoying safety locks. It's a one-stop activity—POW! POW! POW! HASTA LA VISTA BABY! End of argument.

6. It's legal to carry a loaded gun in a public place?

TRUE

FALSE

(I'm confused. I always thought it was OK to wave your gun around in public, in order to let everyone marvel at it.)

7. Which of the following is best qualified to repair your handgun:

Yourself

A friend

A gunsmith

(I chose b) A friend. You know, that ambiguous friend, the guy you lent your powerdrill to and whose name is, perhaps, Morty, is best qualified to fix your gun. This is also a trick question, because what if "your friend" is also a gunsmith. Then what?)

8. It's OK to leave your gun lying around the house if you forbid children to touch it?

TRUE

FALSE

(I'd actually say true. If your pesky kids accidentally shoot themselves, big deal—they disobeyed! It'll just save you all that trouble down the road when they grow up and start asking for the car and stuff.)

When I took the Gun Safety test, I was amazed to discover I got 28 out of 30 correct on my first try. And I wasn't even trying very hard. I was so happy, I couldn't wait to get home and fire off my guns in celebration.

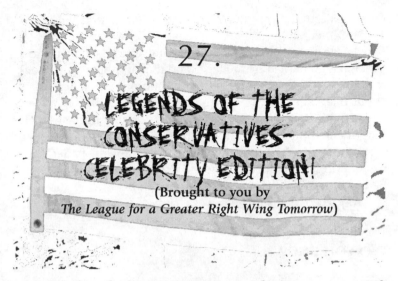

27.
LEGENDS OF THE CONSERVATIVES- CELEBRITY EDITION!
(Brought to you by
The League for a Greater Right Wing Tomorrow)

Legends of the Conservatives salutes................Mel Gibson!!!! Yes, who would have thought the star of such action-packed blockbusters as *Mad Max*, *Mad Max II*, *Lethal Weapon*, and *Lethal Weapon II* would go on to become one annoying conservative mofo?

BORN: January 3, 1956

BIRTHPLACE: Peekskill, NY

OCCUPATION: Actor/Director

At one time Mel Gibson spoke with an Australian accent. Then one day he just suddenly stopped. Although born in America, while still a child, Mel's family moved to Australia after his father won as a contestant on *Jeopardy*.

DID YOU KNOW?

Did you know that Mel Gibson's father believes that the Holocaust, which took the lives off 6 millions Jews, never happened? Yes, Mel Gibson's father, Hutton Gibson, is a notorious Holocaust denier! Not only that but he also claims that the World Trade Center was destroyed by remote control and not by Al Queda. He also contends that the Second Vatican Council was a Masonic plot backed by the Jews, and that all popes going back to John XXIII have been illegitimate "anti-popes." When asked about this, Mel Gibson was quoted as saying in the *New York Post*, "That's bullshit...I don't want to be dissing my father. He never denied the Holocaust; he just said there were fewer than six million. I don't want them having me dissing my father." Mel went on to say, "My dad taught me my faith, and I believe what he taught me. The man never lied to me in his life."

Way to go Mel Gibson!

DID YOU KNOW?:

Did you know Mel Gibson was named *People* magazine's Sexiest Man Alive and also once said, "There is no salvation for those outside the Church...I believe it."

MEL SETS THE RECORD STRAIGHT

"Scholars always dick around with the Gospels, you know? Judas is always some kind of friend of some freedom fighter named Barabbas, you know what I mean?" Mel Gibson said in an interview with the *New Yorker*. "It's horseshit. It's revisionist bullshit. And that's what these academics are into. They gave me notes on a stolen script. I couldn't believe it. It was like they were more or less saying I have no right to interpret the Gospels myself, because I don't have a bunch of letters after my name."

MEL GIBSON FUN FACT!

In *The Passion of the Christ*, many felt Mel Gibson portrayed Jews as Christ Killers. This could not be further from the truth. In fact

Mel Gibson puts the record straight, "It's not meant to. I think it's meant to just tell the truth. I want to be as truthful as possible. Anyone who transgresses has to look at their own part or look at their own culpability."

Way to go Mel!

NO STEM CELL RESEARCH FOR MEL GIBSON!

Did you know that Mel Gibson is adamantly opposed to stem cell research? That's right, Mel Gibson is against the very research that Superman's Christopher Reeve fought for until his dying breath. Mel Gibson told ABC's *Good Morning America* that he has an "ethical problem" with the research that could potentially make crippled people walk and possibly find a cure for such things as Michael J. Fox's Parkinson's, and Alzheimer's, the disease that inflicted now-dead conservative president Ronald Reagan.

The Passion of the Christ director told *Good Morning America*, "I found that the cloning of human embryos will be used in the process and that, for me, I have an ethical problem with that." Gibson told ABC, "Why do I, as a taxpayer, have to fund something I believe is unethical?"

Way to go Mel Gibson!

MEL GIBSON ON BIRTH CONTROL

Did you know that Mel Gibson opposes birth control? "God is the only one who knows how many children we should have, and we should be ready to accept them," Mel Gibson once said. Way to go Mel Gibson!

MEL FUN FACT

Mel Gibson is only 5'9 and is a big fan of *The 3 Stooges*!

DID YOU KNOW?

Did you know Mel Gibson attained a brief notoriety for his loud and crude attacks on gays? When Mel Gibson was asked by the Spanish magazine *El Pais* what he thought of homosexuals, Mel Gibson replied, "They take it up the ass!" He then got out of his chair, bent over and pointed to his butt. "This is only for taking a shit," he explained. "With this look, who's going to think I'm gay? It would be hard to take me for someone like that. Do I sound like a homosexual? Do I talk like them? Do I move like them?"

Way to go Mel Gibson!

MEL GIBSON FUN FACT!

Mel holds extreme conservative views on religion. He quit the Roman Catholic Church because he believes the reforms of the Second Vatican Council in the 1960s went too far. "For 1,950 years [the church] does one thing and then in the 60s, all of a sudden they turn everything inside out and begin to do strange things that go against the rules."

MEL ON MEL

"Everything that had been heresy is no longer heresy, according to the new rules. We Catholics are being cheated. The church has stopped being critical. It has relaxed. I don't believe them, and I have no intention of following their trends. It's the church that has abandoned me, not me who has abandoned it."

Thank you Mel Gibson. We salute you. We thank you for all your movies (especially the action ones), but most of all we salute you for spreading the word nice and thick, and being one conservative mofo.

28.
CHRISTIAN IS THE NEW LATINO!

B ased on the success of the box office smash, *The Passion of the Christ, People* magazine—that vast vessel of knowledge and style—declared that Christianity is not only *hot* but also *sexy*. So what they're saying, as far as trends go, *Christian is the new Latino!*

The Passion of the Christ was the number #1 hit at the box office (well surpassing *Scooby Doo 2*). It grossed close to a billion dollars. Yet, I don't know a single damn person who's seen the movie. Who the hell are these people? It just goes to show that Christianity, and all things Christian, are big, big business, catering to a select, insular audience. It makes you think that there's a whole parallel universe out there that we don't know about. And in that parallel universe, it's just like this universe, except in that parallel universe everything (music, movies, ventriloquists, etc.) are all Christian-bent in Bush's sterile America.

Back in the past, Jesus, alone, was the only selling point needed to get people hooked on Christ. Now, in this modern age, that's not good enough. It's all about marketing; marketing in order to bring *The Jesus* to people in ways we'd never fathom.

And just like in Chaucer's *Canterbury Tales*, I shall set out on a pilgrimage into the heart of darkness of Christian culture USA, sharing my stories with you, my amiable host, letting you decide over a cup of mead which is the best of these Christian tales.

JESUS WAS A BREAKDANCER!

Once on a time, as old tales tell to us,
> *There was a concert hall in the tow n of Davis*
> *A rapper took in guests and $32.50 he charged us,*
> *As he rapped and spoke in street-slang for Jesus!*
> *In the capacity arena, on stage is the Christian equivalent of Justin Timberlake. He wears a basketball tank top and twisted baseball cap, doing ghetto–rap arm motions while a DJ scratches on the turntables.*

"This is from the first book of John, Chapter One, Verse 5!" spouts the Christian Justin Timberlake, with his faux street attitude, doing a song off his new CD called *Freaks* (because he's so craaaaaazy!).

Huge applause. Huge screams. The DJ scratches. He moves with blatant sexuality, making the teenage Christian girls in hip-hugger jeans shriek with the kind of excitement that they will most certainly have to repress in the eyes of God. There's a lot of emphasis put on getting everyone to clap their hands in the air (like you just don't care!). His energetic band kicks into some hip-hop. At one point, the Christian Justin Timberlake does a flip off of a speaker (maybe, as suggested, it's to drive home the point of the first book of John, Chapter One, Verse 5?!). It's a big production with large video monitors on each side of the stage capturing intimate close-ups. This is just like some weird scenario seen on the Simpsons-but without the irony. It's like N'Sync gone God crazy.

Who are these people? Where did they come from to see two bands I have never, ever heard of in my whole entire life? Sponsored by K-LOVE radio, I think this musical Jesus-fest might be close to being sold out. Yes, the place is packed—the entire UC

Davis Recreation Hall. Upper and lower levels (not to mention the floor) are full. This is Christian parent-approved music. You can almost imagine the parental lecturing, "I won't allow you to listen to The Backstreet Boys, but you can listen to Toby Mac [the Christian Justin Timberlake]." It's like having to buy the Walmart knockoff version of Nikes (Wikes?). Like an actor in adult films, Christian musicians still have the driving goal of wanting to crossover to a mainstream music audience. Yes, having a #1 Christian album is like being the #1 band in Finland; you may not make money outside the circle of Finnish people, but no one will really know you.

Meanwhile, thepeople here know all the words to these hip-hop songs for the Lord. They're singing along. Where am I? The crowd is white and whiter. Well-scrubbed, smiling, and of all ages. These are the people that put born again Bush in office. These are the people who thought Gore tried to steal the last election. There's a slight feeling of tensed repression. Yes, Bush has won the war and this is his sterile America.

"Take us to church one time!" the Christian Justin Timberlake commands his dredlocked bass player, who then gets "funky." There's thunderous applause and a display of lasers and lights. They mix up the set with covers of '70's funk songs to get the crowd going, and when they least expect it, cunningly slip in Jesus.

"Thanks for praising God with us in a different sort of way!" shouts the Christian Justin Timberlake with fist in the air, praising the same Jesus found by serial killers while in prison.

Between acts, hoards of very white fans fork over handfuls of cash to buy the tie-in Christian music merchandise with prices not very Christian on the wallet. A T-shirt of Toby Mac doing a gangasta pose costs 25 bucks. A huge line careens around the corner for the band, the entire Toby Mac Experience, to autograph posters ($15). My concert ticket cost me $32.50. Christian merchandising has gone way beyond the sale of that one, best-selling book. Christian is not only the new Latino, but also big, big business.

I go in the bathroom. Written on the wall of the stall is "Fuck

Her Bush!" Did some repressed Toby Mac fan scrawl this in haste as a temporary satanic possession?

> The musician from stage, while the reeve yet spoke,
> Patted his back with pleasure at the joke.
> "Ha, ha!" laughed he, "by Christ's great suffering,
> I shall rock out with a mighty guitar solo ending

Back outside, the headlining band is called Third Day. I think they're named that because something significant involving Jesus must have happened on a third day. These guys have been around for eleven years. They have seven albums out (including Offerings I & II), and yet I have never for the life of me heard of them until tonight.

With their indie-guitar sound, Third Day's mainstream counterpart would be hard-drinking, Jack Daniel's swilling southern good-ole-boys. But this is the parallel universe of Christian rock, and they, in turn, are only swilling the Jesus.

It's music you can clap along to while swinging your hips and occasionally bending your knees. Or at least that is what this crowd is doing. Sons smile at dads. The lead singer looks just like Jesus (if Jesus had a short haircut and played indie-rock).

"Are you ready to rock?!" asks Rock-Jesus. "This is a new single for you called *I Believe*!"

I soon learn that the answer to what they *believe* in is *love*. Yes, that's what they believe in, alright. Go figure. To be brutally honest, Third Day's music is shit. At times it sounds like watered down Pearl Jam. The lyrics are a pure cliché-fest.

Then there's a song about climbing the highest mountain. On the ballad "Wire," the subtle video shows a man in a suit walking across a tightrope over a large city. Yes, very subtle, not to mention metaphorical. Some of the fans put their hands up in the air, stick-em-up style in order to channel the Jesus. People are having spiritual experiences here, much like mullet heads would have a different kind of spiritual experience at an AC/DC concert—after doing several lines of crystal meth. It feels like a Pepsi commercial in here. Breaking into what I assume is one of their "hits," the crowd goes more wild. Flames and fire erupt on the large video screen, all to the sounds of hard rock guitars. This should be good—perhaps leaving a minor warning of sorts. Rock-Jesus croons with the songwriting prowess of, say an early Dylan, " Flames burn deep in my soul..."

But there is no sympathy for the devil here. Again, everyone, in this whole entire damn concert venue, seems to know the words. The next song is about believing, but this time, not in love, but in Jesus.

"I believe! I believe! I believe!" rings the chorus, emoted by Rock-Jesus as the guitarist, wearing a cowboy hat, does classic cock-rock poses. And then, "On the third day he rose again...."

Wait, thus the name of the band, Third Day. Now it's all coming together. Then there's the request to grab your neighbor's hand and the raising of it high in the air. My hand is grabbed by a man whose shirt reads "You Have a Choice. Choose Christ!" I somehow feel dirtied by being here.

"We got to come together...."

The Christian Justin Timberlake is brought back out on stage (Hurrah! I like the Christian Justin Timberlake!). Again, he tries to act all streetwise in his very white Christian way.

"What's going on?!" he asks the screaming crowd.

The Christian Justin Timberlake and Rock Jesus do a big power Christian rock/rap finale.

"I got a message! I got a song! Everybody help me sing along!"

There's nothing like a packed arena of Christians wanting an encore (or 2nd coming). Watching this concert is becoming like some weird David Blaine endurance test. I can't take anymore as Rock Jesus comes back out and does a rock song called Hallelujah.

"Sing Hallelujah," requests Rock Jesus.

Yes, hallelujah indeed. That's what I'll be singing when I start running from the building towards my car.

CHRISTCORE!

There was a good man of religion, too,
A punk rocker, with thrashing guitars, I warrant you;
Who Christ's own gospel truly sought to preach;
While screaming into a mike as those moshed in a pit he'd teach.

I'm a huuuuuuuge fan of Christian hardcore punk. Huuuuu-uuuuge! I love this genre of music because it's that perfect marriage of Christian (happy, happy, happy), meets angry, go-fuck-the-establishment, punk. It just doesn't make sense. It's like vegetarians for meat. Or Klansmen for big, black booty. Now they're trying to get the kids hooked on

Christ through punk. That's why I went and checked out some Christian hardcore punk at a Christian punk venue called 24/7 (named such, being that's how much you should think about the Lord—24/7).

First of all, Sid Vicious must be vomiting in his grave. What a bizarre turn taken by the music spawned from his lions.

"Anybody a hardcore Christian?" shouts the punk musician tattooed and wearing a wife-beater tank-top.

"Yaaaaaa!" screams the crowd. They go apeshit.

"Alright, this goes out to You!"

The band kicks into a pale *Rage Against the Machine* guitar riff. Christian heads shake to the grinding music.

"Do it for Him, for what he did for you! Do it for Him, for what he did for you," shouts the lead singer. He also does ghetto-rap hand motions. He stage-dives into the Christian crowd. This is the heart of "Christcore." Yes, these punk bands are angry; they're angry for the Lord!

Three Christian punk bands are on the bill tonight, playing in a room, that I guess is normally used for Sunday School. A creepy banner hovering over the stage reads "He Is Risen." The music began at 8:00. I don't imagine this running too late. Church is tomorrow.

The band finishes their three-chord thrash for Christ.

"Was that awesome or what!" says the smiley guitarist Josh,

wearing shorts, with white socks pulled up to his knees.

"This a new song, it's called 'CHRISTIAN ELITE!' 1-2-3-4!"

The punk band kicks into the tune. I can't understand the lyrics, but I occasionally hear the word "Jesus" screamed, a lot. A messiah-mosh breaks out amongst the Christian crowd, who's far from angry, in fact they are down right smiley, and that's a big difference right there; more smiles to be found at Christian punk shows.

I'm their groupie, says a smiley woman standing next to me. Now color me stupid, but what would a Christian punk groupie actually do?

Josh follows this up with a song about having good attendance at school.

"You gotta get an education! You gotta go to school! You gotta get an education! You gotta go to school!" he screams to the grinding music. That's so true. You *do* have to get an education! You *do* have to go to school!

Before the last band comes out, this large, burly Henry Rollins look-a-like, who's covered in tattoos, struts to the mike. I think he's going to instill the fear of the Lord with the threat of whoop ass. But most of all, he's got a big, hardcore Christian attitude.

"All the bands you see here tonight. All of them! Are about-Jesus-Christ!" The crowd gets weirdly quiet. Some people go "Sh-sh-sh-sh!" A few even stop smiling. The Rollins doppelganger gets intense.

"You won't leave a show here without hearing about Jesus Christ. If you want to know who he is, I'll tell you, HE'S ABOUT LOVE!"

Is it just me, or has punk has greatly changed since the days of Johnny Rotten calling the Queen a cunt!

The final Christian punk band comes on stage, and they're like guys you'd trust to baby-sit. I don't catch their name, but if I had a Christian punk band, I think I'd name it *Burning Bush*. Or my second choice for a name, *Him/Hymn*.

"Hey come up front! We can't have you moshing, but we can have you dancing, having a good time!" remarks the smiley guitarist.

They kick into their tune.

"DON'T JUDGE US BY THE WAY WE LOOK. WE JUST WANT TO READ HIS BOOK!" The singer rolls on the ground. "I'M ON MY KNEES, BEGGING FOR FORGIVENESS!"

It's all over by 8:50.

"Thank you everyone. We love you! We love Jesus! Goodnight!"

Punk should stay the "devil's music." It's much more fun that way. As the Sex Pistols once said, "Do you ever get the feeling you've been cheated?"

EPILOGUE

Now do I pray all those who hear this little treatise, or read it,

that, if there be within it anything that pleases them, they thank Our

Lord Jesus Christ, from Whom proceeds all understanding and all

Goodness and happens to be also a great entertainment vehicle for hip-hop, sci-fi movies and ventriloquism, not to mention big cash dollars.

And if there be anything that displeases them, I pray them, also, that they impute it to the fault of my ignorance and not to my intention, which is to someday start a Christian Punk band called "The No Sex Before Marriage Pistols."

HERE ENDS THE STORY OF CHRISTIAN AS THE NEW LATINO

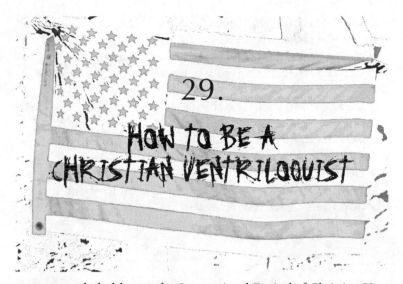

29.
HOW TO BE A CHRISTIAN VENTRILOQUIST

Recently held, was the *International Festival of Christian Ventriloquism and Puppetry* in San Diego. An event where they spread the word of the Lord without moving their lips! Not only does this organized gathering, truly, actually exists in reality, but there was enough Christian ventriloquist in our country to make it a sold out event. The convention's motto, "His Plans....Our Hands!"

For any of you interested in becoming a Christian ventriloquist, I highly recommend a book called, *Church Chuckles.*" It's a Christian ventriloquist script book filed with religious/laugh-provoking routines for every holy occasion. Here's a sample of the zany Christian ventriloquist dialogue to hone with your wooden dummy, concerning themes of salvation, witnessing, and obedience. Remember, God will strike you dead if you move your lips!

VENTILOQUIST: Christianity has been studied and practiced for over 2,000 years.

WOODEN DUMMY: Wow! Somehow I feel it's been studied more than it's been practiced.

VENTILOQUIST: Let's pray people will keep practicing until they get it perfect!

-Amen oh little wooden friend! Insert laughter here-

VENTILOQUIST: Can you tell a Christian by looking at them?

DUMMY: You should be able to see the joy of Christ on their face.

VENTILOQUIST: Sometimes. But sometimes I've seen happier faces in a dentist chair.

DUMMY: Unfortunately.

VENTILOQUIST: I saw a guy the other Sunday that looked like he'd been baptized in vinegar!

Amen!

30.
ONWARD CHRISTIAN EX-GAYS

"**O**K, time to get into the hot seat!" The leader of the Fellow Warrior support group announces. I'm herded over to the coffee table in the center of a small back room in a crappy two-story office complex. I sit down and bow my head. Suddenly, twelve Fellow Warriors—or "ex-gays," as their propaganda calls them — put their hands on my body, most particularly the shoulders and upper-torso, and the praying begins. Like freestyle rappers coming to the mike, each takes a turn praying that my sinful soul stays on the right path. (In order to infiltrate this gathering, I'm going by the pseudonym and persona of Monty, and the Fellow Warriors are praying the Lord will watch over Monty and prevent him from falling back into the gay lifestyle.)

"Yes Jesus. Yes!"

"Monty has a scary journey ahead of him..."

"Evil days! Evil Days!" someone cries.

"...please watch over Monty, oh Lord!"

"Amen! Amen!" someone else cries.

"The righteous man falls several times. Look after Monty

252 Republican Like Me

and guide him!"

"Yes Jesus! Yes!"

This goes on way longer than I feel comfortable with. When the praying finally ends, a box of Kleenex is handed to me; apparently, I'm expected to be in tears.

"Wow!" I remark, moving my hands to emulate some sort of energy field. "Yeah, that was really great. I really felt something there. Yeah, it was like feeling a force or something like that. Yeah, that's it; a force!"

I pause. I can't think of anything else to say except, "Wow!"

Many would think this type of fire-and-brimstone, repent-for-homosexuals, for-they-are-sinners antics would take place only in the Midwest or the heart of the South. Uh-uh. Such religious zealots congregate right outside the gates of the city of sin itself, San Francisco. You can even take the Bay Area Rapid Transit to them.

According to extreme Christian ministries, homosexuality, like poison ivy or frostbite, can be prevented–if you look for the signs. Pick up a copy of *Preventing Homosexuality: A Parent's Guide*; the Christian world provides guidelines for concerned parents who want to prevent their children from entering The World of Gay:

- Masculinity is an achievement. Growing up straight isn't something that happens. It requires good parenting. It requires societal support. And it takes time.
- Dad is more important than mom. Mothers make boys. Fathers make men.
- More often, homosexuals displayed non-masculinity that set them painfully apart from other boys: un-athletic, somewhat passive, unaggressive. and uninterested in rough-and-tumble play.
- A boy needs to see his father as confident, self-assured, and decisive. Mothers need to back off a bit. What I mean is, don't smother him. Tip: Single mothers may need to recruit a trustworthy male role model.
- Be concerned if you see gender confusion or doubt in

your child from ages 5 to 11. There is a high correlation between feminine behavior in boyhood and adult homosexuality.

Infiltration No. 1: Back to Hope
Personae: Carl and Isabella, concerned Christian parents. Which fictional last name do they go by? Why, *the Gaymores*, of course.

Disguises: Isabella is caked with way too much makeup, bright pink lipstick, an over-abundance of eye shadow, and smears of blush. Her hair is a mess that reflects her frazzled state. I adopt the standard Christian male uniform: Dockers' pants, blue sports coat, white shirt, and red tie.

Back story: The Gaymores' are experiencing culture shock; they've just moved to San Francisco from a small town in Minnesota.

The Gaymores' problem: This young Christian couple became frightfully concerned about their son. The little rascal fell within the guidelines of homosexual characteristics on the Web site for the Back to Hope support group. It doesn't help matters that they decide to name him Tobias.

My overused catchphrase: "What do you tell the kids?!"
Approximate distance from San Francisco: 55 Minutes

The Exodus ministry is a Christian-based support group for parents who are concerned and want to take action in regard to their sons or daughters who are, as the ministry puts it, in the gay lifestyle. What separates this support group from others is the firm belief that children who are gay will go straight-to-hell unless they change their ways and embrace the Lord. Why is it those who scream "sinner" are, almost always, the people concealing the deepest, darkest sins?

With the assistance of an actress friend named Johanna, who poses as my fake wife, we enter a classroom that has a large *Jesus Loves You* banner on the wall; it is inside a community church center in the East Bay. We wear funereal expressions.

"We're a limited cozy group this evening," professes Debbie, a woman who exhibits the bobble-headed enthusiasm of an Orange County cruise-ship social director. "We are officially ending our first year as a group."

I take a seat in one of the schoolchild-sized chairs in the semicircle, next to Debbie, Carol, and a large woman, also a first-timer, who has a box of Kleenex, and who appears to have been crying long before we got there. I stare straight ahead, as if I'm harboring a horrible secret.

"Do you have a loved one that's in the gay lifestyle?" asks concerned Carol, a chunky woman who resembles a high school women's softball coach.

I drop my eyes to the ground in shame and answer *yes*.

"I went to the Web site and looked for the signs, and he fit right into that sort of scenario," I explain, highly disturbed. "It said that now is the time to take and action and take the needed steps for prevention."

"Is it a boy or a girl?"

"It's a boy."

"How old is he?"

"He's seven!" I answer in a soft voice.

There's a few seconds of stunned silence; this is obviously a new scenario for participants in their group. Much like parents who want their child to get into a good kindergarten, the Gaymores are taking early steps to prevent their precious son from turning a little gay, since he fits in their definition of the all-important developmental years of 5 to 11.

Debbie bobbles her head and prays: "I like to thank you, Heavenly Father. Thank you for bringing Carl and Isabella to us tonight."

I look at my fake wife with a glimmer of hope. "Thanks for having us," I muster.

Carol takes over with some mean scripture quoting (First Corinthians, to be exact): "Those who won't inherit the Kingdom of God: the sexually immoral, idolaters, male prostitutes, the homosexuals, drunkards, the greedy…"

It's now time for everyone to tell his or her story for being here tonight. First comes bobble-headed Debbie, who says both her children have turned gay.

"I didn't know where to go. I didn't know where to turn. I didn't know what to do. I didn't even know how to say the word *lesbian*," she shares, bobbling her head. "Though working with Carol, I really spent some time gaining knowledge on what little wire could just kind of short-circuit.

"I went to *Parents and Friends of Gays and Lesbians*. That was the only place I knew. 'Cause that's what the kids hear in school (huff); that it's okay; anyone's sexual preference is okay. (More huffing.) If I would have stayed on that path, I probably would have said, it's fine. But I believe now that there is an incredible power, and we *can* change people. I love my children and I'm praying for them. (Nervous cackle.) Because without God, we're all lost." (Big nervous laughs.)

With a bobble of the head, Debbie then directs her attention to the Gaymores. "I don't know at seven I would have recognized the signs, 'cause I don't know at seven that they know. Do you know what I'm saying?"

We, the Gaymores, shake our gloomy heads in unison.

"I believe it takes a lot of guts to walk through that door, to say I even know someone who is homosexual, and I question it. Because socially, it's like drinking," she spews, disgustedly. "Social drinking is very acceptable. They don't know it's wrong."

"We all need God!" exclaims Carol.

"Amen!" someone says.

"What do you tell the kids?!" I throw out as a rhetorical question.

"I sit in the back of the church crying my eyes out," Carol remarks; she's talking about her son, who was kicked out of a Christian college when he was caught in bed with his prayer buddy.

"She's my little prayer warrior," Debbie says.

"I remember standing there, and my son told me he was homosexual. And it's like a death," Carol remarks solemnly "It's like a death in the family."

"What do you tell the kids?!" I repeat again for no reason.

It seems that the large crying woman has a son who recently

moved not just to San Francisco, but to the *Castro District*.

"Right in the heart of it," she says between sobs, going on to explain how shocking it was to hear about the antics of a typical Castro Halloween.

"Halloween is a scary time over there" Debbie agrees, bobbling her head in disapproval.

"I wish he weren't gay. I know that homosexuality is a sin," the large, crying woman says. "It's a sin in God's eyes."

"What do you tell the kids?!" I add.

The large woman's crying intensifies.

"My son designs Web sites. He said to me, 'Mom, look at this Web site I designed.' He brought it up on the computer, and these male figures came up. And it was a gay porn site!" the large woman says. "My mouth had dropped, and I said *Oh my god! What are you doing?*"

"You had to look at them, too," Debbie sympathizes.

"Was there any tea-bagging going on?" I ask, gravely concerned.

Carol sets the record straight. "They do not believe they are living in sin," she says "They live in denial, because they believe what the world has bombarded upon them, and they have bought into it to justify how they live is okay."

Debbie's head-bobbling intensifies: "To them it is not a sin."

Carol poses a little theory. "I pretty much believe that the Christian world has created the Castro, because that's the only place they can go for their sins and live in denial," she says. "Do you know what I'm saying? And I'm not saying it's right, it's just as wrong as any other sin."

Debbie once again turns perky. "When I walked into the Castro, my daughter said she was going to take me to the best taco place around. And I wasn't going to go, but I prayed my way through the Castro," she says. "And I mean it was like, what an experience."

"The kids, what do you tell them?" I ask.

Carl, would you like to share?" Carol asks compassionately.

"I do indeed," I reply solemnly, slowly ticking off the concerns that trouble the Gaymore household. "Nowadays there are so many outside forces. The TV and the movies make it seem like it's acceptable to be gay. Can you believe that?"

As group members nod in agreement, I gesture to my fake wife. "Like we once went to a church that made it seem acceptable to be homosexual. Isn't that something?! Sure, we're all God's children, but what are they going to say next — that necrophilia is okay?!

"We're seeing the gay warning signs! We're seeing the warning signs," I blurt out, hitting the back of a chair. "He doesn't like sports."

"He just ends up playing with the Barbies," adds an almost tearful Isabella Gaymore.

"And he gets picked on by other kids," I state.

"They call him sissy-boy," adds Isabella.

"Yeah, sissy-boy or just plain 'sissy.' They call him..." I declare and then list other examples from the list; the members of the group nod with each new entry. "... homo, felcher, fister, tea-bagger, truck driver on the Hershey highway..."

I elaborate on the evil outside forces descending on our imaginary son.

"Like there's that show *Will and Grace*. We caught him watching that," I spout. "We can only watch him a good 12 hours a day and can't watch him 24 hours day. If there was something we could do ahead of time ... something to prevent it!"

"We're especially, really worried since we're living in San Francisco now," my fake wife says, explaining that the Gaymores just moved one month ago from a small town in Minnesota, located, ironically, not far from the large, crying woman's hometown.

"So you're in gay culture shock!" Carol clarifies.

"I even saw two men holding hands," Isabella Gaymore states with horror. "And our son sees that!"

"What do you tell the kids?!" I remark with a sad, disturbed expression.

"How do you explain that,' the crying woman agrees and then continues to cry. "I'm sitting here thinking we are both orig-

258 Republican Like Me

inally from the same place. God brought us both here for a purpose. I wish I would have seen the signs you've seen."

Carol, who has no counseling degrees of any type, decides it's time to begin discussing the proper ways of dealing with the warning signs of gayness, such as a fascination with long hair, earrings, or scarves.

"In child development there are positive steps you can take," says Debbie, who also is not certified as a counselor. "There are positive ways to make him feel that playing with Barbie dolls is not acceptable."

"What about when he tries on my dresses and makeup?" asks my fake wife. "Should I tell my little Tabby-Wabby that it's not cute?"

"Seems he's bringing that home from those outside influences," Debbie retorts. "There are ways to tell them it's not acceptable to wear Mom's clothes and Mom's makeup, but come in here I'll show you how to put on after-shave! Their little spirits are just so susceptible."

"What about if it's being taught in our schools. Should we change schools?" I cry, slamming down my fist.

"I was just about to say, 'Oh get him into a private Christian school, if there's any way possible,'" Carol counsels.

"The kids! The kids!" I moan. "What do you tell them?"

Carol, who has no medical qualifications whatsoever, explains the science behind homosexuality.

"People are not born gay. The so-called gay gene has not been proven," she says. "People call them sissy boy or queer or fag, and they begin to believe that."

"Not to mention *tea-bagger*," I add, vigorously nodding my head, as my "wife" decides it's time to throw a curve ball at the group's biblical "logic."

"What happens when you are born both man and a woman? A hermaphrodite," she asks. "What then? It seems no matter what they do, they're a sinner."

"Yeah that's a tough thing. Like I said it's a rarity," Carol explains.

"There's deformities of all kinds; some are more visible than others," perky Debbie pipes in. "When my kids ask me about that, I say, 'You can't believe everything you read.'"

"It's actually a medical condition," my fake wife clarifies. "Are you a sinner then because you were born that way and are both a man and a woman?"

"That is the way God created you. And the day will come when you will lean towards one or the other," Carol explains. "They do surgery. It's very common."

"So if you get surgery, and you become a woman, then you're not a sinner if you like men because surgery made you a woman?"

Debbie sheds light on why: "That was not a choice for that child. It was a birth defect."

"As they grow, they will naturally go to what sex they want to go to," Carol says with assurance. "I'm not a doctor so I don't know for certain."

It turns out that dark, dark days are upon us, and prayer is the only hope for homosexuals.

"I believe that our children have been held captive by the enemy. I believe Satan has taken people captive. I believe God has a special calling for us. Because who's going to care for the homosexuals? Who's going to care? Who's going to pray for them?" Debbie says. "A homosexual has to carry that guilt their whole life. Being a Christian, it's just a calling, and we pray for one another to carry each other's burden."

"I think now we have access to the Internet, to television to movies. Now they have banded together to say, 'Hey, we are a force,'" Carol mocks with feeling. "I hate to say this, but the homosexuals do look for kids that maybe don't have a father figure in their life. They look for kids who are susceptible. That fact that you're in your son's life, you're going to guide him ... God will focus you and help guide you."

"Okay," I say.

"The three of us wish we would have known, back then." Carol says, noting, for about the thousandth time, the bravery that we, the Gaymores, are showing in confronting our 7-year-old son's problem so early. "After 27 years I believe that God needs people who are homosexuals so we Christians can pray for them. I see homosexuals and my heart breaks. I think about what's going to happen to them and their families. I think of men who are already married and have kids."

"Carol will close us in prayer?" Debbie suggests.

"I want to ask, 'What's your son's name?'"

"Tobias!"

"Oh, I love that name."

As my fake wife and I clasp hands and lower our heads, Carol brings us home with some Bible verses.

"God, thank you for bringing Carl and Isabella here tonight. God, look after their son, Tobias. Lift him up, God, and surround him with your angels. Reclaim this young boy for your Kingdom. We say that Satan shall not have this young boy. Show him that he is created to be the boy that YOU want him to be, God. And you are molding him into that young man," Carol prays. "We thank you, God, that you have a special plan for Tobias."

If Carol says Tobias one more time I'm going to lose it.

"Father, keep Tobias as secure as he was when he was in Isabella's womb," Carol says. "Father, help Tobias to grow into his masculinity..."

"You got to pray for him every day," Debbie adds as the prayer appears to conclude and the large crying woman hands us the box of Kleenex.

But there's more.

"God, we believe that you are going to redeem them from the land of sin," Debbie prays. "Father, we know that once they become Christians, they won't stay gay. Because they will be lifted by your spirit.

"Father, we thank you and praise you, and you will bring our children through this dark valley we are walking through."

"Amen!" I proclaim, wanting to get the hell out of here. Churches are recommended to the Gaymores, particularly, one led by a "recovered homosexual" named Pastor Brian. Advice is also given on what churches to avoid, and how to behave in the presence of gays.

"When you encounter a homosexual when you are walking on the streets, try to see them through the eyes of Jesus, and be prayerful," Debbie says, neatly wrapping up the double-standard of Christian tolerance: Do not judge, but banish people to Hell, nonetheless. "Just try to be open, because there might be nobody praying for them."

"And we'll be praying," expresses Carol. "Tobias is now on our prayer list!"

"Cool!" I say.

"And you're invited back any time to share all your learnings."

"Now's when the work really begins." I announce with a nervous chuckle. "You know what? For Christmas I'm going to get little Tobias a baseball mitt, boxing gloves, a football, a hockey stick..."

Carol bursts my bubble. "Well, even sports' athletes can be homosexuals," she notes.

"You're kidding?" I exclaim, shocked. "Who? Don't tell me Shaquille O'Neal."

"My son dated a cop, a marine, a construction worker," Debbie proclaims, almost proudly.

My face drops.

"What do we tell the kids?!"

INFILTRATION NO. 2: A COUNSELING SERVICE

Persona: A gay man who needs a hearty dose of The Jesus.

Pretext: I need an initial consultation about becoming ex-gay.

Approximate distance from San Francisco: 58 Minutes

Here's the irony: As far as homoerotic images go, Jesus on the cross is probably one of the most alluring known to humanity. Think about it: an almost naked guy, draped in a skimpy cloth, with long hair and ripped washboard abs, apparently into blood sports.

On the other hand, what Christian anti-gay groups stress as the reason for falling into a gay lifestyle is a lack of Jesus in one's life.

But what if Jesus was the source of the problem? Let the phone consultation begin!

"Are you professional counselors?" I ask a man named Jose.

To my surprise, Jose acknowledges his lack of credentials. "No, we are not professional counselors. We're people who have dealt with same-sex attractions ourselves. Or we are people who have a desire to help people that do."

I tell Jose that I started in the gay lifestyle when I was in the military. "It happened with my commanding officer during the Gulf War," I explain. "That was the first time, when I was in the U.S. Army!"

In response, Jose explains *the cure*: "Recovery is not something that happens overnight. Yes, there have been people who have said yes, it's happened for them overnight. Some people think if the sexual side of things is gone, then they are cured more or less.

"[But] we call it the process, because it is a process of recovery."

"Do you think it's like envy?" I ask, interrupting him and referencing the Exodus Web site, which says that male homosexuality can start because of envy of the size of someone else's Johnson.

"You know, just from reading up," Jose explains, "I think it could be envy of other guys, like if they are more well-endowed … that could be an envy trait."

"For me, it's the complete opposite," I say. "I was much laaaaaaarger than all the other kids in that department, and it was kind of a bragging, showing off type of thing. You know, to show how large I am."

"Uh-huh. Uh-huh."

"I mean, I've always been huuuuuuuge!" I say. "I'd always be whipping it out and waving it around when I got a chance, like a 'Look at me! Look at me!' type of scenario."

"Uh-huh," Jose says, then quickly changes the subject.

"Heterosexuality is not our overall goal, because we have a lot of married people come to us. And they've been married for many years, and they still come to us," Jose says. "They would pretty much confirm that heterosexuality is not the goal because they would say 'I'm pretty much a full heterosexual.' Our main goal is to help them with their relationship with Christ, and from their, sexuality will change them into the person that God created us to be."

Now it's time to turn the religious tables.

"It's kind of weirdly religious based for me," I say, bringing the focus back to my problem."

"Uh-huh," Jose responds.

"It's kind of a messed up sort of scenario. It's really complicated."

"There's actually different roots and different causes," Jose says, elaborating to the point that I think he's reading from a written script. "Some people stem from a sense of envy. Some stem from a sense of anger and rejection. Some stem from other areas. It would really depend on each individual person. Though the roots are somewhat similar, those roots can tap different branches of the same root and splinter off into different areas."

"Well I became aware of my present condition when I was a kid."

"Go ahead."

"Okay. Has this case ever come up?" I ask. "The first time I ever felt attracted to a man, this sounds kind of weird, but it was from seeing pictures of Jesus when I was little. I would have this picture of Jesus hanging in my room and it would get me really, REALLY aroused!"

Long silence.

"Uh-huh," Jose says.

"Has that scenario ever happened to others? How do I deal with that?" I ask. "Every time I go to church, I get really turned on!"

More silence.

Then Jose says, "These are unique cases, but different people can respond to different images differently. (Pause.) Some people are terrified of Jesus because they can use Jesus as a man, a godly man, and they can transform that on to other men in their life or maybe their own father."

"How would you take the steps if that is the sexual image in my mind, and when I try to go to church and pray, I only end up being really aroused?" I ask. "You know, like fully erect?"

Silence.

"Uh-huh." Jose says. (Pause.) "Is that what you're obsessed with currently?"

"Yeah, it's this weird scenario. I want to go to church and get close to Jesus, but these sexual feelings come up, and it's really inappropriate."

(Pause.) "Okay."

INFILTRATION NO. 3: BACK TO HOPE SUPPORT GROUP

Persona: Monty Lamar

Game plan: Posing as someone who wants to become an ex-gay, I decided to dress *really* gay. This will show how much help I actually need.

Disguise: A very tight Enrique Iglesias T-shirt with his large, hunky head blazoned on the front. An open, pink, buttoned-down-the-front shirt. Leather pants. Rings on every finger. A cowboy hat. Most important, a neckerchief. I also wear a large 49ers football jacket, so they'll cut Monty some slack and see at least he's trying to make an effort to be straight.

Approximate distance from San Francisco: 42 Minutes

I'm directed to Marin County and "A Christ-CENTERED MINISTRY designed to help people struggling with homosexuality leave their past lifestyle and to fully EMBRACE THEIR TRUE IDENTITY IN JESUS CHRIST." Here's what the group's Web site professes:

- The homosexual lifestyle often proves to be a painful and unrewarding way of life, particularly for older gays who are no longer desirable sexually.

- Thousands have left homosexuality behind and become "new creations in Christ." Many have married and raised families, while others remain celibate, yet lead joyful lives devoted to God's service.
- Satan is not pleased when someone sees through the deception of homosexuality and discovers the way out.

If there were ever a group to organize a Gay Shame parade, this would be it. The group's monthly, Friday night meeting is held in a crappy, two-story office complex that resembles a meth-addict trucker motel. As I enter a cramped back office that has a large shelf filled with numerous books centered on the subject at hand, about a dozen Fellow Warriors, mostly older men, are gathered in a circle.

"Welcome Monty and Steven," announces the second-in-command, who has excited eyes and wears a large wooden cross. "It's their first night. Make them feel welcome."

After being trumpeted as *fresh meat*, I take my lead from the other new guy — Steven, a teenage kid with tattoos on all his knuckles who's gripping a Bible and looking really intense, to the point of psycho — and stare straight ahead with a distant look in my eye.

For the most part, it's a congenial bunch. I'm offered tea and cookies and note only two really old guys who would be described as "creepy." (They remain silent throughout the whole meeting.) I'm instructed to take my place on the cozy couch next to the second-in-command. As laughter and then concerned of a *fallen member* who is *back in the lifestyle* die down, the meeting begins.

"Father, thank you for turning my life around..." prays the leader, who wears a Promise Keeper T-shirt and mildly resembles a Mel Gibson with 30 years of hard living under his belt. Like a wise, ex-gay prophet, he tells how the "program" began in 1995, bitterly noting, "That's when I started my walk out of this mess."

The group's goal isn't necessarily for members to become heterosexual, but for them to become Holy in God's eyes. "I know straight guys who are screwed up as Grogan's goat," the leader admits with arms folded. "The focus right now is walking with the Lord." He then adds about the heterosexual path, "When it's time, God will pray my wife into me."

The leader asks the others what they've found to have been the hardest thing to deal with; for him, it's been the visual. "Several years ago, there was some construction going on down there. And there was this kid down there. Really nice body," he vividly describes. "And he would have the jackhammer going and have his shirt off..."

Laughter erupts amongst the group. I sense some are slightly aroused.

"It's important to recognize that men are attracted to men. We're drawn to masculinity. There's nothing sexual about it," explains the leader, prompting me to wonder, *What about guys who are into Thai ladyboys?* "For me, it was to deal with the visual, to get that under control, that was my big first step."

The conversation turns to a heated discussion about masturbation: the number of members of the group that were doing it, when, and that sort of thing. As the talking continues, it becomes clear – surprisingly, or perhaps not so – that most all the Fellow Warriors have had serious drug and alcohol problems, but attributed their most severe problems to being *in the gay lifestyle.*

"I lost my job, my house, everything," the leader says.

"When I first came out of the lifestyle, I was screaming at God all the time, because I didn't have anything," the second-in-command remarks. "I left homes, I left cars, I left jobs, I have left everything, and I moved in with Mom and Dad.

"But He knew where I was and was able to work with me, once I gave myself to him."

"I did a lot of coke," someone says.

"I had a problem with drugs and alcohol."

"I got to go to my 12-step meeting tomorrow," another adds.

"My sexual drive was not normal," yet another Fellow Warrior pipes in. "This plain desire was abnormal whether I was attracted to men or woman or whatever."

"When I was in the deepest darkest depths of my sin, that's

when Christ died for me!" adds the leader.

Clearly, these guys weren't casually gay; these were *extreme* gays, people who had multiple partners in the depths of coke and alcohol-induced blackouts. They are mistaking personal excess and fuck-ups for something to do with gay standards in general.

The leader, who has no psychological degree but who reads a lot of books on the subject, goes on to explain exactly what homosexuality is: "It's not a sexual problem. It's a relationship problem," he explains, stressing each word matter of factly. "Men-feed-off-of-each-other's-masculinity. It's a relationship problem!"

"Exactly."

"Repent."

"Uh-huh."

"And that's the key. God, he accepts me with all my frailty in all my screwed up-ness, but he has the plan, the desire to transform me into something that is going to bring him glory.

"Exactly."

"Repent."

"Uh-huh."

"You go girl!" I add with a finger snap, getting into rhythm.

"One of the problems I seem to have right now," a guy wearing a baseball cap says, "is a thing called intimacy."

"Mm-huh," replies the second-in-command.

"And the renewing in the mind that intimacy is not lust."

"Mm-huh"

"When I had a wife, I was not intimate. When I had a lover, I was not intimate. God was showing me that it was lust. Because you don't know the difference," the guy in the baseball cap says.

"Amen."

"Exactly."

"Repent."

"Uh-huh."

"What about Monty and Steven? Do you want to share anything? You don't have to," asks the second-in-command.

I'm momentarily caught off guard; I forgot I was calling

myself *Monty*.

"I'll share," says Steven, the teenage kid with tattoos on each of his knuckles. He sounds as intensely psycho as he looks. "I will literally sit in a room, and contemplate and soak up as much God as I can, you know."

"If God didn't make his provisions for us during his time of blood on the cross, we're all doomed. We're all doomed," repeats the leader. Steven continues.

"One time this guy called me up late at night. He said he made out with me one time at a club when I was drunk.' I told him I'm a Christian now. He started to get very sexually descriptive, so I just shouted into the phone, 'The Lord rebukes!' and slammed down the phone."

I am imagining how creepy it would be to have a random, drunk, late-night booty call end that way when the second in command turns to me and asks, "Monty, do you want to share?"

Since everyone here has had a drug and alcohol problem and has slept with thousands of partners, I change my game plan for reaction sake. How would they counsel someone who's quite normal, but happens to be gay? I tell the group that I've never touched drugs and alcohol in all my life, and I've been in one long, monogamous relationship.

"CANNIBALISM!" the group shouts in cultish near-unison. Somehow, I've triggered a classic sinner case scenario.

The leader explains *cannibalism*, again slowly stressing one word at a time: "You-take-on-the-attributes-of-the-other-person!"

"I know," the second-in-command turns to me, nodding. "I was in a relationship for 17 years."

"Men want lust, not intimacy," the leader sums up this and all other gay case scenarios.

A guy across the circle leans towards me. With strong, crazed eye-contact, he says it straight: "An erection put into a woman's vagina is like going into the paradise of heaven. An erection put in anything else is unnatural, and it's a sin!"

"Ok," I reply.

Keeping the strong eye-contact, he makes hand gestures and

uses the word "erection" at least six more times. I'm grateful when he stops directing the word *erection* at me.

"Can I still hang around my old friends?" I ask. "We've all got the same taste in music."

"I'll answer that," pipes in the creepy teenage kid with tattoos on his knuckles, suddenly sitting up. "An alcoholic shouldn't go into to a bar!"

"It will be worth the sacrifice," stresses the leader. "You'll find the best relationship you'll ever have will be with God!"

I am feeling bad for these guys. Clearly, they are mistaking drug and alcohol problems, coupled with sex addiction and extreme guilt, for sins against God and the world. Their heartfelt comments are nothing if not depressing.

"To become a heterosexual is not my goal; my goal is holiness, spirituality."

"Images still plague my mind, but I dismiss them at the door."

"I use to take the approach that Jesus loves drag queens, now I know it's wrong."

It sounds really lonely. The option provided by their religion is heterosexuality or complete celibacy, yet, obviously, these men aren't into women, and never will be.

"I work around a lot of homosexuals, so what should I do?" I ask the leader.

"You might consider changing jobs," he advises.

"But I work as a costume designer for musical theater," I retort, throwing a curveball. "That's what I do. I can't really change jobs. That's how I make a living."

"Then I would suggest putting up a barrier," the leader counsels "Because they will try to tempt you."

"Amen!"

"Exactly!"

"I'm confused. First you're saying to develop non-sexual relationships with men; then you're saying to put up a wall?" I ask.

The leader has an easy solution: "Just say, 'Hey I'm a Christian now!" He puts his hand up in a stop motion to illustrate his point.

"I used to be DJ at a top gay nightclub in New York," the former coke-enthusiast in the baseball cap says. "It's worth the sacrifice. Give yourself to God."

"What about gay marriage?" I ask; after all, this was the major moral issue of the last presidential election. "It's legal in Massachusetts, you know? If it's legal, it's not a crime."

"It's a sin in God's eyes," the leader says, ending the argument. "Sure the ancient Greeks said homosexuality was okay, but they also said human sacrifice was okay."

The part of the meeting during which I sit in the "hot seat" unfolds. As the ex-gays put their hands on and pray over me, I swear one is massaging my shoulder. When that's over, a guy with glasses pulls me aside. I think he's going to call my bluff. Instead he says, "The Lord showed me a sadness in you."

The statement is so true, I almost begin to cry.

31.
SLAMMIN' FOR JESUS

Dr. Shock, the southern good-ol'-boy wrestling announcer pimps the crowd surrounding the padded ring. "Are you ready for some good old fashion wrasslin'?" Huge cheers. Big applause. "Around here we spell wrasslin' w-r-a-s-s-l-i-n," And then, "Hey, I just got to say something, how many people love Jesus Christ?"

Larger applause. Bigger cheers. Dr. Shock, on stage in front of a large wooden cross, breaks into a little call/response action to whip the wrestling crowd into to a holy frenzy before the body-slamming begins. In this part of the country, wrestling is religion—literally!

"When I say Jesus, You say Christ: JESUS!"

"CHRIST!"

"JESUS!"

"CHRIST!"

"That's what we're all about!" Dr. Shock proclaims into the PA reverberating through the church's auditorium.

"Amen bro!" screams a wrestling fan, as the crowd is fired up. The bell rings. A 330 lbs wrestler, known as Mr. Evil aka Colt

Derringer, flies off the ropes, delivering a crushing Hangman's Neckbreaker to his unfortunate opponent. THUD! Welcome to the world of Ultimate Christian Wrestling.

THE WRESTLING PASSION OF THE CHRIST

Inside the dressing room, pre-match, bare-chested Christian wrestlers in spandex tights, grab each other, practicing ring moves. Others wrap their wrists with tape. Some have created new moves correlated right from the Bible. "He's going to hit me. I'm going to land on my back and we're going to call that move *The Fallen Angel*," instructs Rob Adonis—the founder of Ultimate Christian Wrestling, a very large man wearing a wife-beater T-shirt who looks like he could squeeze my head like a soft melon (thank God he's really nice).

Yes, Saturday night, at the Harvest Church deep in the Bible Belt of rural Georgia, it's the ultimate battle of good vs. evil (in terms of the ongoing clash with Satan). Southern wrestling alone is weird. Throwing in the element of Jesus brings it to a whole new surreal level.

This perfect marriage of Christian and WWE-style wrestling was resurrected June 2003.

"Our first show was in Canton Georgia at a skating rink. We packed out the place. About 200 people were there," Rob explains, while a wrestler with a paunchy belly behind him places a crown on his head. "We had three people that made a move and were saved that night."

After spending five years wrestling in the mainstream, inspiration for UCW came to Rob in the middle of the night like a "sleeper hold" from above.

"I woke up on my birthday in a cold sweat. Immediately, I called my girlfriend." He told her, "I feel I have something laid on me to do. It's been a stellar ride ever since."

UCW now tours all over Georgia with upcoming out of state gigs planned, and a big 3,000 seat show coming up where fans can take in their vision of a lovable Jesus opening a big can of whoop-ass.

"Typically, in every show, 10% of the crowd will make a move to give their life to Christ. So if we have a 100 in the crowd, 10 people will move. If we have 500, 50 people will make a move."

"What if you have 187?" I ask. "How many people would get saved then?"

"If I had to put it on a scale and show our spiritual progress if you will, I could proudly say that 10 % of the crowd is always reached," Rob explains. "And that's what we're going for. It's the folks that don't know Christ that don't have any idea about salvation or forgiveness of sin, that's the one's we're really trying to go after."

In the wrestling world, there's three categories: *The Major Leagues* (referred to as *The Show*), *Outlaw Wrestling* (untrained, fringe wrestlers who partake in spine-breaking, backyard wrestling), and *The Independents* which UCW falls under. Being it's Christian and wrestling, I note their sizes range from grapplers with big pot bellies to scrawny skinny kids who wrestle in street clothes, portraying "heels" and "baby-faces" (fancy wrestling terms for good and bad guys).

"We got characters at this point that have gotten so much popularity that they've got a following," Rob expounds. "And these people, collectively, they will find people that won't go to church and will not have anything to do with missions or outreach, but they go to wrestling shows and they come in and meet Christ. And it's a life changing experience."

Already a crowd of roughly 100 sits in folding chairs, screaming with wrestling excitement, anxiously waiting for some high-flying, body-slamming action (something I call *The Wrestling Passion of the Christ*). A large burly guy wears a T-shirt that reads *Where the Big Boys Pray*, sold at the concession stand along with other impulse wrestling items like Bibles. Christian intro music, springs spiritually from the DJ table, as hoards of little kids run restlessly around waiting for the grappling to begin. Not to stereotype the South, but there's more than one guy in the audience wearing overalls (and they're not trying to be ironic), as well as guys with no teeth (honestly!) and cowboy hats.

"Let's hit the prayer and let's do it!" large Rob Adonis instructs his crew with a slap of his hands. The wrestlers circle up. There's Mr. Evil, Dustin Powers, Frankie Valentine, and Dixie Dynamite, all in their respective, ridiculous wrestling outfits. They bow their heads as Rob leads them in a little prayer; a prayer for those about to KICK SOME ASS!!!!!

"Thank you God for letting us do what we enjoy. We're doing all this for you and your kingdom God......"

GENESIS CHAPTER ONE: THE ULTIMATE RUMBLE

"LET'S MAKE SOME NOISE!" shouts Dr. Shock as the crowd goes wild. "This is going to be the Ultimate Rumble. The only way to get disqualified is going over the ropes, or like me, being thrown over onto the hard concrete floor!"

Two refs, in striped zebra shirts blazoned with red crosses, take position. Banjo music plays. Out comes Dixie Dynamite, a paunchy shirtless guy, with a graying mullet and Confederate flag blazoned on the ass of his silver spandex tights. The bell clangs. Kids are on the edge of their seats, hungry with excitement.

"Come on Dixie!" screams a chubby kid wearing a Confederate flag T-shirt and the same matching camouflage cap as his chubby dad's. He's so excited, he's out of his chair, jumping up and down as his face drips sweat.

A small cruiser-weight wrestler flies into the ring (he's so tiny that he looks as if he can fit in my pocket), taking to the top of the ropes, diving down, landing with a hard, driving elbow to his opponent's back (just like Jesus would do). Unfortunately the little guy is thrown everywhere. Dixie Dynamite grabs him by the feet and makes him fly through the air, flipping him with a loud WHACK on the mat. Another elbow is driven into his thorax. Irate wrestlers argue with the refs. Under the watchful eye of the Lord is this match fixed? 330 lbs. Mr. Evil picks up the

scrawny guy like a ragdoll and throws him over his head out of
the ring onto the concrete floor.

The Christian crowd goes mental. A guy in a baseball cap
and Cosby-like sweater, holds up a sign that has a bloody cross
and reads, "Real Men Pray," and boasts the names of his favorite
wrestlers. A true Christian wrestling fan, he says, "I drew the
cross from the old psalm, *from the blood of Jesus wash away the
sins.*" He flips the sign over. "The second side says, *Colt Derringer,*" he explains. "I drew a Colt [pause] and sorry, a little gun
there."

"Are you also a fan of the WWE?" I question.

"No," he answers firmly. "I'm a fan of UCW because they're
Christian and they have the little service at the end of it and
that's what pleases me. I'm glad they don't have all the blood
[pause] and the hootchie mamas," he lets out a sly chuckle (fully
knowing Satan is behind the *hootchie mamas*).

Meanwhile back in the ring, it's time for Dixie Dynamite vs.
Mr. Bugaloo; the only black guy in the place and he goes by the
name Mr. Bugaloo (is that a racist thing?). All it takes is a
Swinging Neckbreaker and the match is over.

"Mr. Bugaloo, himself, Ray Brown is the winner," announces
Dr. Shock, once the black man has whooped the paunchy Dixie's
Confederate flag-wearing ass.

"When did your church decide to have wrestling?" I ask an
extremely large southern good ol' boy who's wearing a flaming
motorcycle T-shirt that reads "SMOKE 'EM IF YOU GOT 'EM!"

"I don't know," the large man answers, who if he were in the
Hell's Angels would be ironically nicknamed *Tiny*. "Our pastor
come up with it, told us about a month ago and said we're going
to do this. I thought it was a great idea to get people in here and
maybe get them saved."

"So you think that's the most important thing that it saves
people?" I inquire.

"Saving souls. Saving souls," Tiny repeats twice. "Creating
disciples. "

"Yeah, and great entertainment," I add as yet another
wrestler is bodily thrown from the ring. "Because who doesn't

like seeing somebody body-slammed," I rationalize, "then souls are saved."

Tiny thinks for a moment.

"That's right. Yeah come'on."

Between matches, the Christian wrestlers, now filled with adrenaline, partake in a little Christian dressing room humor. Rob, while putting on a karate robe, shares with the group his run-in with a Pastor who poo-pooed the idea of Christian wrestling.

"He told me, 'Everyone at our church is already saved and we want to keep it that way!' Man, I got to get a copy of that Bible he's using," he says with a laugh, adding sarcastically, "Wow, does God win in his Bible too?!"

Others have also thought it's crazy to mix violence with Christ. Rob, though, assures me: "There were men in the Bible who dressed up in loin clothes and ran through the marketplace all in the name of Christ, "Look at me! Look at me! I look crazy, I look freaky," he explains, waving his hands around. "But now you're listening to me so I'm going to give you some Jesus. Our philosophy is get them in here. Do whatever you got to do and give them the truth. Give them the truth and the truth will set them free, you know, that's our goal."

There are a few moments, though, that might raise Christian eyebrows.

"Every woman's dream," announces Dr. Shock, "Frankie Valentine." When taking to the ring, I note you can fully see his large package in the outline of his very tight tights (he must be thanking Jesus). His tights leave nothing for the Christian imagination (Oh Lord!). Maybe that's why he's every woman's dream?! The crowd screams wildly (is it because of his package?). The chubby kid, sensing some cheating, screams himself hoarse, "CHECK HIS KNEEPADS REF! CHECK HIS KNEEPADS!"

Though a displayed wrestler package might be questionable, during the tag-team match, I can clearly see a biblical correlation as two UCW rookies make their holy-grappling ring debut. The two skinny guys, for some reason wearing street clothes, go at it with basic *clothesline* wrestling moves. The depth of their wrestling characters involves looking like regular guys—but really angry. One of the skinny guys is tagged out. Boom. Here comes paunchy Dixie Dynamite. With the Confederate flag on his ass, the paunchy wrestler's first maneuver causes the new guy's face to start bleeding. He's bleeding from the head. Real Christian blood, perhaps ingenuously preplanned to symbolize Jesus' blood on the cross?! No crown of thorns needed, this dude, wrapped in a Dixie headlock, is bleeding all over the mat.

"Yeah, I kinda got busted open pretty early in the match. I played through it," the skinny guy confesses as he limps back to the dressing room. "I noticed I was bleeding but I covered it up coming back." Obviously he feels the blood of Christ washing away his sins, while getting the shit kicked out of him.

"We always have chairs flying," Rob explains about UCW ring antics. "I've had my nose busted open a couple of times from some miscues or hit the ropes wrong or some chair come in and pop you in the face. We try to avoid the blood. It happens on accident, yeah."

"How does the crowd react?" I question.

"The crowd goes crazy. People like gore," Rob says widening his eyes. Then taking a more Christian approach, "We don't, because one, it's not real sanitary. Two, we don't like to mar up our mat, we like to keep it all nice and clean. And three, most churches don't want to see it, the kids don't want to see it. So if there's any blood it's purely because there's something sticking out of the chair and boom when it hits you and rips you open or you hit the rope wrong."

LEVITICUS VERSE THREE: THE ULTIMATE SHOWDOWN

Before the big Ultimate Showdown, I ask Dr. Shock, "What' the big difference between UCW and the WWE."

"The WWE, that's a whole different realm, a whole different realm. Just in my humble opinion, I don't even watch that stuff on TV. Mainly it's based on how big the guy can be and how good looking the lady can be." Then adding about the biggest difference, "It has nothing to do with Jesus in my opinion."

Formally running *American All Pro-Wrestling*, Dr. Shock has done it all in the wrestling business. "I was in the mainstream. I was being booked in bars, mountain homes, trailer parks. If there's a place to put a wrestling ring, I've put one there." What made him tired of the mainstream? "Just the vulgar, the alcohol, the cursing stuff you'd associate with wrestling nowadays unfortunately. Then I got redirected in church and to Jesus. It was hard for me to go out Saturday night" (apparently, "fussing and cussing" people out the night before, made it hard to go to church on Sunday).

So Dr. Shock made a choice. He sold his wrestling ring and organization and gave himself to the heavyweight champ of all-time—Jesus.

"Wrestling and Christian combined is an awesome combination," remarks a guy, wearing a Confederate flag baseball cap with eyes so close together, they almost kiss. "I'm thinking about going to school to do it," he says in a thick accent that sounds like spoon caught in a garbage disposal.

"Nice, and were you inspired enough to actually become a Christian wrestler yourself," I ask, not understanding his hillbilly drawl.

"Ya, I'm thinking about going to school to do this," he says again. "I got the guy's number right there."

"Will you have a special character in mind to wrestle under?"

He shrugs his shoulders and lets out a toothless smile.

"I don't know, maybe like *Son of God* or something. *Saved By God* or something. (Pause) There'd be something Christian in it somewhere."

Not to rain on his parade, but I believe *Son of God* is already taken. Would there be a special wrestling move he'd put on people?"

He shrugs, "The Flying Angel or something."

Prince Brian Lawler enters the ring. "We got the classic Japan vs. The United States match," Dr. Shock announces. Though paunchy, pot-bellied, missing a few teeth and short, The Prince does sport a crown. His opponent, Karate Man, comes out wearing a black belt, karate top, black mask, and holding a long Kendo stick. Clearly it's Rob Adonis; he's the only one within miles that has the same huge body frame.

"Come on Brian, fight for the USA!"

"USA! USA! USA!" the crowd chants, showing the love of God, country, and American ass-kicking.

Of course the Japanese wrestler fights dirty. He karate chops the paunchy Prince in the shoulders and throat. Chop!

"He just gave him some of that ching-chang–chooey, imported directly from Ching Chang Chongy Japan," is Dr. Shock's innocently racist ringside commentary.

"USA! USA! USA!" The chubby kid is worked up into a frenzy, screaming himself red-in-the-face to the point where there's actually sweat running down his piggy little face, approximately where his mutt chop sideburns will someday be.

Karate Man impales the Prince in the face with his Kendo stick.

"The Oriental Spike. Come on ref. You're going to speak some ching chang choey to him and tell him he can't do that," irate Dr. Shock remarks. Karate Man spins his karate hands. "Here comes the Okinawa Special."

A row of little girls gives a firm thumbs down. "USA! USA!" grows louder. The tables suddenly turn. Karate Man hits the mat with a THUD.

"That's something unusual we have an American doing a Russian leg sweep to a Japanese guy."

Karate Man is taken down and pinned. The crowd goes wild, on their feet, fists pumping in the air. "USA! USA! USA!" Wouldn't you know it, just like those sneaky Japanese, Karate Man hits the Prince in the back with his Kendo stick.

"THAT'S ILLEGAL REF. THAT'S NOT LEGAL!" screams the chubby kid, going directly up to the ring to give a thumbs down. I'm certain he's going to have a heart attack right here and now. His artery's about to burst open.

CORINTHIANS SEVEN: THE MAIN EVENT

"Does anyone know what time it is?" Dr. Shock rhetorically asks. "It's main event time!"

Let the Bodies Hit the Floor blares over the sound system. Enters 330 lbs. Mr. Evil aka Colt Derringer, clad in dark shades, a trenchcoat, and sporting a goatee. He emerges to boos, jeers, and taunts from crowd. By his side is Mr. Evil's manager, who holds a folding chair (surely for Christian wrestler hitting). With the heavyweight belt on his shoulder, it's pointed out that Mr. Evil drove the farthest tonight (31/2 hours).

"Go home!" someone yells. Mr. Evil tells the Christian man to shut up.

"Let me tell you one thing. When Mr. Evil comes through that door, you stand on your feet and pay him the respect that I demand and deserve," Evil screams. "You see that belt right there, I have earned your respect. So I expect everyone out here to stand or I'm going to come out there and slap you upside the head."

Surely Mr. Evil is possessed by Satan himself; he threatens these good Christians with head-slapping. He removes his trenchcoat, revealing his large belly, and warms up on the ropes, preparing for the UCW heavyweight bout.

Out comes Rob Adonis. With a towel around his neck, he high-fives little kids, taking to the ring, mounting the top ropes to greet the cheering fans. The bell rings. With a drop kick and a flip, Mr. Evil lands his fat ass on top of him. The place goes crazy. The little chubby kid is screaming so much I'm almost positive that premature-childhood-heart-attack is going to happen precisely now.

Let's just say, in this match, Rob Adonis gets crucified. It's the Last Supper for Rob Adonis as Mr. Evil comes off the ropes, grabbing him by the knees and BAM, slapping his large body loudly onto his back. Un-Jesus-like, Mr. Evil then strangles him with a towel. Like a fatal kiss from Judas, the champ, Rob Adonis falls victim to the best finishing move in wrestling bar none—*The Guillotine.* Like water being turned into stale urine, adding insult to injury, the champ is handcuffed to the ropes then stomped, choked and kicked by Mr. Evil's manager. The chubby kid screams bloody murder, sweat flying off his chubby face.

Dr. Shock senses the rise of the anti-Christ, "Don't hit the ref whatever you do," he warns. Like bringing a plague of locusts to the earth, Mr. Evil administers the guillotine on the ref as well (he *is* possessed by Satan?!).

Mr. Evil puts his arms in the air to a sea of boos, retaining the Ultimate Christian Wrestling heavyweight belt. If this match was fixed, I guess it was because he drove the farthest. Christians are nice that way. Large Rob Adonis is left handcuffed in the ring.

"Hold on we got a little more," Dr. Shock announces, as a few tired fans head toward the exit (obviously leaving without being saved). "We got autographs afterwards," he entices.

Opie, the red-haired sound guy un-handcuffs Rob Adonis from the ropes. Rob puts his shirt on, takes a swig of water, then paces the wrestling ring. Suddenly it gets weirdly serious.

"As I'm looking at this chain wrapped around my wrist, handcuffed, as I was handcuffed to this, I'm reminded of a message I want to share with you," he tells the crowd while sweating profusely. "I want to tell you, the only purpose we are here is to serve God!"

There's more cheers than when Dixie Dynamite was being dropped-kicked by Mr. Bugaloo. Someone yells, "Amen, bro!"

Rob Adonis points to the handcuff still locked around his wrist; apparently there's deep symbolism here.

"This represents chains of bondage within a person's soul," he explains, holding up his handcuffed wrist (ah, so that's what that was all about). "The position of bondage within your soul, within your heart and life."

This is tying together neatly here.

"Are you living a life right now that's got you shackled in chains?" he asks, ring-center. "There's only one addiction out there and that's the addiction to Christ!"

Clearly moved, the wrestling crowd is once again on their feet. They're hooting, applauding, some with fists in the air. This time, it's not because of a well-executed double-elbow-drop; no, it's because of Jesus.

"Woo!"

"That's right!"

"Amen!'

"USA! USA!" I chant.

"We're going to give you a chance to get addicted. "I'm going to give you the opportunity to make the move. There's no drug out there that will give you the high that getting addicted to Christ can be."

(Rob doesn't mention the potent mixture of a speedball cocktail; that gets you addicted, and awfully fucked up.)

There's one last selling point to get people to sign on the Jesus dotted line. "People see us and think 'Yeah that guy's big, he's muscled, he wrestles, he takes a chair shot to the back of the head. But I hope they can make that correlation that that guy gives 150% every night to his savior."

"Woo!"

"Amen!'

"USA! USA!"

The wrestling crowd now has its eyes closed and is praying. Mr. Evil is praying. Dixie Dynamite is praying. The screaming chubby kid is praying. Little girls have their hands in stereotypical prayer poses.

The church's pastor comes into the ring. In sales vernacular, the pastor would be known as *the closer*. I soooooooo want him to get an unexpected body-slam. It would be the ultimate wrestling villain surprise. ("Take that pastor!" SLAM!) "God brought wrestling to our area!" the gray haired pastor proclaims. "If you want to make that decision tonight to follow our lord Jesus Christ, stand up."

The pastor refers to a guy named Big Jack, and then says, "I got some people right by this door and they're going to give some material about the decision you've made." To sweeten the deal, "UCW has a free bible for you if you commit to Jesus!"

As if following the Pied Piper, a line of little children are led to a small room by trained counselors. The door closes. I peek through the crack. Little kid heads are bowed. They are praying.

(It's kinda weird.) Spiritual Music once again plays ("I love you all of my days...........".). Everyone is encouraged to bring friends to the next wrestling match, especially those who *might not have the faith* (won't they be surprised) in this game of religious smoke and mirrors.

IN THE END, GOD SAID IT WAS GOOD

"How did you like the match?" I ask the chubby little kid, who I was certain was going to burst an artery.

"Oh dude, man, it was awesome. I can barely talk," he says with a huge, grinning smile. "I'm going to go home and rest my vocal-izer so I can be ready for more screaming tomorrow morning at church!"

"Tonight we topped over 300 souls saved!" Rob boasts about the grand saved tally. "8 to10 people made a move tonight!" UCW's 2nd biggest inspiration is Rob's girlfriend. "When my back's on fire from chair shot after chair shot, you know, being pounded off the ropes, she's the little voice that says, 'There's kids out there whose souls are going to need you, that won't go to church, but they will come to wrestling shows.'"

After the soul-saving, manic little kids run around the church's auditorium, amped-up screaming, hitting each other with stuffed animals. Is this extra energy boost of energy from an excessive dose of Jesus or from witnessing two hours of body-slamming?

Mr. Evil is now clad in a casual T-shirt, reminiscent of the Harley Davidson logo, that reads *Jesus-David's Son*. He has an entirely different attitude from his brethren on winning the match against baby-face Rob Adonis. "He had the belt. I wanted the belt, so I came and got the belt. And that's the bottom line. That's what I'm here for. It's all about titles," he says while signing autographs for thrilled, adoring Christian wrestling fans.

As Dr. Shock packs things up, I question, "If Jesus wrestled Satan, how would he whip his butt?" He ponders this for a moment then lets out a chuckle.

"Let's see. Man that would be hard to say. It would be over so quickly. It would be over in a blink of an eye."

"Then how about Goldberg vs. Jesus?" I throw out.

Most likely Jesus would finish off Satan with the fatal guillotine, regaining his title as the undisputed heavy weight spiritual champ. "Everywhere we go it's gotten bigger and better. And it's because of Jesus," Dr. Shock summarizes. "Put him first and you ain't got a problem. So as far as wrestling goes, it's Christian wrestling or no wrestling at all."